Special Ops Heroes

MICHAEL ASHCROFT

FOREWORD BY ANDY MCNAB

headline

First published in 2014 by
HEADLINE PUBLISHING GROUP

First published in paperback in 2015 by
HEADLINE PUBLISHING GROUP

1

Cataloguing in Publication Data is available from the British Library

Paperback ISBN 978 1 4722 2395 1

Picture research by Jane Sherwood

Typeset in GaramondThree by Avon DataSet Ltd,
Bidford-on-Avon, Warwickshire

Printed and bound in the UK by Clays Ltd, St Ives plc

www.hachette.co.uk

CONTENTS

Acknowledgements

My numerous 'thank yous' begin with the fifty-four brave men featured in *Special Ops Heroes*, without whose courage this book could not have been written. For virtually all of my life I have had a fascination with bravery, and the nature of the raw, premeditated courage displayed by members of the SAS and other Special Forces units who are the subjects of this book sends a shiver down my spine. Most of the individuals whose lives and careers are written up here are, sadly, dead. Of those who are very much alive, many provided me with their time and their memories in order to expand upon their individual stories.

Three decorated men – Ian Bailey (Falklands War), Bill Pickering (Special Operations Executive) and Graham Watts (a pseudonym, Northern Ireland) – gave face-to-face interviews, while two others – Bill Bentley and Bill Nicol, who live in Germany and Northern Ireland respectively – could not have been more generous in their efforts to help me with details of their brave exploits during the Falklands War. Indeed, Bill Bentley kindly provided me with a previously unpublished write-up of his experiences during the Battle for Goose Green, which I quote, at length, in this book. Similarly, Graham Watts let me have a lengthy account of a major incident during his time in Northern Ireland that led to the arrest of several key IRA suspects. Other decorated men were good enough to read and correct their entries, while the families of some of the men who feature in this book, but who are now dead, supplied me with details about their lives. I am particularly grateful to the family of 'Tobruk' Lowenthal, one of the 'SAS Originals', for their help, given from as far away as Australia. I also thank the family of Vincent Hoey, who served in the Raiding Support Regiment (RSR) during the Second World War, for their assistance in providing information about his life and career.

I am enormously grateful to Andy McNab, the SAS hero turned bestselling author, for writing the Foreword to *Special Ops Heroes*. It is totally fitting that such a distinguished former member of the SAS should carry out this task. Former members of 'the Regiment', as the SAS is known by insiders, do not come any better known or more courageous than Andy McNab. Before leaving the SAS in 1993, he was Britain's most highly decorated serving soldier, having been awarded the Distinguished Conduct Medal (DCM) and Military Medal (MM). He led the famous Bravo Two Zero patrol behind enemy lines during the First Gulf War, which, after he had left the SAS, led to him writing a bestselling book about his exploits, and a host of other non-fiction and fiction books.

My thanks go to Angela Entwistle, my Corporate Communications Director, and her team for helping me to get this project off the ground and for their assistance in promoting the book.

I am grateful to Michael Naxton, my medals consultant, for helping me to build my collection of Special Forces' decorations. Michael, who is the curator of the Ashcroft VC Collection, also provided invaluable advice for this book.

Two more medals experts were generous with their time in assisting me with the book: Pierce Noonan, of DNW (Dix Noonan Webb), and Richard Black, of The London Medal Company, provided help and advice with my research. They also read, and corrected, the original draft. However, if there are errors (and in a project of this size, there will inevitably be some), they are entirely down to me.

I am grateful to the various auction houses and dealers whose cataloguers have researched the lives of some of the medal recipients who appear in these pages. Their research has been diligent and in some cases I have relied heavily on it for my own write-ups. It is impossible to know all those who assisted with this 'cause', but the auction houses include DNW (Dix Noonan Webb), Spink, Bosleys and Bonhams. Individual cataloguers whose work I have benefited from include Pierce Noonan, David Erskine-Hill, John Hayward, Mark Quayle, Oliver Pepys, John Millensted and Richard Black (albeit in his capacity as a dealer).

My long and happy association with Headline now goes back nearly a decade. This is the fifth book of mine on gallantry that Headline has published and once again it has enabled me to bring my passion for bravery to a wider audience. I thank Emma Tait, my publisher at Headline, and her team for their professionalism and support.

Many publishers and authors have also allowed me to reproduce parts of their work in this book – and all of these, and more, are listed in the Bibliography at the back of *Special Ops Heroes*.

They say a picture tells a thousand words and, in a book of this nature, photographs are all-important. I am therefore grateful to Jane Sherwood, the picture editor of the *Sunday Express*, for carrying out such extensive picture research. I also thank Christopher Cox, a freelance photographer, who photographed both my medal groups and some of the medal recipients themselves.

I am grateful to the Defence Press and Broadcasting Advisory Committee and its secretary, Air Vice-Marshal Andrew Vallance, for providing me with initial guidance on potential pitfalls when writing a book of this nature. Furthermore, Air Vice-Marshal Vallance and his deputies, Air Commodore David Adams and Brigadier Geoffrey Dodds, also provided me with specific advice after reading the first draft of this book. I have gone to great lengths not to reveal sensitive information about national security or to endanger the safety of any individual former servicemen. For security reasons, I am not giving many details that are in my possession of Special Forces and intelligence operatives who served after the Second World War. In the case of one former soldier who operated undercover in Northern Ireland and who asked to be given a pseudonym, I have happily granted that request.

FOREWORD
by Andy McNab

Like many serving and former members of 'the Regiment' – as the Special Air Service (SAS) is affectionately known – I became a great fan of Lord Ashcroft's book *Special Forces Heroes*, first published in 2008. It did exactly what it said on the 'tin', by telling extraordinary true stories of daring and valour carried out by the SAS and other Special Forces units.

I was therefore delighted to learn that, just six years on, Lord Ashcroft has been able to write a second book about the remarkable exploits of decorated Special Forces men. As with *Special Forces Heroes*, *Special Ops Heroes* is based solely on the gallantry medals in Lord Ashcroft's extensive collection.

Once again, Lord Ashcroft has produced a page-turner. After telling the story of how the Special Forces originated and developed, he recounts the adventures of many of the 'SAS Originals', founder members of the Regiment. Wonderful characters such as Major Bob Lilley and Major 'Pat' Riley were as tough as they come and their repeated exploits behind enemy lines during the Second World War defied belief.

Lord Ashcroft then goes on to tell more amazing stories of courage by other members of the Regiment later in the war, along with the adventures of SBS (Special Boat Service) members, Commandos and SOE (Special Operations Executive) members. These were individuals who time and again displayed premeditated – or what Lord Ashcroft likes to call 'cold' – courage.

It was, however, the chapter on post Second World War

heroes that particularly caught my eye because some of the write-ups involved theatres in which I had served and also some men I had served alongside for many years. Trooper Bob Consiglio served with me during the Bravo Two Zero mission that I led deep into Iraq during the First Gulf War. Bob was a great guy and a truly professional soldier, but sadly he was one of the ones who didn't make it back. I am delighted that his courage has again been highlighted nearly a quarter of a century after the events.

Having carried out covert operations with the Regiment in Northern Ireland, I was fascinated by some of the accounts in this book of serving soldiers during 'the Troubles'. I was riveted by the story of the undercover work of Sergeant Graham Watts (like me, because of his role in Northern Ireland, he has adopted a pseudonym). Back in 1973, Watts was responsible for the most successful surveillance coup during the entire period of the Troubles. In fact, he was at the heart of an undercover operation that virtually wiped out the entire IRA command structure in Belfast.

Special Ops Heroes ends with stories of derring-do from a theatre that I would have liked to have served in, but never got the opportunity to be present at: the Falklands War. Here, men from the Parachute Regiment and many other regiments repeatedly put their lives at risk during the push to recapture the islands from the invading Argentinian force.

I, like many others, am grateful to Lord Ashcroft for his continuing efforts to highlight the bravery of men from the Regiment and other Special Forces units. We should all be grateful that his lifelong passion for bravery in general, and gallantry medals in particular, has been put to such sterling use. I was fortunate enough to be a guest in November 2010 when HRH The Princess Royal opened the Lord Ashcroft Gallery at Imperial War Museums, London, thereby making the world's largest collection of Victoria Crosses (VCs) accessible to the public for the first time. Over the past four years, the gallery has undoubtedly become a centre of excellence for bravery, and one that is respected worldwide.

Lord Ashcroft is to be commended for his continuing efforts to champion bravery. I have no doubt that *Special Ops Heroes* will bring the gallantry of members of the Regiment and other Special Forces units to a global audience. Lord Ashcroft's latest book has been diligently researched and the exploits in it are superbly told. *Special Ops Heroes* tells the inspirational stories behind some of the bravest men ever to put on a British military uniform. I have no doubt that it will be read and enjoyed for many years to come.

AUTHOR'S ROYALTIES

Lord Ashcroft has decided that all his author's royalties from *Special Ops Heroes* will be donated to the Special Air Service (SAS) Regimental Association and Walking With The Wounded.

The SAS Regimental Association is the only official organisation that represents the Special Air Service Regiment and its affiliated units, and that incorporates its benevolent fund.

Walking With The Wounded was established in 2010 to support British wounded servicemen and women back into the workplace after they have left the military.

LORD ASHCROFT
AND BRAVERY

All the write-ups in this book are based on medal groups that were collected by Lord Ashcroft KCMG PC. They form part of the world's largest private collection of British and Commonwealth Special Forces gallantry decorations.

Lord Ashcroft also owns the world's largest collection of Victoria Crosses (VCs), a substantial collection of gallantry medals for bravery in the air and some George Crosses (GCs). His collections of VCs and GCs are on display in the Lord Ashcroft Gallery at Imperial War Museums, London, along with VCs and GCs owned by, or in the care of, the museum.

For more information visit: www.iwm.org.uk/heroes

For more information on Lord Ashcroft's five books on bravery visit:
www.victoriacrossheroes.com
www.specialforcesheroes.com
www.georgecrossheroes.com
www.heroesoftheskies.com
www.specialopsheroes.com

For more information on Lord Ashcroft's VC collection visit:
www.lordashcroftmedals.com

For more information on Lord Ashcroft and his work visit:
www.lordashcroft.com

Follow him on Twitter: @LordAshcroft

PREFACE

My interest in bravery in general, and 'cold' (or premeditated) courage in particular, has always drawn me to the Special Air Service (SAS) and Special Forces units. I have long been in awe of the gallantry of men who are prepared to go undercover, behind enemy lines or to be part of a small, elite unit on a hit-and-run raid against a larger force. The risks associated with such missions are high and, if things go wrong, the men taking part in them know that they face being captured, tortured and killed or, if they are lucky, kept as prisoners of war, often for many years.

This is my fifth book in the 'Heroes' series and follows on from the success of my second book on gallantry, *Special Forces Heroes*, which also concentrated on Special Forces operations. *Special Ops Heroes* is not, in any way, intended to be a history of the Special Forces and the SAS: such formidable tasks have already been undertaken by others. Neither is this a book about *all* the heroes who have served in the SAS – such a task would require a larger tome than this. Instead, this book deals with part of a collection of Special Forces medals that I have built up over the past quarter of a century. It is the largest collection of its kind in the world and it is preserved by a trust that was set up to care for and protect the medals. This book deals with a substantial part of this collection – although obviously not individuals who have already been written about in *Special Forces Heroes*.

As I have detailed in previous books, my interest in bravery dates back to my childhood, and was partly inspired by my late father, Eric, who, as a young officer, took part in the D-Day

1

landings of 6 June 1944. A general interest in courage developed into a more specific passion for gallantry medals. I purchased my first Victoria Cross (VC) in 1986 and now own more than 180 such decorations – which are on display at a gallery bearing my name at Imperial War Museums, London.

My first purchase of a medal group for Special Forces-type operations came in 1988 when I learnt that the gallantry and service medals of a member of the Cockleshell Heroes were to be auctioned at Sotheby's. The raid by just ten men in small canoes into German-occupied France in December 1942 had filled me with wonder ever since I had seen the film *The Cockleshell Heroes* shortly after it came out in 1955.

I was the successful bidder for the medals belonging to Corporal William 'Bill' Sparks, one of only two survivors from the mission. This led me to begin building up a separate Special Forces medal collection, on top of my VC collection. Today, this collection consists of the medal groups of well over 100 men.

Decorations that feature in *Special Ops Heroes* date back to early in the Second World War and cover a period of more than half a century to the First Gulf War. My book also features gallantry medals awarded for courage in Malaya in the 1950s, Dhofar (1975), the Iranian Embassy Siege (1980), 'the Troubles' in Northern Ireland (1969–98), the Falklands War (1982) and the First Gulf War (1990–1).

The length of the individual write-ups varies considerably, often depending on the amount of information that is available about the medal recipient's life and career. If there are gaps in individuals' lives, including details of their births and deaths, it is because, despite extensive research, this information is unavailable. In the panels that begin every individual write-up, only British and Commonwealth gallantry and special service medals are listed. In most cases, other decorations, including those from foreign governments, are mentioned in the write-ups themselves. If an individual has received more than one decoration, they are listed chronologically in the panel based on the dates they were 'gazetted', rather than in the order of the seniority of the decoration. Not all the decorations in this book relate to men who have served in the Special Forces, but all the men in *Special Ops Heroes* have shown outstanding courage either under fire or in highly dangerous situations.

And, finally, some of the language used by the former servicemen in their interviews is a little colourful. As with *Special Forces Heroes*, I have chosen not to censor their words other than to insert some asterisks in place of appropriate letters so as not to cause unnecessary offence.

1

THE ORIGINS OF THE SPECIAL FORCES AND SAS

The very name Special Air Service (SAS) still conjures respect, even fear, worldwide. It is synonymous with qualities such as courage, professionalism and toughness. The SAS is also renowned for its secrecy, which was why, when the world caught a glimpse of how it operated during the Iranian Embassy Siege of 1980, the appetite of outsiders to know more about it grew and grew. Nigel McCrery, in his book *The Complete History of the SAS*, wrote: 'It should also be made clear that the SAS is not a machine; neither is it a clinical force cloned for warfare. It is what it has always been: a collection of dedicated soldiers. They are men who love military life, and wish to reach the pinnacle of their chosen profession. Above all, they are men who have found the true meaning of self-discipline.'

The SAS was formed as a unit in the British Army in July 1941 and was originally called 'L' Detachment, Special Air Service Brigade. Early in the Second World War, British military leaders began to appreciate the value of having a small, elite unit for specialised reconnaissance and for hit-and-run missions behind enemy lines. Until then, the British had only dabbled with Special Forces operations. 'These demand a particular skill, exceptional courage, a certain amount of imagination (but not too much), and the will-power to go on to the end, come what may; all of which are well suited to the British character with its love of adventure, willingness to accept hardship and risk, and propensity for individualism,' wrote William Seymour in his authoritative book *British Special Forces*.

The inspiration for Special Forces actions goes back to the time of legend. Homer's tale of the Trojan Horse, dating back to around 1200 BC – in which the Greeks used subterfuge to enter the city of Troy – was clearly a classic undercover operation. However, it took many centuries for Special Forces operations to become part and parcel of warfare. This was partly because great warrior leaders, such as Genghis Khan – although utterly ruthless – thought it cowardly and lacking in glory to deceive the enemy, or to mount hit-and-run operations against its forces.

There were, however, sporadic examples of Special Forces-style operations carried out by the British during the nineteenth century. I purchased the Victoria Cross (VC) awarded to Lieutenant (later Rear Admiral) John Bythesea for a daring mission during the Crimean War in which he and just one other man intercepted enemy mail on the Russian-held island of Wardo, near Finland. It is a story of a cunning hit-and-run mission, told at length in my book *Special Forces Heroes*. Yet the success of the operation did nothing to speed up the development of separate Special Forces units, and the First World War, which claimed the lives of more than ten million people, will always be remembered for its trench warfare, even if there were the occasional raids, from trench to trench, to capture documents or prisoners.

In the inter-war years, there was some sporadic thought given to using Special Forces. H.E. Fox-Davies, a subaltern in the Durham Light Infantry, wrote a paper in 1935 in which he highlighted the need for small bodies of specially trained men to be used against specific targets. His main point was that such a force would be able to create damage to the enemy out of all proportion to the number of men used.

Nothing really came from the paper but, in 1936, Charles Orde Wingate, a British Army officer, established Special Night Squads (SNS), an effective, but brutal, force that carried out surprise ambushes during the first two years of the Arab Revolt of 1936–9. Controversy over its tactics led to the SNS – a forerunner to the SAS – being disbanded in 1938.

The Second World War broke out in September 1939 and it was only after the start of hostilities that Britain, ahead of its enemies and allies, gave serious consideration to forming small, elite forces that were specially trained and specially equipped for undercover operations. Indeed, throughout the six years of the war, only one German commander, Otto Skorzeny, mounted a series of effective Commando-style raids on the Allied forces. In fact, it was Skorzeny who was personally chosen by Adolf Hitler to lead the successful operation to rescue Benito Mussolini, the Italian dictator, after he had been overthrown and imprisoned by the Italian government in 1943. Yet, by then and afterwards, Germany was lagging well behind the British in its use of Special Forces.

The British Army had formed ten Independent Companies in the spring of 1940. Each comprised some twenty officers and 270 men, and was trained to carry out sabotage raids on the enemy's lines of communications. The reality was, however, that a shortage of troops meant these 'private armies', as they were dubbed, more often carried out conventional infantry roles. When, in November 1940, the companies were disbanded, its members were drafted into the new Special Service battalions that had been formed just months earlier.

Winston Churchill, the great wartime prime minister, was starting to warm to the use of Special Forces in the wake of the evacuation of most of the British Expeditionary Force (BEF) from Dunkirk. Indeed, he instructed his military commanders to form a 'butcher and bolt' raiding force to be used against Nazi Germany. Lieutenant Colonel Dudley Clarke, who at the time was serving as Military Assistant to General Sir John Dill, the Chief of the Imperial General Staff (CIGS), came up with the format for the new force. Clarke, who started using the word 'Commando', had admired some of the guerrilla tactics of the Boer Commando units fighting the

British during the Boer War of 1899–1902. Like Clarke, Churchill favoured the name 'Commando', but other military leaders preferred the phrase 'Special Service'. In fact, both were used, as the public seemed to like the idea of a superior, specially trained force defending British shores.

William Seymour, the author of *British Special Forces*, was one of those who served during the war with 52 (ME) [Middle East] Commando. He and his comrades were trained in physical fitness, survival, orienteering, close-quarter combat, silent killing, signalling, amphibious and cliff assault, vehicle operation, weapons and demolition. Seymour said: 'A man would learn some of these [Commando] skills in his training, but vitality and a zest for adventure must be the well-spring of every one of his actions.'

Furthermore, the Commandos received extra money from which they had to find their own accommodation whenever in Britain. At their inception, each Commando unit was intended to consist of a headquarters plus ten troops of fifty men but, as the war progressed, the size of the units varied. In general, the system worked well, although some commanders resented losing their best men to the Commando units. Many soldiers volunteered to become Commandos, but not all made the grade. Inveraray, in Scotland, was the venue for much of the early training, including the use of fast landing craft.

The first Commando raid of the war took place on the night of 23 June 1940, when 120 men from No. 11 Commando/ Independent Company took part in an offensive reconnaissance manoeuvre on the French coast south of Boulogne-sur-Mer and Le Touquet. In a skirmish, two German soldiers were killed. John Durnford-Slater, who had observed the raid, was given command of No. 3 Commando, the first Commando unit in the field. Soon he was put in charge of expanding the force. Over the summer of 1940, six more Commando units were formed: Nos 4, 5, 6, 7, 8 and 9.

Brigadier J.C. Haydon was appointed in October 1940 to

command the Special Service Brigade. This, in turn, led to the Commandos being amalgamated into Special Service Battalions. However, they were unwieldy and were short-lived: Nos 1 to 5 Special Service Battalions were disbanded in March 1941 – four months before the formation of 'L' Detachment, Special Air Service Brigade. After the disbandment of the battalions, the Commandos, who had kept their own identity within the battalions, were re-formed and expanded to create eleven Commando units (numbered from 1 to 12 with No. 10 missing).

A key area of the early fighting in the Second World War was North Africa, where initially a small British and Commonwealth army faced the Italians, who, though superior in numbers, were poorly equipped. However, as the fighting in this area escalated – the Allies were determined to restrict the Axis Powers' access to the Suez Canal and Arabian oil field – Hitler sent his famous Afrika Korps. Under the command of General Erwin Rommel, the 'Desert Fox', the Afrika Korps soon came up against a British unit called Layforce, commanded by Colonel (later Brigadier) Robert Laycock. This was a Commando brigade attached to General Wavell's Middle Eastern Army: 2,000-strong, it consisted of 7, 8 and 11 Commandos. During his time with 8 Commando, David Stirling, a Scots Guards lieutenant, had begun to appreciate the benefits of attacks on targets behind enemy lines, but he thought such missions would benefit from smaller groups of men than were being used, relying largely on the element of surprise.

As a result of unfortunate circumstances, Stirling, six feet seven inches tall, athletic and solidly built, was given time to ponder such a new unit. Determined to learn to parachute, his first jump, with faulty equipment, left him paralysed from the waist down for days and in hospital for weeks. As he lay recuperating, he contemplated a new form of strategic warfare. Stirling wanted a force that, like the early Commando raids, would be aimed at specific targets. However, as stated, he wanted to use far fewer – around one twentieth – of the men. He believed four-man airborne units could cause havoc by employing surprise and guile behind enemy lines.

Once he became mobile with the aid of crutches, he met and won over British military commanders in the area to the idea and, in July 1941, he was given the go-ahead to form 'L' Detachment of the Special Air Service Brigade (which formally came into existence on 24 August 1941). The new force operated from Kabrit (later renamed Kibrit) Air Base in Egypt, close to the Suez Canal. Stirling initially recruited sixty-five Commandos and was provided with five aircraft and limited amounts of other equipment. From these modest beginnings, the SAS was born.

After rushed training, their first mission was disastrous. Some fifty-five men were dropped on the night of 16 November 1941 in support of 'Operation Crusader', an offensive from the Eighth Army. The aim was to attack five airfields in the Gazala–Timimi area of Libya, destroying as many enemy aircraft as possible. However, appalling weather – including winds of up to Force 8 – scuppered the plan. Just twenty-two of the men (numbers vary in different reports) reached the pick-up point agreed with the Long Range Desert Group (LRDG); five men died and twenty-eight were taken prisoner. However, the SAS was soon operating effectively in the area as part of the desert war, and performed many successful and daring long-range insertions to destroy aircraft and fuel depots. Stirling was, according to folklore, reputed to have strangled forty-one of the enemy himself, while, in the fifteen months before his capture, the SAS had destroyed more than 250 aircraft on the ground, dozens of supply dumps, put hundreds of enemy vehicles out of action, and wrecked railways and telecommunications centres.

Field Marshal Montgomery, of Alamein, once described Stirling as 'mad, quite mad', but he acknowledged his great worth as a wartime soldier. Stirling was a formidable, but unassuming, character with a tremendous sense of adventure.

After his capture in January 1943 his brother Bill Stirling and Robert Blair 'Paddy' Mayne took over command of the SAS, which continued to succeed with its hit-and-run tactics. As the war progressed, 'the Regiment' was used in numerous successful operations outside North Africa, including the invasion of Italy. Before and during the Normandy invasion, the SAS was used to help the French Resistance and to strike at targets.

As spelt out in the Preface, this book is not a history of the SAS, or the British Special Forces. Those wanting to read more about the SAS during its first four years should study the *SAS War Diary 1941–1945*. Written in 1946 and then kept secret for six and a half decades, it was finally published in 2011 to mark the seventieth anniversary of the founding of the SAS. Weighing nearly 30 lb, bound in leather and some 600 pages long, its contents tell of deeds of derring-do in the Western Desert, North Africa, Italy, France, Holland and, finally, during the last months of the war, in Germany. Once Germany was defeated, the SAS helped to disarm and control 300,000 Germans in Norway.

The diary is undoubtedly one of the most remarkable documents to emerge from the Second World War: a private history of the SAS by the SAS for the SAS. In a short introductory section headed 'Birth, Growth and Maturity of 1st S.A.S Regiment', it says: 'In this Diary, the reader can obtain for himself some small idea of the part played by the 1st S.A.S. Regiment in the overthrow of Germany. It has invariably fought under the most daring conditions and often against heavy odds, added to which the members of the Regiment were fully aware of the German order stating that Special Air Service Prisoners of War (PoWs) should receive no quarter and that on capture they would be sentenced to death. This never proved a deterrent to the Regiment.'

As with the SAS, the origins of the SBS go back to early in the Second World War. The Special Boat Section (which became the Special Boat Squadron in 1977 and the Special Boat Service in 1987) was formed by Roger Courtney, a Commando officer, in June 1940. In fact, for the first few months, it was known as the Folbot Troop, a folbot being a folding boat or kayak. As with the SAS's first operation, the SBS's initial mission got off to a troubled start due to adverse weather. The intention had been to target German operations on the Dutch coast. The men were taken to their targets on motor torpedo boats (MTBs), but their folbots could not be launched. The mission was, eventually, aborted, but not before 'Jumbo' Courtney learnt a lesson: that submarines were preferable, as carriers, to MTBs. The SBS, however, made its mark during the remainder of the war, including when, in February 1941, it sailed with No. 8 Commando for the Middle East. It carried out similar roles to the SAS, except taking on more amphibious assignments. The SBS today – motto 'By Strength and Guile' – is a highly respected fighting force and it has taken part in operations all over the world.

During the Second World War, the SAS, SBS and other groups sometimes worked closely with the Special Operations Executive (SOE), which was formed on 22 July 1940 as a British Second World War organisation. It was established to conduct espionage, sabotage and reconnaissance in Occupied Europe, working both against the Axis Powers and in support of local resistance groups. The SOE controlled or employed some 13,000 people, including 3,200 women, and it is estimated it supported or supplied a million operatives worldwide.

Since the end of the Second World War, members of the SAS have also seen action all over the world. Britain has certainly made more use of its Special Forces than any other military power. For the remainder of the book, I will use brief introductions to each chapter to detail how, since the end of the Second World War, the SAS and other Special Forces units have been, and still are being, used in countless theatres of conflict all over the world.

I have always considered it unfair that, despite innumerable courageous actions from the SAS/SBS, only one of their members – Major Anders Lassen, a Dane – has been awarded the VC, the UK and the Commonwealth's most prestigious bravery award. This is partly because so many SAS/SBS missions have been carried out in secret and were unseen by officers who have to recommend gallantry awards. It is partly, too, because the SAS/SBS like to operate in the shadows: the award of a VC to a serving Special Forces soldier would turn him into an instant celebrity and make it hard for him to do his job properly in the future.

Today the SAS is based in Hereford, where its members still fondly refer to the fighting force as 'the Regiment'. Its selection process and its training, often in and around the Brecon Beacons, remain brutally harsh. In his book *The Complete History of the SAS*, Nigel McCrery says that an average of three SAS soldiers die every year, though in a bad year the total can be as high as twenty. The names of those men who have died carrying out their SAS duties are engraved on the clock tower at the SAS's headquarters. It means that when an SAS man retires he is said to have 'beaten the clock'.

The SAS remains the principal Special Forces unit of the modern-day British Army and it acts as a model for similar units in other countries. William Seymour concludes his book *British Special Forces* by saying that 'it is doubtful whether even the percipient genius of David Stirling could have foreseen how the fortunes of his small force would have broadened through the years. Always faithful to its founder's principles, the SAS has become a renowned regiment with worldwide commitments and a broadening story of achievement, whose greatness lies not in its tradition – for that will come later – but in the superb training, discipline and spirit of its soldiers.'

The *SAS War Diary 1941–1945* concludes its introduction with a summary of the ethos of the Regiment and all it stands for: 'Much has been written about the S.A.S. and the daily papers and weekly periodicals have attempted to glamorise it. However it has always remained first and last, a Regiment composed of officers and men who have fought with the true offensive spirit and outstanding esprit de corps. Unfortunately no matter how much is written about 1st S.A.S. Regiment, the spirit and bond between officers and men can never be expressed. This is the true explanation of its greatness and it is only to be hoped that the Regiment has always lived up to its motto:-"WHO DARES WINS".'

2

FOUNDING FATHERS OF THE SAS

As explained in Chapter 1, David Stirling was given the authority to form the SAS in July 1941 and 'L' Detachment of the Special Air Service Brigade officially came into existence the following month. Initially, it comprised 100 men of all ranks who were tasked with carrying out raids behind enemy lines and with striking at communications and aerodromes of the Axis Powers in the Western Desert. Over the next four years, the SAS grew in size and expanded its boundaries, operating more widely in North Africa and, later, mainland Europe.

The SAS War Diary 1941–1945 *credits Stirling and other men with the Regiment's early successes: 'Stirling gave birth to the idea, but found in men like Paddy Mayne and Jock Lewis [sic – Lewes] the ideal leaders to enable him to put these ideas into practice. The other ranks which made up "L" detachment were volunteers recruited from Commando Units which had been disbanded in the Middle East. They were men who possessed the qualities of responsibility, initiative, individualism, and a strong sense of discipline. It is important to remember from the start that toughness was in no way a passport into the S.A.S., invariably volunteers with the above characteristics coupled with a strong will power and stamina were selected.'*

Stirling is given a short write-up in the introduction to the SAS War Diary 1941–1945 *in which his qualities as a soldier and a leader are highlighted: 'During the North African Campaign there appeared in the newspapers a few occasional and rather vague stories about a British officer known to the Axis troops as the Phantom Major. He was an incredibly successful raider behind the enemy lines. His command destroyed hundreds, if not thousands, of* enemy planes and vehicles. The information he supplied to the British General Staff in Cairo was invaluable, sometimes decisive. He was Major David Stirling of the Scots Guards, and of the old Scottish family of Stirling of Keir.

'It's now possible to tell a little more – but not yet all – about David Stirling and his merry men; about a man who, an awkward and sensitive boy of artistic tastes, made himself into a most desperate and successful soldier; a man who chafed under Regimental discipline but was the happy warrior, and more than a regiment himself, when he got loose in the Desert with a handful of fighters, and a jeep to take them about.'

Stirling's vision of using a small number of men to target enemy resources in a massive desert led to the formation of the Special Air Service, so-called because the original intention was to drop the raiders from aircraft by parachutes. However, after early problems caused by the weather and other issues, the trusty combination of the American Jeep and the Long Range Desert Group (LRDG) became the preferred method of getting a small number of men behind enemy lines and back again to the safety of Allied lines.

The LRDG had been formed in June 1940 and was primarily intended to carry out reconnaissance patrols and intelligence missions. However, the group also carried out daring raids of its own behind enemy lines and, because of its expertise in desert navigation, it also brought SAS operatives and secret agents to and from their targets, sometimes several hundreds of miles behind enemy lines. After the surrender of the Axis forces in Tunisia in May 1943, the LRDG switched its activities to the eastern Mediterranean, carrying out operations in the Greek islands, Italy and the Balkans. After the war in Europe ended, the LRDG made a request to the War Office to be transferred to the Far East to take part in operations against Japan. However, this was turned down and the LRDG was disbanded in August 1945, having been active for more than five years.

The introduction to Stirling in the SAS War Diary 1941–1945 concludes: 'S.A.S. was never a large outfit. Each party in its jeep *consisted only of three to four men. But a moderate calculation is that the hunting of David Stirling and his lads and defence against his darting forays, immobilised at least 5,000 Axis troops of quality. They got him at last. He was caught by the Germans, escaped, and was subsequently recaptured by the Italians, having been betrayed to them by an Arab.'*

Ultimately, however, any leader is only as good as the men who serve under him. The founding fathers of the SAS were men of outstanding qualities and, almost to a man, strong characters too. It is many of these incredibly brave individuals, who fought shoulder to shoulder with Stirling, who will feature in this chapter.

A strict interpretation of the 'founding fathers' of the SAS, or the 'SAS Originals', refers only to those who served in 'L' Detachment SAS. I confess, however, that I have been a little more liberal in my use of these terms, including in this chapter not just men who served in the early years of the SAS but also those who served in the LRDG on whom the early members of the SAS relied so heavily.

CORPORAL (LATER SERGEANT) JOHN VINCENT BYRNE
AWARD: DISTINGUISHED CONDUCT MEDAL (DCM)
GAZETTED: 7 OCTOBER 1943

By any standards, Sergeant John 'Jack' Byrne had a quite remarkable war: being left for dead at the time of the Dunkirk evacuation, seeing action in the desert, being captured, shot and beaten, and escaping from a German prisoner-of-war (PoW) camp in time to serve as a Commando on D-Day. When Christopher Hill, of auctioneers DNW (Dix Noonan Webb), was preparing Byrne's medals for sale, he said: 'If I could have only one Second World War medal group, I would be hard pressed to come up with a better one than this. One could not wish for a more representative medal group to capture the iconic image of your Second World War Commando hero than this man.'

Byrne was born on 1 April 1921 in Preston, Lancashire, and educated at Army Apprentices College, Chepstow, Monmouthshire. He enlisted into the 1st Battalion, Gordon Highlanders, in February 1939. Byrne saw action with the British Expeditionary Force (BEF) in France, where he was twice wounded, first by shrapnel and then, in desperate hand-to-hand combat, by a deep bayonet thrust just above his groin. His latter injury took place during the 51st Highland Division's rearguard action on the Dunkirk perimeter. Byrne was left for dead at the bottom of a trench but was found, semi-conscious, by two French civilians who carried him to the beachhead, where he was evacuated to England.

After making a quick recovery from his injuries, Byrne became a founding member of 'L' Detachment. In his wartime memoir *The General Salutes a Soldier*, published by Robert Hale Ltd in 1986, Byrne explained how this came about:

> When France fell in 1940, I transferred to 11 (Scottish) Commando and served with them until the unit was disbanded after storming the beaches north of the Litani River during the invasion of Syria. By this time 7 Commando and 8 (Guards) Commando, their ranks depleted by the fighting in Crete and Tobruk, had also been disbanded. It was from these remnants of the Middle East Commandos that Captain David Stirling selected the original members of 'L' Detachment, the 1st Special Air Service Brigade, myself among them, which he founded in July 1941. Later the unit became the 1st SAS Regiment.

After completing his parachute training, Byrne took part in 'L' Detachment's first operational jump on the night of 16 November 1941. Their aim was to destroy enemy aircraft on five airfields between Timimi (sometimes also spelt 'Timini') and Gazala on the eve of 'Operation Crusader', the British offensive to relieve Tobruk. However, conditions on the night chosen for the mission were entirely unsuitable: there was no moon and high winds whipped up clouds of dust, which made accurate navigation impossible. None of the parachutists landed within ten miles of the pre-arranged drop zones, and weapons and other vital equipment needed for their mission also went astray. At least two men were killed on landing by being dragged along the ground and many others suffered broken bones and other injuries. Stirling was forced to cancel the mission and instead struck out for the rendezvous with the Chevrolet trucks of the Long Range Desert Group (LRDG). Only four officers and eighteen other ranks, out of a total of fifty-three men, returned to the safety of British lines.

A month later, however, Byrne was involved in a much more successful mission, this time a raid on Agedabia airfield when five men successfully destroyed thirty-seven enemy aircraft. The mission took place the night before an offensive by a battle group of armoured and motorised infantry codenamed 'E' Force. 'L' Detachment's surprise attack took place when it was based at the oasis of Jalo in the Western Desert. In his memoirs, Byrne vividly describes what happened after they were dropped some fifteen miles south of their target:

When it was dark, we set off, the others taking turns leading, marching soundlessly at about one mile per hour. Maintaining complete silence the whole time, we stopped for a moment in each hour, for our bladders were proving troublesome. Three hours later Philips, the man I was following, passed back a signal for me to go forward. On reaching the front, I found Bill Fraser and Bob Tait kneeling before a two-strand wire fence, presumably the outer perimeter of the airfield. Standing up, Bill put his hand on my shoulder and pointed into the darkness. It was my turn to take the lead.

Stepping over the fence, I strode onto the airfield, the others following. Moving swiftly, we soon reached the runway, on the other side of which was the first batch of aircraft, a mixed bag of fighters and bombers of all types. Losing no time, we set to work placing our bombs high up on the wings of the bombers and on the noses of the fighters. Jeff du Viviex [Vivier] and I wasted a few minutes inside a huge transport plane hunting for souvenirs but it was too dark to search properly. We left the plane together just in time to stop Bill Fraser climbing on the wing with a bomb, for Jeff had left one inside.

The aircraft were parked close together in clusters, each group about 200 yards apart. Keeping together, we dealt with every plane in each batch before moving on to the next. During all this time we saw no sign of any enemy personnel. When it was thought there were no more planes, Bill Fraser and Bob Tait put bombs on a tractor and a covered lorry which were parked together in the centre of the runway.

Punctually, the first of our time-bombs exploded and the aircraft burst into flames. Other bombs followed, exploding in quick succession until the centre of the airfield was one great forest of fires. Then, as enemy machine-guns began firing tracer bullets on fixed lines down two sides of the airfield and partly across our escape route, searchlights probed the sky, mistakenly believing the RAF were overhead. Their anti-aircraft guns too soon joined in sending up great sheets of exploding flak. There was the most tremendous din, with ammunition crackling in the exploding and burning aircraft, the continuous rattle of machine-guns and, noisiest of all, the rapid-firing flak-guns. The enemy, convinced that they were being attacked by bombers of the Royal Air Force, made no attempt to save their aircraft and wisely remained in their bunkers and foxholes, for not one aimed shot came our way.

It was at this moment that we spotted the eight German fighters. They were about fifty yards away to our right, clearly visible now by the light of the other burning aircraft, all eight being parked very close together, nose to tail. Bill Fraser shouted to me above the din, 'Collect all the remaining bombs.' I counted them into my haversack as the others reluctantly handed them over. There were seven, for I had used all my own bombs. To the others, Bill shouted, 'You three make your way back to the rendezvous. Bob you're in charge.'

Bob answered for all of them: 'Get on with it. We'll wait here.'

Whilst Bill and I were running hard towards the fighters, I squeezed the time-pencils of two of the bombs and for good measure jerked the pull-switches: the bombs should now explode in fourteen seconds. It took only a moment to place a bomb on each plane – all ME 109 Fs, apparently brand new, each one having a canvas-type horseblanket strapped around its fuselage.

Bill stood watch at the wingtip of each plane whilst I placed the bombs. Twice he held out a hand to take the tommy-gun from me but I pretended not to notice. When we got to the seventh fighter, I ran straight past it, putting the last bomb on the eighth whilst Bill remained standing by the seventh, shouting his head off until I displayed an empty hand. As we turned to run back to the others, the first four of the fighters went up in flames almost together, and within seconds all eight were burning fiercely, the planes being so close together that one well-placed bomb in the centre of the row would probably have destroyed the lot.

Together again, all five of us added to the bedlam by shouting to each other, pointing out the destruction all around. The whole area was light as day, and we must have been clearly visible to anyone who wanted to see. Spreading out in one long line, we marched off the airfield in style, taking giant strides. We made for a point well to the left of the entrance to the desert track in order to avoid the position of a possible enemy fort. As we went, we heard unmistakably above the din the droning engines of the RAF bombers. There were three of them high overhead and as they stooged around, dropping their bombs, the fort at the entrance to the desert track fired on one of them, briefly giving its position away, enabling us to enter the desert well clear of it.

Many other missions followed: some successful, others less so. After one missed rendezvous with the LRDG, Byrne and four others had to embark on a 200-mile desert trek before hijacking a German staff car. In March 1942, another desert mission – an attack on Berka airfield – went wrong when bombs the men had planted went off early. Having missed his rendezvous, Byrne struck out alone, but on the fifth day, and desperately short of water, he was captured by an enemy patrol just seventy miles from Allied lines. A German officer emerged from the turret of a tank and ran towards him.

Byrne wrote: 'He stopped about three feet away, breathing heavily, his pistol held in front of him within inches of my face. As I yanked my revolver from its holster and flung it on the ground, the German, either nervous or sensing defiance, drew back his pistol to strike at me, then fired point-blank into my face. I fell, half stunned, face down in the sand, blood spurting from nose and temple.'

In fact the bullet had only brushed his face and, after some medical assistance from the Germans, Byrne was able to prepare for the ordeal ahead: he was savagely beaten by an Italian officer and guards when they discovered he had been concealing his fighting knife following his capture. In his memoirs, he describes one beating that took place just three days after he had been captured and shot in the face:

> With blood spurting from my nose, there was barely time to put my tunic on before I was struck on the head by an officer with a long black cane whilst two soldiers held my arms. From that moment there was no let up, for the officer continued to strike at my face, knees, shins and ankles with all his strength. He struck anywhere and everywhere as I tried to escape the savage blows by twisting and turning, flinging myself from side to side, stamping on the feet of the men watching and kicking out at the thug in front. It was hopeless. The pain was unimaginable, and I began to retch and vomit in my agony . . .

Flown to Athens, Byrne was taken by rail to Dulag Luft, the Allied aircrew interrogation centre near Frankfurt, from whence he was sent to the NCOs' compound at Stalag Luft III at Sagan and, later, to other PoW camps. In October 1942 and March 1943, he made two unsuccessful escape attempts, receiving twenty-four days in the 'cooler' for the second one.

On 16 July 1943, Byrne and five RAF aircrew spent the night at a transit camp at Königsberg while en route to Stalag Luft VI at Heidekrug. Next morning, he lowered himself into a latrine drain and passed into a neighbouring Russian compound from which he escaped by breaking through a rusty fence with his bare hands, the whole procedure taking about five minutes. That night he made his way to Königsberg docks and fell in with some French forced labourers, who supplied him with a suit of blue overalls, food, money and advice. Byrne stole a bicycle on the 19th and, two days later, arrived in Danzig at dawn, having spent the intervening nights up a tree and in an old signal box. With help from another Frenchman he reached the docks and, mingling with a working party, slipped past a German guard and boarded a Swedish ship. Byrne hid in the bowels of the ship for the next two days until at last it began to move. A few hours later he revealed himself to the crew and demanded an interview with the captain, who duly congratulated him on his escape. Byrne eventually returned to the UK in an unarmed Mosquito aircraft on 14 August 1943.

It was for his escape that Byrne was awarded the DCM on 7 October 1943 after his once-confidential recommendation stated:

Corporal Byrne was captured by the Germans in Libya while returning alone from a special sabotage mission. He was sent to a Prisoner of War camp in Germany where he volunteered to act as an Officer's batman as he thought this would give him a better opportunity of escaping. He was, accordingly, transferred to Oflag XXIB, an Officers' camp, where he made two attempts to escape but, unfortunately, was recaptured on each occasion. On 18 July 1943 [the citation is not quite accurate here: see account of his escape above], while being transferred to another camp, he escaped from a transit camp at Koenigsberg [Königsberg] and succeeded in reaching Danzig, where he boarded a Swedish ship and finally arrived at Goteborg [Gothenburg] on 25 July 1943. This N.C.O. showed courage, pertinacity and initiative of the very highest order under the most trying circumstances.

A period of recuperation and re-training followed before Byrne was posted, with the rank of lance sergeant, to 6 Commando, part of Lord Lovat's 1st Special Service Brigade. In September 1943 he was chosen to take part in a promotion of National Savings certificates with General Sir Frederick Pile, the commander of the City of London. On one occasion, Pile saluted him in front of a large crowd, thereby giving him the name of his wartime memoir, *The General Salutes a Soldier*.

On 6 June 1944, having been in a sealed camp with 6 Commando since the previous month, Byrne took part in the D-Day invasion, landing on Queen section of Sword Beach (incidentally exactly where my father, Lieutenant Eric Ashcroft, landed on D-Day with the South Lancashire Regiment). Along with his fellow Commandos, Byrne was tasked with infiltrating through enemy defensive positions in the landing area and linking up with the 6th Airborne Division, which was being dropped in darkness to secure bridges over a river and canal. He advanced to the beach and then to a partly demolished building with two comrades, one of whom (Private Graham) was shot dead. In his memoirs, Byrne takes up the story:

> Whilst I was off guard, two of the dead Germans in the trench behind me decided to come to life. Corporal Todd, reacting like lightning, ran up and, firing from the hip with his rifle at point-blank range, shot one dead. At the same time Private Croal, who was almost facing me, unable to aim because I was in his line of fire, lunged forward with the utmost violence and, shouldering me aside, bayoneted the second German in the upper part of the

throat, impaling him on a wooden stake in the back of the trench. The point of the bayonet entered the neck just above the chinstrap and came out at the side of the face through the cheek in front of the ear. When Private Croal tried to jerk the bayonet free, the enemy soldier's helmet fell forward and, with the chinstrap fouling the end of the rifle, swung beneath it. The German, far from dead and still holding a Schmeisser sub-machine gun, tried to grip the bayonet but somehow got one hand entangled inside his own helmet. Shouting 'Wait!', I tossed my tommy-gun to Corporal Todd, then, drawing my fighting knife, bent down and with one swift movement slit the German's throat, his warm blood spurting into my face, up my sleeves and over my trousers. Cutting the helmet free, I struck the wooden stake with the flat of my boot, causing the bayonet to come away easily.

As Byrne and his comrades advanced inland over the next day or two, he was shot in the knee, a serious wound that resulted in him spending six months in hospital. However, he recovered in time to join the re-forming brigade and go with them to north-west Europe. Byrne was involved in the heavy fighting to take Maasbracht, Holland. Later, after being promoted to sergeant, he was involved with 1st Commando Brigade, as it was now called, in fierce close-quarter fighting after crossing the Rhine and advancing to capture Wessel. His last front-line action came on 29 April 1945 when he was involved in capturing a vital bridge over the Elbe–Trave Canal.

After serving with the 4th Norfolks in Greece and the 2nd Royal Fusiliers in Egypt, Byrne was demobbed in February 1947, when he joined the Kenya Police. Following the 'Malaya Emergency' in 1948, he answered the call for volunteers and was posted to the Kulai Police District in Johore on internal security duties. In 1953 he was shot in the stomach at point-blank range and received injuries that ended his service. After being discharged from hospital, he returned to Kenya to work in the prison service. He married in 1955 and he and his wife,

Mary Hayes, went on to have three daughters. He retired from the prison service in Kenya in 1958 before settling in Shropshire, where he built up a drapery business that he ran until his retirement in 1986.

Byrne died on 10 January 2007, aged eighty-five.

2ND LIEUTENANT (LATER CAPTAIN) RICHARD PHILLIP CARR

AWARDS: MILITARY CROSS (MC) AND ORDER OF THE BRITISH EMPIRE (MBE)
GAZETTED: 27 AUGUST 1940 AND 1 JANUARY 1946

Richard Carr has been likened to 'the Cooler King', the charismatic character played by Steve McQueen in *The Great Escape*. In the 1963 American film set in 1944, McQueen plays Captain Virgil Hilts, who kept being returned to solitary confinement after repeated attempted break-outs as a prisoner of war. In real life, Captain Carr was equally vigorous in his escape bids, making no less than four determined attempts to gain his freedom and rejoin the war effort. Carr himself was modest about his escape attempts, describing them as 'four real breaks and a few minor ones'.

Carr was born in 1920, the son of a businessman who ran a large biscuit-making company. Little is known about his younger years but, by early in the Second World War, he was serving with the Royal Artillery in France, where he proved to be a regular and quite splendid letter-writer. If ever there was a man relatively unfazed by the horrors of war it was the cool, calm and collected Carr, as his informative letter to his father, dated 22 May 1940, testifies:

> I am dreadfully sorry that I have not written before, but we have been terrifically busy. It's extraordinary how used you become to being shot at, bombed by, machine gunned and shelled at by those bloody Germans, but the more they do it the less it worries.

I can't describe the things I've seen because it's all so absolutely amazing, but I am well and feeling in cracking form and I must say we laugh a lot.

For instance, the other day 42 German aircraft attacked the building I was in, making the most frightful din but not hurting anyone! Where I am now is like a city of the dead, not a soul about; you just go into any house you want to and take what you want; stray dogs are wandering about; everything half in ruins; it's all so grotesque. But it's such a rest from the last few days that it feels marvellous.

A Spitfire is at this moment in the process of bringing down one of those bloody Germans. Ah yes! I can see the smoke going up where he crashed – just one more out of his many hundreds.

Don't worry about this War since I am sure that at the moment it's not as bad as that of 1914. I felt sorry for the German Tanks that come under my gunfire since it will put them straight out! The weather is superb and I am sitting out in the open at 4 a.m. writing this. The War has certainly made me see the dawn!

It would be terrific if you could send me some Bourbon and Chocolate Biscuits as soon as possible since one never seems to have enough food on these occasions. I simply must stop now since I must go on my rounds and see what's going on this morning.

Incredibly, just six days after writing this boyish and enthusiastic letter, Carr, still only twenty years old and a 2nd lieutenant, was involved in the action for which he would later receive the MC. It was for his outstanding bravery during the retreat to Dunkirk that he was awarded his decoration, which was announced on 27 August 1940, when the recommendation stated: '2nd Lieutenant Carr was left in command of his Battery on the 28th May 1940, when his Battery Commander and Battery Captain became casualties, and he showed great qualities of leadership and initiative during that day and during the subsequent withdraw from Ypres Comines Canal. 2nd Lieutenant Carr has throughout displayed great powers of leadership and by his coolness under fire and contempt of danger has set a high example to all ranks.'

Following a period at the 42nd General Hospital as the result of an apparent small wound or illness, Carr volunteered for service with the Commandos. He joined 11 Commando on 28 August 1940, serving with No. 1 Troop. After Carr was sent to the Middle East, it is believed he took part in the famous Litani River Raid of 9/10 June 1941. It was during this raid that his Commanding Officer, Lieutenant Colonel Richard Pedder, was killed. In a letter to a friend – dated 3 July 1941 and giving his address as 'C' Battalion, Layforce, Middle East Forces – Carr says Pedder is 'a great loss to us, life is very different without him.' Carr wrote: 'I have travelled thousands of miles by air, sea, land,' but added 'I am beginning to dislike the Middle East intensely.'

Carr appears to have served in Layforce, the British Commando unit commanded by Colonel (later Brigadier) Robert Laycock, during September 1941 and then transferred to the Long Range Desert Group (LRDG), where he was appointed as adjutant. In January 1942, Rommel's Afrika Korps made a surprise attack, gaining ground quickly, resulting in a rapid withdrawal of the British forces. Carr was given command of a seven-vehicle patrol ordered to Msus, Libya, to collect valuable stores and to carry out a reconnaissance of the area. However, the German advance was so swift that it had captured Msus and Carr's patrol drove straight into them. Carr was taken as a PoW to Italy: it was here that he wasted no time in trying to escape, making his four determined, but eventually unsuccessful, break-outs in just over two years. A letter home, dated 17 January 1944, while he was still a PoW, indicated how hard it was for him as he tried to keep up his spirits: 'I must say that letters from me have, after two years, become rather pointless, except to tell you that I am safe and well. After a few days in hospital with a touch of 'flu, I am both "Safe and Well"!

'. . . There are a few lines left and I find it very hard to know what to say. My experiences would fill a book, so many worlds have crashed about my head during the last six months that sometimes I lose faith and hope in everything; but of course that is ridiculous.'

Even as a PoW, he was a regular letter-writer and a considerate son. On 1 November 1944 he wrote to his father: 'Many congratulations on completing 40 years in the business. How I wish I had lunched with you on that day. We'll have just as good a celebration on my return won't we?' In the same letter, Carr tries to be optimistic about his life after the war ends: 'But here's to the future; the past is dead. I've all my life ahead. A wonderful job, independence, security; surely with those ingredients I can make happiness? It is that thought which makes the next few days, weeks, months, whichever it may be, bearable, because viewed dispassionately what are a few weeks out of a lifetime?'

Carr was eventually freed as the Germans retreated in the face of the Allied onslaught in April 1945. His MBE (Military Division) was announced on 1 January 1946, when his citation stated:

Captain Carr was captured at Msus on the 26th January 1942. At Camp 35 Padula on 13th September 1942 he and thirteen others escaped through a tunnel which had taken them 1½ months to construct. Outside the camp the party split up and Captain Carr with one other started out in the direction of Switzerland. They were recaptured by Carabinieri 7 days later when forced to seek shelter at a farmhouse in the hills near Titopotenza. As a result of his escape Capt Carr was sent to Camp 5 Gavi and did one month's cells as punishment. His second attempt was made after the Germans took over camp 5. In September 1943 he and another Officer had prepared a small hideout beneath the stairs and were sealed in an hour before the camp was due to move. About 58 others had also hidden themselves and at the last

29

moment their absence was noticed. After a hunt lasting all day and most of the night, during which the German guards threw hand grenades indiscriminately, Captain Carr and his companion were dragged out of their cramped and airless quarters at 3 am and beaten up before being taken to Mantua and thence with others by train to Stalag VII A Moosburg. On the 5th October 1943 Captain Carr and an American Officer walked out of this camp dressed as French workers and walked to Munich, where they parted and Captain Carr with the assistance of French workers, boarded a goods train bound for Strasbourg. He had been given the address of a helper at Vendhelm but was unable to get in touch with him and while trying to find him in one of the barges on the cannel [canal] at Detweilie, was arrested by a German Policeman. Taken to Oflag VA Captain Carr took part in digging a tunnel, but before they could use it 120 Officers including Capt Carr were moved by train to Stalag VIIIF. On the second day of the journey (6th January 1944) while the train was going fairly fast Captain Carr and another Officer escaped through the netted window of their truck and jumped from the train. Captain Carr broke a finger and was completely winded but his companion's face was so badly cut that he had to give himself up at Neurode next day. Captain Carr who was wearing his battledress was arrested at Oppeln and after an unpleasant interview with a Gestapo agent in Neurode and time in the cells at Gorlitz, he was returned to Stalag VIIIF, given five days hospital treatment and a week in the cells. In May 1944 all the prisoners were loaded onto trucks, handcuffed together and taken to Stalag 79 at Brunswick. Almost immediately Captain Carr walked out of the camp through a partially finished sewer but was caught when he returned to fetch his kit. He remained in this camp until his final liberation in April 1945.

Carr left the Army at the end of war and joined his family business, Carr's Biscuits. He also became a keen sailor and a member of the Royal Yacht Club. He died, aged fifty-eight, on

24 December 1977 after a brief illness. An unidentified friend wrote a short obituary that was published in at least one national newspaper early in 1978:

> The death of Mr Richard Carr, MBE, MC, on Christmas Eve at the age of 58 came as a great shock to his friends. He faced his short illness with the same courage that he faced life, and those who took part with him in his many escapes as a prisoner of war marvelled at his physical courage in the face of danger. He won the Military Cross at Dunkirk before he reached the age of 21.
>
> In addition to his physical courage, those who worked with him in business equally admired his moral courage. Calm in the event of any disaster, no matter whether he was at the helm of his yacht in a Channel race or solving the problems which inevitably face any large business, he had the ability to see the best course to follow and he followed it with complete integrity and honesty.
>
> He had little ambition for himself, and yet his life was crowned with success, taking him through various responsibilities in his family firm (Peek Frean & Co) to chairman of the group (The Associated Biscuit Manufacturers Ltd). Never, however, did that success alter his outlook or his way of life, and he remained modest and unassuming throughout, with a touch of diffidence which endeared him to those who knew him well.
>
> He had a particular way with him when talking to the younger generation and an ability to see things from their point of view, with the result that many young people benefited from his wise counsel.
>
> A member of the Royal Yacht Squadron, he was probably happiest when sailing his yacht Amokura with his devoted wife, Susan, who was his constant companion and help at every stage of his career.

SERGEANT (LATER MAJOR) CHARLES GEORGE GIBSON RILEY
AWARD: DISTINGUISHED CONDUCT MEDAL (DCM)
GAZETTED: 26 NOVEMBER 1942

'Pat' Riley, as he was known to one and all in the Army, had many claims to fame. He was one of the founding fathers of 'L' Detachment, SAS Brigade, having joined as one of the legendary 'Tobruk Four', which also included Bob Lilley, Jim Almonds and Jim Blakeney. Furthermore, he was a renowned pugilist and is believed to have been the only man to have got the better of both 'Paddy' Mayne and Reg Seekings, two truly formidable SAS members, in fierce fights. During the war, Riley established himself as one of the SAS's greatest heroes and he was awarded the DCM for gallantry during the Bouerat Raid of 1942 in North Africa.

Riley had an interesting childhood: he was born in Redgranite, Wisconsin, USA, on 24 November 1915 into an Irish-American family. However, when Riley was just seven, his family moved to Haltwhistle, Cumbria. The eldest of five children, he attended local schools until he was fourteen, but then went to work in the same granite quarry that employed his father and grandfather. He left his manual job at the end of 1933, aged eighteen, and on 15 January 1934, having already served with the Territorial Army, he joined the Coldstream Guards. While celebrating joining up, he missed his last bus home, 'borrowed' a local farmer's horse and rode it bareback to his home, tying the animal to a neighbour's fence.

Riley served with the Coldstream Guards in Palestine from October to December 1936 and then transferred to the Army Reserve in December 1937, after which he joined the Wisbech Division of the Isle of Ely Constabulary (now part of Cambridgeshire). He served as a policeman until he was mobilised for service, again with the Guards, in September 1939. Before the outbreak of the Second World War, when both were serving in the Army, Riley confronted Reg Seekings in the ring. Indeed the two men fought twice at the Women's Institute Hall, Alexandra Road, Wisbech, with Riley winning on points on both occasions. After being mobilised, he volunteered for service with 2 Troop, 8 Guards Commando, as part of Layforce, Colonel Robert Laycock's elite Commando unit. Riley's troop was commanded by Jock Lewes, who was destined to become the principal training officer of the SAS. The troop was operating in the Western Desert in 1941 when it launched a surprise raid in the Fig Tree sector, as part of the defence of Tobruk, the besieged Libyan port, causing considerable casualties. It was during this action that Lewes developed and instigated the new tactics of using a four-man operating team behind enemy lines. As stated earlier, his foremost team of Riley, Almonds, Blakeney and Lilley became known as the 'Tobruk Four'.

With the disbandment of Layforce, Riley was due to be returned to the 2nd Battalion, Coldstream Guards, but David Stirling, the SAS founder, invited Lewes, together with the 'Tobruk Four', into 'L' Detachment on the basis of their reputation, enthusiastically describing them as 'pure gold dust'. Stirling wanted to use small raiding parties to infiltrate behind enemy lines and destroy Rommel's aircraft and supply dumps.

Riley arrived at the 'L' Detachment camp at Kabrit (later renamed Kibrit) in the Canal Zone, Egypt, in September 1941 and quickly settled into the rigorous training regime implemented by Stirling. This included parachute training, which, due to a lack of available equipment, meant back rolls from lorries and trucks travelling at 30mph. Inevitably, several men had bones broken during their training.

Riley took part in the first raid carried out by the unit in November 1941; the attack was supposed to be on the five advanced airfields in the Gazala–Timimi area. However, appalling weather conditions led to a disastrous result: of the fifty-five individuals who took part in the parachute drop for the raid, only eighteen men and four officers survived death or captivity. However, 'L' Detachment recovered with successful raids, including those on Sirte and Tamit, before embarking on the Bouerat Raid in January 1942.

The backdrop to this raid was that, due to a successful offensive move by General (later Field Marshal) Claude Auchinleck, the Axis forces had been driven out of Libya and the capture of Benghazi was imminent. Stirling assessed the situation and concluded that the enemy supply ships would be re-routed to Bouerat, which would, in turn, then become an important harbour for fuel tankers to supply Rommel's advanced forces.

Stirling proposed to Auchinleck that 'L' Detachment should enter Bouerat and blow up whatever ships they found, also taking the opportunity to destroy petrol dumps and tankers. Permission was granted and the raid was scheduled for the night of 22/23 January, with the RAF due to bomb Bouerat the following night. On 17 January Riley set off with Stirling from Jalo as part of the raiding party. They were conveyed by the Long Range Desert Group (LRDG) and accompanied by two members of the Special Boat Section (SBS), who were equipped with a canoe and the necessary explosives and limpets to blow up enemy shipping. Bouerat was some sixty miles west of Sirte and thirty miles from Tamit, so for most of the journey the SAS men were travelling over the same terrain that they had crossed twice the previous month. They had to keep fairly south to avoid detection by the enemy, and for the first four days saw no sign of life at all. Sometimes they were able to travel at thirty miles an hour, but the terrain was rough and punctures and repairs slowed their average speed to around 100 miles in a long day's drive.

On the evening of 22 January, the convoy reached the edge of the Wadi Tamit as the light was fading. Because of the growing darkness, Captain Hunter, of the LRDG, decided that it would be better to leave the descent until morning and so the men pitched camp where they were. The next morning, at first light, Hunter assessed that the party must take cover in the *wadi* (dry gully) as rapidly as possible, but no sooner had they done so than an Italian plane appeared on the scene. Corporal Reg Seekings, one of those on the raid, later recalled: 'We sat and prayed it had not seen us but no such luck. It banked steeply and came straight for us. The rocks which I was sitting by suddenly became as small as peas . . .'

As the recce aircraft headed off, Riley and the others scrambled for what cover they could find, knowing that enemy bombers or fighters would soon be in attendance. Initially, six bombers came and flew up and down the *wadi*, bombing and strafing for over an hour. After an hour's relief, three more bombers appeared, and it began all over again. This went on until the middle of the afternoon. In her book *The Phantom Major*, Virginia Cowles wrote: 'At six o'clock Hunter gave the signal to reassemble. The men came out of their hiding-places in twos and threes, each little group looking surprised that the others had survived. None of the trucks was damaged and the party appeared to be wholly in tact.'

However, it was then realised that the wireless truck and its three operators were missing: it was never discovered whether the men had been bombed and killed, or whether they had driven into the desert and been taken prisoner. Yet the result was the same: no further intelligence, including where to place the petrol dumps, could be received and the raiding party had to search for their targets in the dark. The group pressed on, and three hours later they reached what was to be their main rendezvous area. Weapons were checked, the canoe was constructed and at 8.45pm twenty men proceeded in one vehicle.

Hunter planned to drive the raiding party of sixteen men to within one mile of the port. They had twenty-five miles of rough desert to cross before reaching the surfaced road that led to Bouerat, and then a further fifty miles on the better road. At

10.15pm the truck was within five miles of the surfaced road when two wheels struck a cavity, causing men and boat to crash against the side of the vehicle. The canoe, of vital importance for getting to the big tankers believed to be in the harbour, had split in two and was useless. Despite this disastrous turn of events, Stirling decided to press on. 'We will have to reorganise a little,' he said. 'There are plenty of targets waiting for us at Bouerat. If we can't get the ships we'll get the harbour installations instead. They are almost as important. If the enemy can't unload his supplies they'll be as useless to him as though we'd sunk them.' Stirling also instructed three men to target the wireless station two miles away on the other side of town: 'It's a splendid target. The idea of passing it up was worrying me, but we didn't have time for both jobs.'

Once on the surfaced road, the men made good time and arrived just outside Bouerat shortly after midnight. Stirling told them they had just under two hours to carry out the raid and make it back to the rendezvous. However, it was decided that three men attacking the wireless station would not have time to get there and back by 2am. Instead, Stirling arranged to return the next night and pick them up at a point on the track, marked by stones and twigs, eight miles from Bouerat.

The remaining men were divided by Stirling into two groups of six and seven each: he would lead one and the other would be led by Riley, and each would approach the harbour from opposite sides. Stirling issued a series of strict instructions: stealth was essential and no one was to use a gun unless absolutely necessary. They were to set all their explosions for 2.30am, which would give them plenty of time to get away and meet at their rendezvous point.

Stirling's group set off first, five minutes ahead of the second group. Advancing in single file, he and his men found themselves at the warehouses on the quay without being challenged. Stirling positioned look-outs, whilst the others placed their bombs. Moving from building to building, they set up their bombs on pumping machinery and vast stores of army food rations.

At one point, Stirling disappeared down an alleyway between buildings and then heard someone approaching. He pulled himself close to the wall and stood still as a figure turned the corner and a body pushed against him. 'What the hell . . .' said an English voice. It was Riley, and the rest of his party was with him, having finished planting their bombs. However, they had come up against a wire and could not find their way out and had decided to try this side of the harbour. Stirling said the two groups should make their way back independently, with his moving off first.

On their way back, as they kept close to the road, Stirling's group came across an enormous car park, with rows of giant petrol carriers, each able to hold some 4,000 gallons of fuel. It was impossible to resist, and soon they had deposited nine bombs in five minutes, using one-hour fuses so that these devices would also detonate at 2.30am. As Stirling adjusted the tenth bomb, he again felt a body beside him – and once again it was Riley's. For Riley and his men had spotted the same target and were also unable to resist it: their bombs had been placed further away from those of Stirling's men. The rendezvous point was reached at 1.45am, shortly after Riley had placed one bomb beside an enemy anti-aircraft gun emplacement and further bombs had been laid on some supply trucks.

As the men headed away in their LRDG escort, they heard explosions shortly after 2.35am and soon the sky in the distance turned a grey-pink. The operation, which only hours earlier had been in danger of turning into a shambles, had ended as a significant triumph: the harbour at Bouerat would be unusable for weeks and many petrol tankers, which were already in short supply, had been destroyed.

As dawn broke, enemy recce planes could be seen and heard scouring the desert for the raiders. The LRDG trucks were draped in camouflage nets and the men took cover as the search went on and on. However, some time after midday a sandstorm blew up, forcing the aircraft to give up the search. At 9pm, Stirling left with a small group of comrades to meet up, as arranged, with the three men who had targeted the wireless station. They all met and Stirling was told that the wireless station had been successfully destroyed and the RAF had bombed the harbour too. Stirling was reluctant to leave the area without a final parting 'gift', and they eventually came across an unguarded petrol carrier that was despatched using two bombs. Some fifteen minutes and eight miles further on, they heard a click and saw a piece of metal spinning in the air. It was a telemine but, fortunately, it had not exploded. Shadowy figures then emerged on both sides of the road and they realised that they were heading into an ambush. Although Stirling shouted at the driver to swerve off the track, he ignored the order and put his foot on the accelerator. The truck sped into a curtain of machine-gun bullets and several grenades exploded in mid-air but, miraculously, the SAS team emerged unscathed from their ordeal and raced off. 'Not even a ruddy tyre punctured,' said Reg Seekings, after inspecting the vehicle later that night.

It was for his courage during the Bouerat Raid that Riley was awarded the DCM on 26 November 1942. The recommendation for his award – originally for a Military Cross (MC) – read: 'This N.C.O. led a party on the first Bouerat raid Feb [*sic*] 1942. The party placed demolition charges on many heavy enemy transport vehicles and on various dumps. By skilled and daring leadership he succeeded in bluffing the enemy sentries. Thereby he avoided giving any alarm which would have interfered with the work of other parties operating in the same area. He has shown the greatest gallantry and the highest qualities of leadership in other raids at Slonta and Nofilia in March and April 1942.'

After the success of the Bouerat Raid, Stirling returned to Kabrit, where he had left the training of the new recruits in the hands of Paddy Mayne. However, Mayne had quickly tired of his new role and resented being away from the action. When Stirling saw that Mayne had effectively downed tools, the two men had an angry argument. However, Stirling also saw that it was pointless trying to turn a brilliant combatant into an administrator. Instead, Riley was put in charge of training, a role he embraced from the start, fathering and giving confidence to the young soldiers.

Despite this new role, Riley was still scheduled to take part in the next planned series of raids that were due to take place in March 1942. The aim was to target a string of airfields in the Benghazi area but, eventually, most attacks proved unsuccessful: for example, Riley and Lieutenant Dodds were unable to get to Slonta because of the heavy defences.

Whereas Riley was well liked by officers and men alike, Mayne had as many detractors as he did supporters. Mayne was terrifying in battle but, in drink, he could be terrifying off duty too. Indeed, some men lived in terror of his violent mood swings, but Riley was not one of them. In his book *The Regiment: The Real SAS*, Michael Asher wrote:

> Big Pat Riley, the Wisconsin-born ex-Coldstreamer, was perhaps the only SAS man who ever knocked Mayne down. He once found him drunk, beating someone so savagely it looked as if he might do him real harm. Without even thinking about it, Riley – who had been a champion boxer in the Guards, and had fought Reg Seekings in the ring before either had joined the Commandos – walloped Mayne with a massive fist and flattened him. 'I thought I was in for a rough time,' Riley said, 'but not a bit of it. He stood up, looked at me for a while and then quietly went off.'

In September 1942, Riley was heavily involved in the large-scale raid on Benghazi harbour. However, the enemy had been alerted and it proved almost impossible to penetrate the harbour. In the fierce fighting, the SAS lost 50 out of the 200 men involved.

After being promoted to regimental sergeant major (RSM), Riley was posted to Officer Cadet Training Unit (OCTU) in March 1943. He was commissioned into the Queen's Regiment the following month before returning to the SAS. By the beginning of 1943, with Stirling now a PoW and Jock Lewes dead, Paddy Mayne took command of the SAS. Riley, who had returned from the OCTU at the end of April, was appointed commander of 'C' Section, No. 1 Troop. According to Asher, No. 1 Troop was 'a repository of all the skills and experience the SAS had acquired since its inception' and was extremely highly regarded.

On 12 May 1943, the war in North Africa officially came to an end, and the Allies landed on Sicily a month later. Riley continued to serve with the Regiment during the Italian Campaign. On 10 July 1943, the SAS – now designated 1 Special Raiding Squadron (SRS) – destroyed a coastal battery at Capo Murro di Porco on Sicily's eastern coast. The following day the squadron took part in the first opposed daylight landing of the war – on the beach of Augusta. On 4 September, they landed at Bagnara on the Italian mainland, taking the town and securing a bridgehead in preparation for the landing of the main Allied force a few days later.

After these successes, the SRS took part in the Special Service Brigade raid on the coastal port of Termoli on 3 October. As part of a thousand-strong Commando raiding party, they carried the town, but during the day's fighting the squadron had one man killed, three wounded and twenty-three missing. Yet the SRS had taken out twenty-three enemy killed, seventeen wounded and thirty-nine captured.

However, the 16th Panzer Division were in the vicinity of Termoli and the enemy launched a formidable counter-attack on 5 October. The Allied forces were temporarily without tank support and had to hold out against the overwhelming German firepower. From first light, when half a dozen tanks had rumbled towards the Eighth Army's defensive ring north of the town, British units had been pulling back. Indeed, according to Asher, the infantry were so shell-shocked that the CO of 1 Special Service Brigade, John Durnford-Slater, had apparently threatened to have retreating British officers and men stood against a wall and shot. One of the few units to hold its ground, 40 (Royal Marine) Commando, had taken heavy casualties as a result of being hit by 88mm anti-tank shells.

In Termoli, Italian civilians had been given confidence from the force of the German attack and they started dropping grenades and taking pot-shots at British soldiers from their windows. Indeed, Durnford-Slater called the entire male population together in the piazza and promised mass executions unless these irritations ceased. However, at 1.30pm, an 88mm round hit Brigade HQ, killing a staff captain. Around this point, Mayne had been playing a game of billiards with Riley, Bill Fraser and Phil Gunn in an abandoned palazzo. Asher takes up the story: 'While panic reigned and shells were crumping into the streets outside the palazzo, Mayne chalked his cue with Francis Drake-like insouciance. "He just carried on with the game," Pat Riley recalled. "I thought to myself, 'Well, if you can do it, chum, I'll do it with you.' And we did. We finished the game, and then went outside to get things sorted."'

However, once they started fighting, Mayne took things very seriously and a ferocious battle for the town ensued. Riley, now a lieutenant, was hurrying back towards the palazzo with his batman when a spot close to him was struck by a 105mm shell that caused a massive explosion. 'The next thing I knew I was halfway down the street,' Riley recalled, 'lying on my back, laughing like hell. It must have been [the] shock.' In one strike, eighteen men had been killed or mortally wounded, the largest mortality from a single incident that the SAS had ever suffered.

In three days, 1 SRS had lost sixty-nine men, killed, wounded and missing: a third of the 207 who had come ashore. When casualties from the previous three operations in Italy were taken into account, the SRS was down some fifty per cent on its initial strength. However, in Termoli and on other occasions, the men had fought with astonishing courage and determination, filling Mayne with pride and, at the same, making the Army hierarchy fully aware that Mayne himself was a brilliant leader of men as well as a formidable combatant. The SAS had fought bravely, but their leader knew that they were not using traditional SAS tactics; they were simply fighting like any other troops, although rather better than most.

Termoli proved to be Riley's, and the SRS's, last action in Italy. He went to Scotland to help set up a camp at Mauchline, in east Ayrshire, before moving to its permanent camp nearby in Darvel. By this point the SAS had grown to the size of a brigade, with two British battalions, two Free French battalions and a Belgian squadron. When the SAS moved south to their new headquarters at Highland House in Chelmsford, Essex, Riley was in charge of recruiting and training. After the D-Day landings of 6 June 1944, mobility for the military was key. Riley, still based at Chelmsford, ensured that all the new jeeps were properly equipped for action behind the enemy lines. The SAS, now 2,500 strong under Brigadier Roddie McLeod, was to form a number of bases from which to harry enemy communications, and to work with the French Resistance, blowing up roads and railway lines and reporting to the RAF suitable areas to bomb. Although Stirling was not around to direct operations, the tactics they used were very much his favoured ones of inflicting damage, casualties and confusion. After the Armistice, two battalions of the SAS were airlifted to Norway, where Riley, based at Bergen on the west coast, assisted with the disarming of the occupying German forces.

In September 1945 the SAS was disbanded and Riley was released to Army Reserve in November of the same year. He moved back to Cambridgeshire and rejoined the police, serving as a police constable in March and Wisbech. Post-war life, however, proved to be too sedate for his liking and he volunteered for service as a captain with the Malayan Regiment, working closely with the newly formed Malayan Scouts in their actions against communist insurgence. In fact, the Malayan Scouts became 22 SAS in 1951. By now a major, Riley liaised and worked with the SAS in the persecution of the terrorists, more than 100 of whom were killed or captured.

In late 1955, and having just turned forty, Riley decided it was time to leave Malaya and he retired from the Army in July 1959. After military service, he purchased the Dolphin Hotel, essentially a pub, in Colchester, Essex, and ran this for a number of years before taking a managerial role with Securicor. By the time he retired in 1980, he was living in Hastings, East Sussex. Although slowed down by poor health, he continued to be a stalwart of organising regimental reunions. His wife, Kay, whom he had married in 1940 and with whom he had a son, died in 1996 and he never really got over her death.

Riley, one of the first and most remarkable men ever to serve in the SAS, died in Hastings on 9 February 1999, aged eighty-three. Even on the very last day of his life, he had been reminiscing about his wartime experiences – and quite rightly too.

CAPTAIN (LATER LIEUTENANT COLONEL) JOHN EDWARD HASELDEN
AWARDS: MILITARY CROSS (MC) AND BAR
GAZETTED: 12 FEBRUARY 1942 AND 18 FEBRUARY 1943

John Haselden was awarded the MC and Bar for his courageous work with the 'Libyan Taxi Service', the affectionate name given to early members of the Long Range Desert Group (LRDG) who were responsible for operating behind enemy lines in the North African desert. Because of his early upbringing in Egypt, Haselden understood the Arab mentality and forged excellent links with the tribes who lived behind the Axis lines. Although he was neither an early member of the SAS nor of the

LRDG, I feel the story of this wonderfully courageous man best fits in this opening chapter.

Haselden was born in Ramleh, near Alexandria, Egypt, on 10 August 1903 to a family with long connections to the area. His grandfather, Joseph Haselden, had moved to Egypt in 1863 and had married the eldest daughter of the British Consul in Alexandria; they went on to have nine children together. Haselden's father, Henry, married an Italian, Maria Ester Cazzani, in Milan in 1902. Haselden was educated at The King's School, Canterbury, Kent, but 'left early' – a euphemism for being expelled (apparently for striking up a teenage liaison with the daughter of a local greengrocer). He returned to Egypt, where, in 1922, his father died as the result of a hornet's sting to the back of his neck. In 1931, Haselden married Nadia Szymonski-Lubicz, of Polish and Italian descent, and the couple had a son, Gerald, who was born in Alexandria on 15 April 1932. After Nadia was killed in a car crash in Egypt in March 1936, Haselden arranged for their son, aged just four, to be sent to live with his wife's aunt in Oldham, Lancashire. Before the Second World War, Haselden worked for Anderson, Clayton & Company, the Houston-based US cotton house, and benefited from speaking fluent Arabic, French and Italian. However, after the outbreak of war in September 1939, he joined the British forces with the blessing of his employer.

After hostilities with Italy began, Haselden was originally posted to the Libyan Arab Force. However, on 15 July 1940 he was commissioned as a 2nd lieutenant in the Intelligence Corps, working with a branch of the General Staff Middle East, which dealt with raiding forces and prisoner-of-war rescues. Next, he became Western Desert Liaison Officer with the Eighth Army, where his job was to gather intelligence from the local Arab population. He spent much of his time behind enemy lines disguised as either an Arab or an Italian, and operating under the name of 'Hasel'.

By this point, he had established a formidable reputation

with the LRDG, which was usually responsible for dropping him behind enemy lines and retrieving him after his mission was completed. Bill Kennedy-Shaw, the intelligence officer with the LRDG, said: 'Haselden was the outstanding personality of the dozen odd men who worked with the tribes in Cyrenaica behind the Axis lines. Untiring, strong, courageous, never without some new scheme for outwitting the enemy, yet with a slow and easy-going way of setting about a job which was far more successful with the Arabs than the usual European insistence on precision and punctuality which they neither like nor understand.'

In late 1941, Haselden is understood to have parachuted out of a Wellington bomber and landed in the desert. He buried his parachute and, having dyed his skin a darker colour, he dressed as a Senussi tribesman and made his way on foot to Beda Littoria. It was in this town that General Erwin Rommel was rumoured to have his headquarters, and Haselden had been tasked with trying to confirm this. He spent several weeks watching a whitewashed building in the town that appeared to be a large German command post, while at the same time posing as a trader in ostrich feathers. Over the several weeks, he observed a large number of officers and despatch riders coming and going, along with several sightings of Rommel himself, who was protected by heavily armed guards. He radioed his findings to British Intelligence in Cairo.

However, it was for other courageous actions in October 1941 that he was awarded the MC. The once-confidential recommendation to his gallantry award, formally announced on 12 February 1942, stated:

Captain Haselden was landed from a submarine behind the enemy's lines on Oct. 10th 1941 to reconnoitre for a possible operation in conjunction with local Arabs. In order to decrease the risk to the boat crew, this officer swam ashore in the dark and, after reconnoitring, signalled that it was safe for the boat to come ashore. He remained in enemy territory until picked up by one of our patrols at a given rendezvous on 19 October (R-Patrol under Capt. Jake Easonsmith). During this period, in which he was in constant danger of being arrested and shot, he collected valuable information both regarding the local Arabs and the movement of enemy troops. The success of the reconnaissance was largely due to the high degree of courage, determination and clear-thinking possessed by this officer.

As a result of Haselden's earlier intelligence on Rommel, the British forces planned 'Operation Flipper', an attempt by a Commando raiding party to attack Rommel's supposed head-quarters in Beda Littoria. Haselden, along with three officers and two Arabs, was dropped by the LRDG in the Slonta area in order to carry out further reconnaissance for the raiding party. After walking nearly 100 miles through the heart of enemy territory, Haselden signalled the 'all clear' for two submarines and men led by Lieutenant Colonel Geoffrey Keyes to come ashore. However, bad weather and Rommel's absence from Beda Littoria conspired to turn the mission into a fiasco: one in which Keyes was awarded a posthumous VC after he and most of the raiders were killed or captured.

Haselden, however, was able to make his way through enemy territory to his appointed rendezvous with the LRDG, but not before successfully disrupting vital enemy communications. He escaped despite a fierce encounter between his LRDG patrol and Italian forces prior to him being collected. For this bravery, he was awarded a Bar to his MC, after his recommendation for a gallantry award from the Controller of the Special Operations Executive (SOE) concluded: 'I consider that Capt. Haselden's fearless action is worthy of the highest praise. Such success as was achieved in the operation was largely due to information which Capt. Haselden had gained during his reconnaissance. I cannot recommend too highly Capt. Haselden's outstanding endurance, his cool and calculated bravery, and his unswerving devotion to duty.' However, the Bar to his MC was not formally announced in the *London Gazette* until 18 February 1943.

In January and February 1942, Haselden had worked with a LRDG patrol and two Arabs to conduct a valuable Axis traffic census in Libya. For example, they reported that one in five Axis vehicles using the northern route was captured from the British and that most seemed in better condition than enemy vehicles. By August 1942, Haselden was preparing for another dangerous mission: the planning for the attack on the Libyan city of Tobruk that had been recaptured by Rommel in May of that year.

The aim of 'Operation Agreement' in September 1942 was to destroy oil-storage tanks, ammunition dumps and various enemy defences. Haselden was put in charge of the ground force (Force B) that was tasked with assisting a squadron from 1st SS (Special Service) Regiment. After entering the port, the force was to attack anti-aircraft and coastal defence batteries at the south-east end of Tobruk harbour, with the intention of creating a bridge for Force C. The approach march of 700 miles from Kufra went undetected and, after gaining entry to Tobruk, the immediate objectives were achieved.

However, then things started to go wrong: the eighteen motor torpedo boats (MTBs) carrying Force C lost touch with each other in the dark and few troops managed to make it ashore. Furthermore, Force A, mainly Royal Marines, embarked in two destroyers, also encountered major difficulties as a result of navigational and weather problems. This meant that all who landed from Force A were killed or captured and both destroyers were lost. Shortly before dawn on 14 September, Haselden succeeded in getting several wounded soldiers on to a truck and he jumped into a second one. Both vehicles headed down hill through the enemy in an attempt to get the wounded out of the area, before going on to try to capture enemy guns along the southern shore and then to attack the oil-storage tanks.

As the enemy closed, Haselden tried, along with some comrades, to hold them off so that the wounded could escape. He led a charge with five other men against the Italian forces, but was killed by a hand grenade. The date was 14 September 1942 and Haselden had died at the age of thirty-nine. Only six members of his ninety-strong raiding party that had left Cairo on 6 September made it back to British lines more than two weeks later.

Two decades after his death, a Norwegian officer wrote a treatise about Special Forces operating in the desert and devoted a two-page write-up to Haselden which he sent to Brigadier David Lloyd Owen, the one-time leader of the LRDG, who, in turn, forwarded it to the Haselden family. The unidentified Norwegian officer began his write-up: 'This officer was one of the most colourful personalities of the SF.' He described his early years in Egypt as living 'like a feudal lord, courteous and smiling, and with charm of manner. As many Englishmen abroad he was more British than most stay-at-home Britons. At the same time, he spoke Arabic fluently and could pass as an Arab even among the Arabs themselves.'

The Norwegian officer was rich in his praise for Haselden's wartime exploits, operating behind enemy lines in Cyrenaica: 'He was known to Arab tribes for hundreds of miles up the desert, and because of his old desert friendships could rely upon protection and hospitality even where it was dangerous for his host to extend it. Although there was a big reward for his betrayal, he was never given away. On one occasion he drove a flock of sheep across an enemy airfield, in order to examine the aircraft at close quarters.'

The Norwegian officer also said that Haselden was calm in the face of danger, and eager to pursue calculated risks. The officer concluded that the soldier had died charging a machine-gun nest single-handed. The write-up quoted an unnamed comrade: 'He seemed not to understand fear. It was as though it never occurred to him that things might go wrong, that in some way the enemy would detect him.'

In another tribute written long after Haselden's death, David Lloyd Owen said: 'He was a man many years older than myself and I admired him intensely. He had become a kind of legend to me for he had spent months with the Arabs in Gebel [usually spelt 'Jebel'] Akhdar where he lived as one of them. They, too, trusted him and loved him for he was sincere in all he did.'

LANCE SERGEANT (LATER REGIMENTAL SERGEANT MAJOR) ERNEST THOMAS LILLEY
AWARDS: MILITARY MEDAL (MM) AND BRITISH EMPIRE MEDAL (BEM)
GAZETTED: 26 NOVEMBER 1942 AND 1 JANUARY 1952

Ernest 'Bob' Lilley was one of the legendary 'Tobruk Four', whose tactics behind enemy lines were adopted by David Stirling when he formed 'L' Detachment of the Special Air Service Brigade. Lilley was awarded his MM for single-handedly strangling an Italian soldier who had tried to capture him after the raid on Berka aerodrome in May 1942. He went on to have a distinguished career in 21 Special Air Service Regiment, being awarded the BEM for his services in the aftermath of the war.

Lilley was born in Wolverhampton on 10 February 1914. He was twenty-five at the outbreak of the Second World War and, in September 1940, he enlisted in the Coldstream Guards. Later he served with 8 Commando before becoming a member of the legendary Tobruk Four. Along with Jim Blakeney, Pat Riley and 'Gentlemen Jim' Almonds – and under the leadership of Lieutenant Jock Lewes – the men caused mayhem to the enemy around the besieged Libyan city of Tobruk. Operating mainly at night and hiding out during daylight hours, the Tobruk Four reconnoitred enemy positions as well as making sporadic hit-and-run attacks.

It was on the basis of their formidable reputations that David Stirling brought Lilley and his three comrades into 'L'

Detachment in September 1941, the SAS founder describing them affectionately as 'pure gold dust'. In his book *Daggers Drawn: Real Heroes of the SAS & SBS*, Mike Morgan describes Lilley as 'one of the toughest original members of L Detachment'. In particular, Lilley was an expert in unarmed combat – a skill that he did not hesitate to use, if necessary. Moreover, his speed of thought was astonishing, as were his reactions and his determination to fight harder than any opponent he was likely to meet. Like his fellow Commandos, Lilley had been taught a variety of lethal martial arts, silent killing with the knife and various skills that were designed to get an SAS operative out of a tricky encounter. Because of their talents and keenness for battle, Lilley and his fellow 'SAS Original' NCOs from the Commando were among the first volunteers that Stirling recruited when he formed 'L' Detachment. Perhaps unsurprisingly, many of these men subsequently received gallantry decorations and soon became experienced veterans who helped to train new SAS recruits. While under the command of David Stirling and Paddy Mayne, Lilley was involved in numerous series of successful raids along the Axis-dominated coast of North Africa.

Lilley was present when Jock Lewes, the principal training officer for 'L' Detachment, was killed in action on New Year's Eve 1941 during a raid on Nofilia airfield, Libya. Lewes had been close to David Stirling, who later said, generously: 'Jock could far more genuinely claim to be the founder of the SAS than I.' In Virginia Cowles' book *The Phantom Major*, Lilley described the scene as their first bomb went off soon after they placed the second bomb on an enemy aircraft. As all hell broke loose, the SAS men retreated and were spotted by a low-flying Savoya aircraft: 'He circled over us and came in with all guns firing. We blazed away at him with everything we had, but our fire didn't seem to affect him. We abandoned the trucks and tried to find some cover. The pilot came gunning for us. He attacked twice. Jock Lewes was hit. We bandaged him with field dressings, but he died about five minutes later and we buried him in a grave about two feet deep.'

In May 1942, Lilley was forced to fight for his life after a mission. This was the incident for which he was awarded the MM on 24 November 1942, after a recommendation from Stirling, then a lieutenant colonel, that was marked: 'Most Secret – Not to be Published'. It read: 'Lance Sergeant Ernest Thomas Lilley, "L" Det S.A.S. Bde (Coldstream Guards). This NCO was cut off and captured by the enemy when returning from a raid on Berka Aerodrome, in May 1942. Although completely unarmed he subsequently managed to surprise and strangle his guard and to return by himself to the RV [rendezvous]. He has distinguished himself by great coolness and calmness in other raids.'

In his book *The Special Air Service*, Philip Warner also refers to this incident involving Lilley: 'Looking for a way back [from his mission], he wandered inside the perimeter of a large German camp. After a short time he realised that it would be impossible for him to slip unnoticed through the German lines so he stood up and walked for two miles. He was dirty and dusty and no one noticed he was not a German until he met an Italian outside the perimeter; the latter unwisely tried to arrest him but had his neck broken for his trouble.'

It was much later that Lilley described this incident in more detail. In Virginia Cowles' book *The Phantom Major* he is quoted as saying: 'I was near the road which ran parallel to the railway and suddenly I saw an Italian soldier coming along on a pushbike. He slowed up when he saw me, staring at me very hard. Then he got off his bike and came over to me leaving his rifle on the crossbar. He indicated to me that I was his prisoner and that I had to go back with him to Benghazi. This I had no intention of doing, so we got to wrestling. I got my hands round his throat and strangled him.'

There were numerous other dramas and on one night, after a hit-and-run bombing mission on Bernina airfield, Lilley eventually made his rendezvous with the Long Range Desert Group (LRDG). However, a group of men, including Stirling, 'Paddy' Mayne and Lilley, insisted on going back in a LRDG vehicle to assess how successful their bombing mission had been, only to be halted by a road-block where an enemy Non Commissioned Officer (NCO) held a grenade in one hand and a pistol in the other. The hidden British soldiers prepared for a shoot-out, only to be waved through. After attacking some more targets, the Britons withdrew, hotly pursued by the enemy in a high-speed chase. The SAS band lost their pursuers and made it to their *wadi* (dry gully), where they were hidden.

In his book *Daggers Drawn: Real Heroes of the SAS & SBS*, Mike Morgan describes how Lilley shouted a warning for everyone to jump out of the truck. This was prompted by the fact that, rather alarmingly, he had detected the distinctive smell and heard the click of acid starting to eat through one of their time pencils. Lilley was aware that, as they were still carrying upwards of 40lb of high explosive, this development demanded evasive action – and quickly. He and his men jumped out of the truck and raced away from it as fast as their legs would carry them. No sooner had they reached safety than the bomb detonated and their LRDG truck was totally destroyed. Without a vehicle, the men continued the journey back to their base on foot. However, before long they met some friendly Senussi Arabs who, in turn, sent a message to the LRDG. As Morgan noted, the raiders were collected by their LRDG comrades, who brought back 'the dishevelled SAS party, minus, unfortunately, their shiny LRDG truck'. Much later, Stirling recognised their achievements and their courage by ordering a vast round of drinks for his men in the bar at the famous Shepheard's Hotel in Cairo.

Lilley continued to serve with distinction throughout the war and was Mentioned in Despatches (MiD) – on the first of two occasions – on 13 January 1944 'in recognition of gallant and distinguished services in the Middle East'.

After the war he remained in the SAS and completed at least two operational tours of Malaya with his parent unit, before switching to the South Staffordshire Regiment. He was promoted to regimental sergeant major (RSM) in 1950 and was awarded the BEM on New Year's Day 1952, after his recommendation from Lieutenant Colonel Augustus Newman stated:

> RSM Lilley was appointed RSM of this unit in September 1950 and for some considerable time before his appointment was carrying out the duties of acting RSM under difficult circumstances in connection with his taking over the appointment. He weathered this period in an extremely resourceful manner.
>
> RSM Lilley has served with SAS troops since they were first formed in 1941. He has a very distinguished war record and was awarded the Military Medal for outstanding bravery in the field, by this outstanding example he has contributed to a very great extent to the reputation earned by SAS troops during the war.
>
> His name is legendary throughout the Regiment and since taking over as RSM of 21st SAS Regiment, his qualities of tact, understanding and unswervable loyalty combined with firmness, have been invaluable in a unit combining the SAS role with the previous traditions of the Artists Rifles and containing ranks representative not only of all corps of the Army but of other services and other countries and including a high proportion of ex officers.
>
> He has carried out the difficult job of RSM to a TA [Territorial Army] unit magnificently and continues to be an example to all ranks. I strongly recommend that he be awarded the BEM for his outstanding services to the Regiment.

Lilley, who was discharged from the Army in 1958 after seven years of service with newly created 21 Special Air Service Regiment, died in Folkestone, Kent, on 14 August 1981, aged sixty-seven. His funeral a week later was attended by Stirling and other 'Originals' from 'L' Detachment.

CORPORAL (LATER SERGEANT) HAROLD WHITE
AWARD: MILITARY MEDAL (MM)
GAZETTED: 26 NOVEMBER 1942

Harold White was a superb athlete who, after a successful career as a professional footballer, became a fine soldier, serving with 'L' Detachment, SAS, from September 1941. He displayed bravery time and again during the Second World War, being awarded the MM for an act of outstanding gallantry during a raid on an enemy airfield that resulted in a life-or-death shoot-out.

White was born in 1916 and grew up in the Black Country in the West Midlands. He dedicated the early part of his life to his passion for football, playing for both Wednesday Town and Darlaston before signing for West Bromwich Albion – then, as now, a professional team – as a full-back in 1938. According to the club's records, White was 'one of our full-time professional players prior to the war in 1939 and was a regular first team man'. However, his promising career as a sportsman was interrupted by the outbreak of war in September 1939.

White enlisted with the Royal Army Service Corps on 24 January 1940 and was originally part of Layforce, the British Commando unit commanded by Colonel Robert Laycock. He began his service with 'L' Detachment on 6 September 1941, the day after the legendary 'Gentleman Jim' Almonds, one of the 'Tobruk Four', arrived in Kabrit, Egypt. White took part in 'L' Detachment's first major raid as part of 'Operation Crusader' when, after appalling weather and other setbacks, just twenty-two of the fifty-five men (numbers vary in different accounts) reached the pick-up point agreed with the Long Range Desert Group (LRDG): five died and twenty-eight were taken prisoner (see the Byrne write-up, page 17, for more details). White had been part of a nine-man section led by 'Paddy' Mayne, which had held up remarkably well given the difficult scenario.

However, Mayne, White and the others were shocked and dejected by the outcome of the raid, and at losing so many comrades. Furthermore, they had been disappointed at their failure 'to get a good crack at the Hun'. After the failure of their mission, tactics were reassessed. 'L' Detachment realised for the first time that the LRDG was operating up to 400 miles into enemy territory and it was decided that it offered the SAS teams a better chance of getting in and out of the desert than parachuting into enemy-held areas.

From December 1941, raids by 'L' Detachment, operating from Jalo Oasis, proved far more successful as they targeted enemy airfields using adapted Lewes bombs as aircraft demolition charges. On 8 December Mayne led the first raid on Tamet airfield, with seven men, including White, destroying approximately twenty-five aircraft on the ground and several fuel dumps. Next, on 27 December, Mayne, with five men – again one of them was White – returned to Tamet airfield for a second raid. On this occasion, twenty-seven aircraft, three lorries and several fuel dumps were all destroyed. It was as a result of shooting his way out of a tight corner during this raid that White was later awarded the MM. His decoration, however, was not announced until nearly a year later, on 26 November 1942, after the once-confidential recommendation, signed personally by David Stirling, read: 'This NCO has taken part in five raids and has himself destroyed more than 20 aircraft. During the second raid on Tamet Aerodrome Dec 1941 this NCO carried on with his task while visible to the enemy and under heavy fire from automatic weapons. He succeeded eventually in shooting his way out from a position in which he was apparently hopelessly surrounded. It is requested that no details of these operations should be published owing to their secrecy.'

At some point, possibly during the second raid, White, then a corporal, was wounded: an article that appeared in the local newspaper, which mentioned he had written home to his parents to inform them that he was to be awarded the MM, noted that he was in hospital. However, the paper added that 'he is well on the way to recovery and he hopes to be back to duty soon'.

After recuperating from his wounds, White returned to 'L' Detachment, serving, in addition to North Africa, in Crete, Italy and France, often well behind enemy lines. He was involved in the landings on Sicily in July 1943, when the Allied forces captured two coastal gun positions and some 300 Italians at Capo Murro di Porco. This was followed by the capture of the town of Augusta a few days later. In September and October he and his comrades were again in action, once more in Italy, landing and attacking the coastal towns of Bagnara and Termoli; the latter involved three days of severe fighting, with the loss of twenty-nine men killed when a shell fell on a lorry carrying reserve men to the front line.

After action in Italy, White's unit returned to North Africa before moving to the UK for new training; the unit was sent to Darvel in Scotland to practise for missions in which they would be dropped behind enemy lines on the Continent, and then meet and lead the French Resistance against the Germans. One of these operations in which White, by now a sergeant, was involved was 'Operation Houndsworth': this took place in the Morvan Hills, west of Dijon, for three months from 5 June 1944. Houndsworth's patrols covered 6,000 square miles, cut twenty-two railways, killed or wounded 200 Germans, and reported thirty targets for Allied bombers.

Indeed, an extract from Derrick Harrison's book *These Men Are Dangerous* provides an insight into an episode involving White that occurred during Operation Houndsworth while they were trying to contact a Resistance leader who had some information for the SAS:

Just after eight in the morning they passed through the village of Lucy, and turned right along a secondary road. They had not gone more than a hundred yards when they came face to face with a German officer and a Sergeant. The officer, not realizing they were British, signalled them to halt. For answer Sergeant White gave them a burst with his guns. Suddenly, round a bend fifteen yards further on, they came on a truck-load of Germans halted at the side of the road. The Germans immediately opened fire. Returning their fire, the jeep swept past only to realize, too late, that they were passing a stationary German convoy of considerable size. It was too late to turn back. They decided to shoot their way out. They were now coming under heavy fire from the troops in the trucks and in the fields on either side of the road. Raking the trucks with fire, they raced on. Roy Bradford [one of White's comrades] had been wounded in the left arm and the mechanic killed. The situation was desperate but they could only carry on. They were passing the last truck of the convoy when a heavy burst of machine-gun fire hit the jeep, killing Roy and wounding Sergeant White and the maquisard [French Resistance fighter]. They managed to get out of sight of the convoy before the jeep packed in. Hearing the Germans running down the road the three survivors, two of them wounded, made a dash for the woods, where they threw off their pursuers.

White was discharged from the SAS on 16 November 1945, returning home hoping to resume his career as a professional footballer with West Bromwich Albion. However, the club noted: 'Unfortunately, injuries received in the services, prevented him playing regularly for us when he came back and eventually brought about his retirement from first class football . . . We believe but for these injuries, he would have been an International Footballer, of the top grade, he was certainly a regular first team man with us in professional football with very bright prospects to his future.'

White, who lived his later years in Great Barr, West Midlands, died in 1982, aged sixty-six. He left a widow, a daughter and a granddaughter. Shortly after his death, his widow, Ruby, successfully asked a local newspaper to publish a photograph of White and his teammates from the 1946 West Bromwich Albion team, asking if the picture brought back memories for anyone.

LIEUTENANT (LATER MAJOR) BERNARD BRUCE
AWARD: MILITARY CROSS (MC)
GAZETTED: 22 APRIL 1943

Bernard Bruce was a close friend of David Stirling, the founder of the SAS. He distinguished himself several times with his bravery during the Second World War and served in both the Royal Air Force Volunteer Reserve (RAFVR) and the Army, eventually receiving the MC for his courage while commanding a Long Range Desert Group (LRDG) patrol that carried out a lengthy recce behind enemy lines in North Africa.

The Honourable Bernard Bruce was born in Aberdour, Fife, on 12 June 1917, the son of the Earl of Elgin and Kincardine and his wife, Gertrude Bruce (*née* Sherbrooke). He was educated at Eton and New College, Oxford, before being taken on as an articled clerk with a firm of chartered accountants. Having gained his pilot's certificate with the Oxford University Air Squadron, he joined the RAFVR of Officers in 1937. After serving as a pilot officer, he transferred to the Supplementary Reserve of Officers, Scots Guards, the following year and was commissioned a 2nd lieutenant in this regiment on 23 February 1938. On the outbreak of war, he was posted to the 2nd Battalion, Scots Guards, in April 1940 and served in Egypt and Libya. In October 1941 he joined the headquarters of 13 Corps as GSO [General Staff Officer] III (Liaison) and later as GSO III (Air). However, he rejoined the 2nd Battalion, Scots Guards, in July 1942, and in September of the same year joined the headquarters of 30 Corps as aide-de-camp (ADC). He was Mentioned in Despatches (MiD) in the *London Gazette* of

15 December 1942: 'In recognition of gallant & distinguished services in the Middle East for the period November 1941 to April 1942.'

Two months before the announcement of his MiD – in October 1942 and when apparently eager for greater adventure – he had joined the LRDG and served as a patrol commander in Egypt, Libya, Tunisia and Algeria. More specifically, from late 1942 to early 1943, he commanded 'G' (Guards) Patrol, which included missions deep behind enemy lines.

A crucial part of Bruce's role was to write long, detailed reports on his findings during the recces so that the information could be used by Allied forces operating in North Africa at the time. These reports, highly confidential at the time, have been preserved and provide a fascinating insight into the vital part played by the LRDG during the war. Bruce had a natural talent for penning lengthy, but clear, reports, one of which was an account of a patrol that took place from Christmas Day 1942 until 23 January 1943. It came at a time when General Montgomery had started to turn his attention towards Tripoli and the best way of reaching the city and attacking the enemy. At a meeting with Lieutenant Colonel G. Prendergast, the Commanding Officer of the LRDG, Montgomery ordered that the whole force should be tasked with the reconnaissance of a little-known desert that lay inland from the main coastal road between Sirte and Tripoli. Montgomery wanted to piece together an image of the terrain so that he could plan his renowned left-hook movement on the enemy to attack it at a vulnerable flank.

The Italian maps of the area had proved to be inaccurate and so Prendergast set about the task of following Montgomery's orders, dividing the long coast into six parts. Each area was designated to a patrol: some embarked on their role immediately, others once they had finished the task that they were midway through. Bruce and his men fell into the latter category because he was in charge of a composite of G1 and G2 Patrols, which were taking part in the final Road Watch of the African Campaign. During this operation, Bruce had a meeting with Major Vladimir Peniakoff and his force, the Eighth Army's No. 1 Demolition Squadron, always known as 'Popski's Private Army'. At another point, 'G' Patrol had an uncomfortably close encounter with enemy armoured cars that gave chase but were eventually shaken off. After making it back through enemy territory, Bruce prepared a report that later helped considerably in Montgomery's advance on Tripoli and the successful capture of the city.

Subsequently, however, Bruce led one of the last LRDG patrols in North Africa, which covered a record distance for the area. In his book *Providence Their Guide: The Long Range Desert Group 1940–1945*, Major General David Lloyd Owen takes up the story:

Bruce had left Hon on 3 February [1943] to report on the going between the Shott Djerid [a large salt lake in southern Tunisia] in the north and the Grand Erg Oriental [area of sand dunes in the Sahara] in the south. He took some time to get to the area he had been given, because of the appalling ground and the greatly increased enemy activity, which all our Patrols were meeting at that time. They found the country very rough, and were continually badly struck. During one of these really bad moments, they were attacked by some Arabs, but their superior fire-power enabled them to get clear without casualties.

They moved on to the west, only to be attacked again that night, with two men wounded. Bernard pressed on again towards Tozeur in order to find help, and was quite ignorant of the fact that First Army had been forced to withdraw from the place the day before, when the Americans had been badly mauled by German counter-attacks.

But the French were helpful, and sent Bruce on his way westward, after he had stocked up with abandoned American fuel and rations. He was aiming for El Oued [in Algeria], some 120 miles away. Here there was help, and Bruce got the wounded flown to Touggourt [Algeria], where he then went to try to get spares for his vehicles. These were not available there, but were flown from Tripoli to First Army, and so Bruce went on to Constantine – 250 miles to the north – to collect them.

In order to avoid the trouble he had run into on the way he decided to return south of the Grand Erg via Fort Flatters and Ghadames [in Tunisia]. He reached Hon on 12 March, having covered altogether 3,500 miles. He had sent his report back by air from Constantine, and his information was just another part of all that was being poured in every day by the LRDG Patrols, operating on a carefully worked-out plan of Guy Prendergast.

Bruce's MC was announced on 22 April 1943, after his once-confidential recommendation stated:

Lieut. Bruce commanded a patrol of L.R.D.G. which carried out a recce of the area Bir Dufan-Bir Tala-Beni Ulid before it had been evacuated by the enemy. With a complete disregard of personal safety he spent seven days behind the enemy lines, during which time he collected a vast quantity of information which was of paramount importance to the comds [commanders] who planned the advance and to those leaders whose task it was to execute the resultant plans. During the actual advance Lieut. Bruce went forward with the advanced elements in order to be in a position from which he could amplify the information he had previously sent in. Lieut. Bruce's bravery was largely responsible for the speed with which this part of the advance was carried out.

With the war in North Africa over, Bruce attended the Staff College Course at Haifa, Palestine, in April 1943. In August of that year he joined HQ 78 Division and served as GSO III (Operations) in Sicily and Italy. In January 1944 he joined the (Tactical) HQ Eighth Army and served as GSO II (Operations) in Italy. He returned to Britain in December 1944, having been selected under the 'Python' scheme, whereby long-serving soldiers on overseas duty were granted home-service postings because the end of the war was in sight. Once back on home soil, Bruce rejoined the Training Battalion, Scots Guards.

Bruce was released from military service in 1946 with the honorary rank of major and became one of the founder members of the Long Range Desert Group Association. He married three times after the war, in 1958 (divorced 1968), 1970 (divorced 1976) and in 1976. Bruce died in 1983, aged sixty-six.

TEMPORARY CAPTAIN (LATER MAJOR) WILLIAM JOHN CUMPER
AWARD: MILITARY CROSS (MC)
GAZETTED: 14 OCTOBER 1943

Bill Cumper took part in scores of clandestine operations during the Second World War and was, in the words of SAS founder David Stirling, 'the best and most ingenious explosives man' serving with 'L' Detachment, Special Air Service Brigade. As an early member of 'L' Detachment, his bravery was matched by a relentless cheerfulness and he was renowned for eccentric behaviour and his witty, sometimes barbed, comments. Despite being in his forties when he was still carrying out raids, Cumper was always keen to be involved at the sharp end of the SAS's activities. Yet, on the eve of such operations, he could often be heard saying: 'Not for me, mate. I'm too old . . . What time do we start?'

Cumper was born in Hawick in the Scottish Borders and he enlisted in the Army as a boy soldier in January 1924. When the war broke out in September 1939, he was serving as a lance sergeant with No. 1 Field Squadron, Royal Engineers, and he was older than many of his comrades. In May 1941 Cumper was granted an emergency commission and was posted as a lieutenant to 143 Field Park Squadron. After working to ensure that his men were ready for combat, he sailed with them to the Western Desert to join the 7th Armoured Division.

On 30 December 1941, Cumper was Mentioned in Despatches (MiD) for distinguished service. He was described as a 'tall, erect 16-stone man . . . who asked no quarter and gave none to his men'. In May 1942 he was selected by David Stirling for 'L' Detachment as an explosives expert and wasted little time in seizing opportunities to deflate the egos of his fellow officers. On one occasion, Cumper walked into an ex-ranker's office for the first time, and saw the man was still wearing the rather ostentatious uniform insignia of his previous unit. He shouted, 'My God, look out, the Commandos are here!' before diving for his captured Luger and attempting to shoot one of the office lights. However, John Lodwick, a member of the SBS, recalled in his book *Raiders from the Sea* that Cumper could be verbally intimidating too. In a reference to David Stirling, he wrote: 'Naturally, he had the best Royal Engineer officer in the Middle East: Captain Bill Cumper, a regular soldier with the bite of a centipede. I know this to my cost. Once, much later, I stole some explosive from Cumper. He caught me.'

In his book *The Special Air Service*, Philip Warner tells an amusing story about Cumper:

In one raid on Benghazi Captain Cumper's jeep was knocked out and he leapt on to the one driven by Sergeant Bennet; his hold was not very secure and after a while he fell off. Bennet stopped the jeep and ran back. Cumper was lying in the middle of the road, head supported on arm, as if on a vicarage lawn. All around was an inferno of fire and explosion. As Bennet came up – to find Cumper unhurt – Cumper said: 'Now, look here, Bennet, if that's the way you treat your passengers I'm going to stay here and have a nice quiet read until you've learnt to drive properly.'

Cumper was awarded the MC on 14 October 1943 for an act

of great bravery during the famous Benghazi Raid in Libya the previous year. This was codenamed 'Operation Bigamy' (later also known as 'Operation Snowdrop') and coincided with raids on Tobruk and other enemy-held cities and towns. Cumper personally led members of 'L' Detachment to the gates of the enemy's position, having previously crawled around in the dark to investigate the mines and other hazards. As he unhitched the bar on the road-block, it swung upwards and he announced: 'Let battle commence.' Soon all hell had broken loose and Cumper retired to Stirling's jeep as heavy machine-gun and mortar fire went off around them. However, Cumper kept his calm and told Reg Seekings, another 'L' Detachment 'Original': 'If this is the bloody SAS, you can keep it, you crazy bastard.' However, despite the intensity of some of the fighting, all the raiding party made it home.

The recommendation for Cumper's award stated:

On 14 September 1942, the 1st S.A.S. Regiment raided Benghazi. From information received on the previous day it was believed that the Benghazi garrison had fortified their position by mines, wire and other entanglements. These obstructions to a night raiding party without artillery or tanks might have proved disastrous. Captain Cumper volunteered to lift the mines and clear a way through the entanglements and so lead the raiding party in. He picked a way which avoided mines and got the party to within thirty yards of the enemy's positions. He carried on and managed to open the gate which allowed the attacking force to get at the enemy. All through the operation, Captain Cumper's cheerfulness and bravery had a magnificent effect on the morale of the troops, and although faced with an extremely dangerous and difficult job, he showed no regard for his own safety.

Several books about the SAS mention Cumper in their pages. In his *Born of the Desert: With the SAS in North Africa*, Malcolm James (Pleydell) wrote: 'He would step in where angels feared to tread and carry it off each time . . . Bill came from the ranks: he knew it, rejoiced in it, and pushed it straight in front of your face to see how you would take it.' David Stirling, in Alan Hoe's authorised biography of the SAS founder, described Cumper as 'a very likeable and professional chap. He took on all the explosives training and improved our techniques tremendously. He also had the happy knack of getting on amazingly well with our new French contingent.'

In his memoir *Eastern Approaches*, Fitzroy Maclean, a former member of the SAS, was equally fulsome in his praise of Cumper:

> He knew all there was to be known about demolitions. He arrived straight from the desert in a fifteen-hundred weight truck full of high explosive. As he got out, I noticed that he was wearing a detonator behind his ear as if it were a cigarette. He had sandy-coloured hair and a jaunty appearance. His hat was worn well over one eye. He had a loud and penetrating voice. His pockets were bulging with explosive devices of one kind or another.
>
> Soon it became clear we had made a remarkable acquisition. In addition to his knowledge of explosives, Bill had a gift for repartee which pricked anything approaching pomposity as though with a pin. He was never bad-tempered and never at a loss . . . Soon the whole camp echoed with the crash and thud of exploding charges. When at the end of a fortnight he left us, our knowledge of the theory and practice of demolitions had increased out of all recognition and Bill had become an important part of our lives.

The pressure of continually operating deep behind enemy lines would have proved too much for many men, but Cumper kept his sense of humour throughout. When he went on the daunting six-jump parachute course attended by all would-be SAS officers, he cut up a pair of parachute wings into six pieces and, after each jump, entered the Mess with another small piece stitched on to his tunic. The arrival of the SAS's cap badge with the motto 'Who Dares Wins' was greeted by Cumper with the words: ''Oo cares 'oo wins.' On another occasion, David Stirling was haranguing officers about everything needing to be ready for a pending operation. Cumper had already answered in the affirmative to a string of equipment when Stirling asked when the moon would rise. 'Sorry, sir, I forgot to lay that on,' was Cumper's mocking apology.

Cumper joined HQ Raiding Forces in September 1943, serving with them for a year and taking part in thirty clandestine operations. His missions included a raid on the Greek island of Symi in July 1944. John Lodwick, a former SAS soldier, described how the explosives and canoe expert got to work after the German garrison had been seized. 'General demolitions were begun by Bill Cumper and installations as varied as 75mm gun emplacements, diesel fuel pumps and cable-heads, all received generous charges. Ammunition and explosive dumps provided fireworks to suit the occasion. In the harbour, nineteen German caiques [sailing vessels] some displacing as much as 150 tons, were sunk. At midnight the whole force sailed, the prisoners being crowded into two "Ems" barges . . .'

Cumper survived the war and was re-employed in the SAS between August 1945 and January 1946, before returning to regular duties with the Royal Engineers. He was released from military service in December 1948, with the honorary rank of major. He retired to Rhodesia, but died suddenly from a stroke in December 1954, leaving a widow and a son whose godfather was none other than David Stirling.

In Cumper's obituary in the *Regimental Gazette of the Special Air Service Association* of March 1955, it stated: 'He was insistent about his Corps, for this ex-boy regular was intensely proud of being a British soldier and, in particular, a sapper. He was intelligent rather than intellectual, simple in taste, almost spartan, shrewd and generous, and intensely fond and proud of his wife and family; no one knew him who didn't know them. Britain has lost a great patriot, the SAS a great leader, and we, a great friend.'

CORPORAL (LATER LIEUTENANT COLONEL) DAVID LAMBERT PAXTON DANGER
AWARDS: MILITARY MEDAL (MM) AND ORDER OF THE BRITISH EMPIRE (MBE)
GAZETTED: 29 MARCH 1945 AND 13 JUNE 1964

The appropriately named David Danger was awarded his MM for bravery as a corporal while serving with the SAS. Yet, as one of the 'SAS Originals', he went on to rise swiftly through the ranks so that he retired with the rank of lieutenant colonel. In 1968, fully twenty-three years after receiving his gallantry medal, he was awarded the MBE in recognition of his distinguished military career in general, and his work during the Cyprus emergency in particular.

David Lambert Paxton Danger was born in Heswall, Wirral, on 1 March 1923. He left school, aged sixteen, for an apprenticeship with a bank in Liverpool. However, in 1941, and having lied about his age, he volunteered for the Army and was accepted.

Danger served with the Royal Corps of Signals and was posted to Egypt, where he was recruited into 'L' Detachment, Special Air Service Brigade, the forerunner of the SAS Regiment. After training at Kabrit, near the Suez Canal, he served with the Special Raiding Squadron (as 1st SAS had briefly been renamed). Unlike other radio operators who served with 1st SAS between 1942 and 1945, who were usually attached, he underwent SAS training and became a full member of the Regiment.

In July 1943, Danger landed with the squadron at Augusta, Sicily, and subsequently took part in the assault on the Italian east-coast port of Termoli. In June 1944, then a corporal, he was dropped near Dijon as a member of the main reconnaissance party for 'Operation Houndsworth'. The mission's objective was to disrupt enemy lines of communication and prevent German units from moving up to Normandy to reinforce their offensive against the Allied bridgehead. Danger's team established base camps and ammunition dumps in the forest and was constantly being hunted by the enemy. Medical facilities were very basic and, in the early weeks, those who were badly wounded and could not be evacuated were operated upon on a kitchen table by a French surgeon.

According to an undated letter sent to Danger's father, he was parachuted into Occupied France shortly after D-Day. Headed from '1st SAS Regiment', it said simply: 'He was dropped into France on 10.6.44. and up to the time of writing was quite safe and well. You may take it for granted that he is safe unless you hear to the contrary from us. He will not be able to write to you for some time but will be able to receive your letters so please keep writing. Cheerio, keep smiling and don't worry.'

It was the legendary Lieutenant Colonel 'Paddy' Mayne who put forward Danger for the MM, when his once-confidential recommendation stated:

Corporal Danger parachuted into France in July 1944 as Signaller on an Advance recce team. On Aug 20 1944 German troops surrounded the area of his base camp while he was at Maquis [Resistance] camp about two miles away. Hearing that his own group was encircled, Corporal Danger made his way at great personal risk through the cordon of German Patrols to warn his comrades. His clear situation reports, and the energy he put into organising the defence of the camp was instrumental in foiling the German surprise attack. He then volunteered to return for more information, passing through the German Cordon twice more to accomplish his mission successfully. Throughout he showed high qualities of leadership and initiative, and a complete disregard of danger. It is also impossible to speak too highly of the way in which he kept communications with England during the four months he spent behind the enemy lines.

This recommendation was approved and his award formally

announced in the *London Gazette* on 29 March 1945. Earlier, at the end of August 1944, Danger had accompanied Mayne, the Commanding Officer of 1st SAS, to the Morvan area in central France to link up with other SAS groups. In May 1945 he accompanied the SAS Brigade sent to Norway to assist in taking the surrender of German forces there and in 1946–7 he served with the Parachute Regiment in Palestine. After leaving the Army, he worked for a printing and publishing firm before joining 10 Parachute Regiment, Territorial Army. In 1949 he married Beryl Morris, and they went on to have one son (who predeceased his father) and a daughter.

However, when still only twenty-eight and bored with civilian life, Danger returned to regular service and took a commission in the Royal Army Ordnance Corps. He served in the British Army of the Rhine (BAOR), Hong Kong and Cyprus. He was appointed MBE (Military) on 13 June 1964 and the next year was promoted to lieutenant colonel, aged forty-two. Danger left the Army in 1978, but served as a retired officer until finally retiring for good in 1986.

Danger died on 27 February 2009, aged eighty-five.

PRIVATE WILLIAM MORRIS
AWARD: MILITARY MEDAL (MM)
GAZETTED: 20 SEPTEMBER 1945

By any standards, Bill Morris had a remarkable war in his role as a founder member of 'L' Detachment, Special Air Service Brigade. He took part in the ill-fated raid on the enemy airfields of Gazala and Timimi, where he was wounded and captured. However, as a prisoner of war, he escaped and joined Italian and Yugoslav partisans fighting against the fascists, before eventually reaching the safety of Allied lines early in 1944.

Morris was born in Glencraig, Fife, and, during the 1930s, joined the Black Watch. After the outbreak of the Second

World War he served in Layforce Commando with the British Expeditionary Force (BEF) in 1940, including during the retreat to Dunkirk and then behind enemy lines following the evacuation. In the summer of 1941 Morris was selected to join the fledgling SAS. After undergoing training at Kabrit camp in Egypt – close to the Nile – he was chosen to take part in the SAS's first parachute operation. The aim had been for five groups of SAS men to drop by parachute and attack five enemy airfields in the Gazala and Timimi areas. Two nights later, the British planned to launch 'Operation Crusader', the military attack by the Eighth Army in North Africa.

The men were carried to their different jump-off sites by five Bombay aircraft on 16 November 1941. However, by the time of their jumps the weather had deteriorated and they were forced to leap from only 500 feet into gale-force winds. Both the men and their equipment were scattered over a large area and there were many casualties. Morris was wounded in the fighting and was one of those taken prisoner. As described earlier in this chapter (see pages 18–19 and 33–34), only twenty-two of the fifty-five men who took part in the raids made it back: David Stirling and some other men were picked up by the Long Range Desert Group (LRDG) and transported 250 miles out to their Siwa Oasis base in the Libyan desert. The experiences of the SAS men on the night of 16/17 November convinced Stirling to rethink his tactics and use the LRDG to take them to and from their missions, rather than having them parachute into an area. Subsequently 'L' Detachment was allowed to expand, recruiting further from Layforce Commando, which, by then, was in the process of being disbanded.

It was for his successful escape attempt and his fighting with the partisans that Morris was awarded the MM on 20 September 1945. His recommendation for the award detailed his activities after the ill-fated November 1941 raid:

Morris was captured near Tmimi [also spelt Timimi] on 14 [*sic* – 17] Nov 1941, and at the time of the Italian Armistice was imprisoned at Macerata (Camp 53).

Owing to a leg injury he was unable to leave the camp on 15 Sep 43 when the sentries deserted, and was therefore entrained for Germany. He and another P/W jumped from the truck near Ancoma on 21 Sep 43.

After staying at Potenza for two months they joined a band of patriots in the mountains; in addition to participating in actions against the Fascists they assisted in the distribution of grain from the store at Caldarola. On 13 Mar 44 Morris left with another paratrooper to try to cross the lines. They had abandoned this attempt and retraced their steps when they learnt of the spring offensive. They therefore proceeded south again and were recaptured 20 miles beyond Aquila.

When, after they had been imprisoned at Laterina for a few days, the whole camp was evacuated, Morris and four other P/W hid until everything was quiet and then climbed over the wire. Although his companions decided to hide until Allied forces reached the district, Morris proceeded alone and encountered British troops near Peruglia on 28 Jun 44.

Morris returned to the UK but saw no more service overseas. After the end of the war he was employed at the Glencraig colliery. He died in February 1993 and his obituary was published in the December 1993 edition of the SAS journal, *Mars & Minerva*. This short, but affectionate, tribute was submitted by his daughter, who wrote:

My father, I suppose, was rather a wild young Scot in the 1930s when he joined the Black Watch. His spirit plus his commando's experience (which included rearguard action at St Valerie during and after the Dunkirk evacuation) would have made him an ideal candidate and the demands of this newly formed group would have suited him well.

The operation in which he was lost was early on in the history of 1 SAS during an airborne raid in the desert, unfortunately due to weather conditions the airdrop did not go as planned, with tragic consequences, from the little he did say, they landed in a sandstorm, a few men managed to regroup and went on to do some damage to an airfield before capture. The next few years of his life were spent in escaping from prisoner of war camps throughout Italy. In his free time he worked with the Italian and Yugoslav partisans who named him Marco. It was during his final escape from Laterina that he managed to make his way alone back to allied lines.

Post-war years were kind to my father in as much as he enjoyed much better health than expected due to the deprivations he endured (shackle marks were still evident in his 70s if he exposed his ankles to the sun). He enjoyed his whisky, snooker and golf and was a member of St. Annes Old Links [Lancashire] for many years. His sense of devilry was still in evidence and [he] never appeared happier than when he would intentionally drop a volatile comment to his golfing pals that would leave them in a quandary whilst he chuckled into his whisky wondering what he could do next.

My father died in February, a release from his suffering.

SERGEANT JOHN MORRIS LOWENTHAL
AWARD: MILITARY MEDAL (MM)
GAZETTED: 13 DECEMBER 1945

Morris 'Tobruk' Lowenthal was awarded the MM after the end of the Second World War, having served with distinction behind enemy lines in three areas of fighting: the Western Desert, Albania and Yugoslavia. The recommendation for his gallantry award detailed his repeated courage during the final four years of the conflict.

Lowenthal was born in Penza, Russia, in August 1917 before his family moved to Southern Rhodesia in 1928. He was educated at Milton High School, Bulawayo, before joining the Gwanda Regiment (Territorial Force) in October 1936, while also working as a bookkeeper. After the outbreak of hostilities in September 1939, he was posted 'on commitment outside the Colony', enlisting in the 1st Battalion, Cheshire Regiment, at Mersa Matru, Egypt, in early 1940.

Lowenthal initially saw action in Egypt before serving with No 50 Commando ME [Middle East] in Crete until March 1941. However, the next month he returned to Egypt, where he was wounded in action. After a period of recuperation, he was selected for the Long Range Desert Group (LRDG). During the final months of 1941 he took part in no fewer than twelve patrols behind enemy lines and also completed a demanding parachute course at Kabrit, Egypt. During this phase of the war, 'L' Detachment SAS and the LRDG worked closely together. Although 'L' Detachment often received more of the glory than the LRDG, David Stirling, the founder of the SAS, was always quick to acknowledge the vital role played by its support group. Indeed, in a letter written from Stirling to Lowenthal, the officer said: 'The L.R.D.G. had a much larger than minute part in the forming and growth of the early S.A.S. I always state, when asked, that the L.R.D.G. and not the S.A.S. were "Masters of the Desert".' Stirling added that it was the LRDG that taught the SAS about the desert. He explained that the primary role of the LRDG was reconnaissance, but time and again it came to the rescue of 'L' Detachment, recovering its members after its work was done.

While taking part in operations in Albania and Yugoslavia in 1944 and 1945, Lowenthal served in a patrol commanded by Lieutenant Mike Reynolds, a fellow Rhodesian. After receiving intelligence from a Special Operations Executive (SOE) officer, Anthony Quayle – a famous actor who had operated behind enemy lines – the LRDG took part in an operation in Albania in June 1944. Their task was to observe a German coast-watching station that was being established near Valona. By then, the LRDG was commanded by Major General David Lloyd Owen, who once wrote: 'Danger has some sort of satanic appeal to me. I am drawn towards it in an octopus-like grip of fear.' On the morning of 29 June 1944, Lloyd Owen, Reynolds and thirty-three men, including Lowenthal, departed from Brindisi in an Italian MAS torpedo boat. Following a naval bombardment on their target, the LRDG team carried out a classic assault on the enemy's position amidst what Lloyd Owen later described as 'the patter of machine and tommy guns and a few small explosions'. The operation was an overwhelming success and the LRDG raiders returned to waiting destroyers with some useful prisoners. In fact, Reynolds and Lowenthal came back to observe the same enemy position the following month after German attempts to reinforce it. However, in the end, the enemy, fearing another attack, blew up their own watching station and abandoned the position.

In August 1944 Reynolds, Lowenthal and a small group of men landed at a partisan airstrip in Yugoslavia after poor weather prevented them parachuting into the area. On this occasion, he and his comrades were tasked with establishing a shipping watch in Istria between Fiume and Pola. It took them some time getting through German formations near Fiume and, when the enemy became aware of their presence, they actively hunted them down. On 29 September the LRDG team set up a watch on the east coast, but the Germans stepped up their search using a portable detection-finding station, hoping to pick up wireless transmissions. On one occasion, a German patrol got so close to finding them that the LRDG had to fight, ambushing the enemy and killing three of them. Soon afterwards they were ordered out of the area and they made it back to Italy on 17 October 1944 after a successful mission.

However, in February 1945 it was decided that the LRDG needed to resume their coastal-watching duties in Istria with the intention of calling in RAF and Royal Navy strikes at enemy shipping. Once again, Reynolds' patrol was chosen for the role and once again Lowenthal was an important member of the team. Reynolds split his men into sections and Lowenthal remained undiscovered in the area for two months, even though the enemy was billeted just a mile from his hide-out. Once more, the Germans knew the LRDG was present and they made regular searches of the countryside using dogs and setting the bush on fire, while fascist spies were another threat. In April 1945 Lowenthal was eventually picked up in a motor torpedo boat (MTB) after his transmissions had led to many enemy ships being attacked and destroyed.

Lowenthal's overdue gallantry award came with the announcement of his MM on 13 December 1945. The earlier confidential recommendation for the award had stated:

Sergeant Lowenthal joined the Long Range Desert Group in the Desert in 1941 and took part in twelve patrols behind enemy lines in Libya. In June 1944 he was a member of a patrol which carried out a successful attack on an enemy Observation Post in Albania, where his leadership and coolness in this action were outstanding. In August 1944 he dropped by parachute with four men to join another Long Range Desert Group patrol in Yugoslavia and despite a damaged ankle walked over 100 miles before he was evacuated. In February 1945 he was landed by sea on the coast of Istria where his patrol was split into two sections to observe shipping movements. He commanded one section and maintained a watch each day for nearly two months from a point where the enemy were billeted only a mile away. Throughout all these operations Sergeant Lowenthal has shown great courage, enthusiasm, and coolness under fire, and his leadership and ability have set a fine example to all ranks working with him.

Lowenthal was demobbed in late 1945 after the end of the war and was invited to join the Rhodesian contingent at the Victory Parade in London. He then returned to Rhodesia, where he settled in Selukwe (in modern-day Zimbabwe this is known as Shurugwi). Lowenthal received his MM at an investiture held by George VI at Government House in Salisbury in April 1947. In Rhodesia, he pursued a career as a cattle rancher, and he also ran his own butchery, invested in various businesses and played the Stock Market conservatively throughout his life. On 18 March 1956 he married Ethel Bernstein and the couple went on to have one daughter, Jenny. Lowenthal retired from ranching and butchery in 1969, but he remained busy, serving on various committees over the next decade. These included the town council and the Rhodesian Farmers Union (on both of which he served as chairman for several years), the Rhodesian Railways Board, the State Lottery Board of Trustees, the National Censorship Board and five national industrial boards. Furthermore, he played an active role in local sporting bodies and charities. In 1974 he successfully stood as a candidate for the Rhodesian Front, of which he was a founder member, in the Midlands constituency. After being elected to parliament in July of that year, he served under Prime Minister Ian Smith. Lowenthal was re-elected in 1977 and served until 1980, when he retired from politics. After that, he remained active, playing bowls and bridge and maintaining his portfolio of shares. In 2002 he followed his daughter Jenny Joffe and her family to Australia. However, like his late wife, Ethel, who died in 2011, Lowenthal suffered from dementia for the final years of his long life. He died in Sydney, Australia, on 30 March 2013, aged ninety-five.

In the summer of 2014, I contacted Jenny Joffe at her home in Australia with the help of the Rhodesian Services Association. She kindly gave me information on her father's life after the Army and she said of him: 'He was a very special and loving person. He lived for, first and foremost his wife, Ethel, myself, my husband, Ian, and, most of all, for his grandchildren, Jessica, Melissa and Greg. He was always the life and soul of the party, and he gave generously both of himself and financially to what he believed in. He was at his happiest when relating stories of his Army days to anyone that would listen. Strangely enough, even when his mind started to fail him, he still remembered his Army days vividly.'

Left: The SAS badge, with 'Who Dares Wins' motto, as worn by members of 'the Regiment'. The SAS was founded in July 1941 with the formation of 'L' Detachment, Special Air Service Brigade.

Right: Lieutenant-Colonel Robert Blair 'Paddy' Mayne is photographed in the desert near Kabrit, Egypt, in 1942. Mayne, a tough Irishman, became one of 'the Regiment's' legendary figures, taking command of 1 SAS in 1943.

IWM (MH24415)

TOPHAM PICTUREPOINT

:utenant-Colonel (later Colonel) David Stirling (standing), the founder of the SAS, talks fellow members of the SAS in North Africa in 1943. Stirling was captured in early 1943 d, although he escaped, he was later recaptured and spent the rest of the war as a W, latterly in Colditz.

Sergeant (later Major) Pat Riley (centre), a formidable boxer, was one of the founding fathers of 'L' Detachment, SAS Brigade. He was awarded the DCM for his courage during the Bouerat Raid of 1942 in North Africa.

Below left: Captain Richard Carr, 11 Commando, who was awarded the MC for bravery during the retreat to Dunkirk in 1940. After being captured, he was held as a PoW and was later awarded the MBE for his relentless attempts to escape.

Below: Corporal (later Sergeant) Jack Byrne was left for dead during the evacuation from Dunkirk in 1940. He was later captured and held as a PoW. He was awarded the DCM for his successful escape and served with the Commandos during the D-Day landings.

jor Bernard Bruce, a friend
SAS founder Colonel David
rling. In 1943, and while serving
a lieutenant, Bruce had been
arded the MC for his gallantry
leading a Long Range Desert
oup (LRDG) patrol behind
emy lines in North Africa.

low: Captain (later Major) Bill
mper took part in scores of the
rly SAS raids in North Africa. A
nowned wit, he was awarded
e MC for bravery during the
nghazi Raid of 1942 in Libya.

low right: Captain (later
eutenant-Colonel) John
selden was awarded the MC
d Bar for his courageous work
th the Long Range Desert
oup (LRDG), who were
sponsible for operating behind
emy lines in the North African
sert.

THE LIBERATION OF NORWAY · 8th MAY 1945

THE PEOPLE OF

2660913 - WO II E. T. Lilley M.C.

OF THE BRITISH ARMED FORCES

FOR YOUR VALUABLE SE

HELPING TO RESTORE

2660913 SSM Lilley
'B' Sqn. 22 SAS. Ω
c/o G.P.O. Kuala Lu
Malaya.

OLD COMRADES ASSOCIATION
of
THE ARMY COMMANDOS

Regular Army

Certificate of Service

By the KING'S Order the name of
Sergeant (Acting Company Quarter Master Sergeant) E.T. Lilley, M.M.,
Coldstream Guards,
was published in the London Gazette on
13 January, 1944,
as mentioned in a Despatch for distinguished service.
I am charged to record
His Majesty's high appreciation.

Secretary of State for War

1st S.A.S. Regt

This is to certify that
2660913 S.S.M. Lilley E.
served in the 1st Special Air Service
Regiment
from 4.9.41. to 16.11.45
during the following Campaigns:-
Western Desert, Italy,
N.W. Europe.
He was awarded:-
Military Medal 1939/45 Star Africa Star
with 8th Army Clasp. Italy Star. France
& Germany Star. Mentioned in Despatches.

Date 16.11.45   Lieut Colt. Comd.
1st S.A.S. Regt.

Above: The medal group and memorabilia belonging to Lance Sergeant (later Regimental Sergeant Major) Bob Lilley, who was one of the founding fathers of 'L' Detachment, SAS Brigade, and a formidable character.

Left: Lance Sergeant (later Regimental Sergeant Major) Bob Lilley is photographed in the Western Desert where he served with the SAS. He was awarded his MM for bravery during a raid in North Africa May 1942 and, later, received the BEM.

THE ASHCROFT COLLECTION

3

OTHER SECOND WORLD WAR
SAS HEROES

The SAS War Diary 1941–1945 *tells how David Stirling and Robert Blair 'Paddy' Mayne pursued their raids with 'L' Detachment, Special Air Service Brigade, from November 1941 until the beginning of 1943 when, by then 700-strong, it was formed into the 1st SAS Regiment. The Regiment then consisted of four squadrons that operated in a similar way to 'L' Detachment; for example, striking at Axis aerodromes hundreds of miles behind enemy lines. 'Some months later the Regiment underwent a further change when it was split in two, one half being commanded by Mayne (Stirling having been captured) operated as the S.R.S. [Special Raiding Squadron] while the other half under Major Lord Jellicoe was formed into the Special Boat Squadron,' the diary says.*

Under Mayne, the Regiment enjoyed great success, first in attacking deep behind enemy lines and, later, when given the formidable task of assaulting the shores of Italy ahead of the main Army. Soon afterwards, there were further successes on Italian soil. By the New Year of 1944 there were active plans for an invasion of Continental Europe. With the battle for North Africa won, members of the SRS docked in Scotland on 4 January 1944 and were given a month's leave – the first proper break in years for the founding fathers of the SAS.

However, once again the make-up of the Regiment changed: there was an increase in the number of officers, sergeants and troopers, and it grew from four squadrons to five, with Colonel Paddy Mayne in command. While based at Darvel, Ayrshire, SAS members underwent three months of rigorous training that stood them in good stead for their operations in the final two years of the war. There was then something of a lull until the preparations for the D-Day landings of 6 June 1944 got under way.

The SAS War Diary 1941–1945 *largely concentrates on the activities of 1 SAS, rather than 2 SAS. After the capture of David Stirling in January 1943, his brother Bill (2 SAS) and 'Paddy' Mayne (1 SAS) took over command of the Regiment, which continued to succeed with its hit-and-run tactics.*

The SAS War Diary 1941–1945 *says: 'At the beginning of June [1944] the Regiment moved down to Fairford in Gloucestershire where it was placed behind barbed-wire and in the centre of the 38 Group R.A.F. airfields and it was from this barbed-wire camp that the 1st S.A.S. Regiment was infiltrated by parachute into France.' The Regiment's role in this phase of the war, following the D-Day landings of 6 June 1944, was highly successful. Once the operations in France were completed, 'C' Squadron moved up into Belgium and northern France. However, at this point there was a lull in SAS operations until the Allies advanced into Germany in February 1945.*

Once again, the SAS War Diary 1941–1945 *takes up the story:*

Two Squadrons under Colonel Mayne operated with the Canadian Army and two Squadrons under Major Poat with the 7th Armoured Div. The Regiment fought in Germany until the cease fire was sounded on May 7th, and it was withdrawn to Poperinge about 6 miles from Ypres where it consolidated and returned to England by ship.

Although Germany was defeated there came yet another task for the S.A.S., namely that of helping to disarm and control 300,000 Germans in Norway. Consequently on May 15th, within a week of arrival in England, the Regiment, transported in Stirling aircraft, arrived at Stavanger airfield. It travelled overnight to Kristiansand which was the centre of its area of policing. However, the Regiment was destined to make yet another move, for on May 28th it moved North West by ship to Bergen where it undertook a larger and more *difficult policing area. The Regiment while in Norway formed an independent part of the 1st British Airborne Division.*

The SAS returned to Britain in August 1945. Meanwhile, David Stirling had arrived back in London in April of that year, having been held as a prisoner of war for twenty-seven months, latterly in Colditz. He discussed with Winston Churchill his plan to take the SAS to war in Japan, but the Second World War drew to a close before he could implement it.

On top of the Regiment's founding fathers, there were many courageous men from the SAS and the Long Range Desert Group (LRDG) who played a significant and daring role behind enemy lines from 1941 to 1945. This chapter concentrates on some of these heroic characters.

CAPTAIN (LATER MAJOR) RICHARD JELLICORSE HOLLAND
AWARD: MILITARY CROSS (MC)
GAZETTED: 22 OCTOBER 1940

Richard Holland was decorated by the British military for repeated courage prior to the Dunkirk evacuations in 1940. However, after joining the SAS, he took part in daring missions behind enemy lines in the Netherlands in the spring of 1944 and in France shortly after the Normandy landings of June 1944. For this gallantry, Holland received the rare distinction of being decorated by both the Dutch and French governments.

Holland was born in Peterchurch, Herefordshire, on 4 June 1910. He was commissioned into the Royal Artillery as a 2nd lieutenant on 28 August 1930. In 1937 he was posted to the Anti-Aircraft Brigade before being promoted to captain the following year. On 14 September 1939 Holland embarked with the British Expeditionary Force (BEF) for France, serving with 6/2nd Anti-Aircraft Regiment. He fought courageously during the defence of Calais from 22 May to 26 May 1940, which preceded 'Operation Dynamo', the evacuation of the BEF through Dunkirk from 27 May to 4 June. Holland strove tenaciously to bring all his wounded men back successfully to Dover, via Calais, during the German *Blitzkrieg* that overran northern France.

It was for this bravery that Holland was awarded the MC on 22 October 1940, after the once-confidential recommendation for a gallantry award stated: 'Although the gun position was being shelled and bombed on and off all day on 23rd May, and was also under rifle and L.A. [Light Artillery] fire, Captain Holland showed coolness, and after dark succeeded in getting away all the wounded and some others to Calais. After getting to Dover he made two trips back in boats lent by the navy, his object being to try and get in the gun position as he was not certain that a R.D.F. [Radio Detection Finding] transmitter had been successfully destroyed.'

Holland served in Iceland before being posted on 21 March 1944 to 2 SAS Regiment under Bill Stirling, the brother of SAS founder David Stirling. He undertook training in Scotland in March 1944 and, in May 1944, the SAS received plans outlining the use of their troops in the Normandy landings. The training was to enable small SAS units to penetrate deep into France where they could link up with the Maquis, the French Resistance, and set up bases for larger groups. The men were also taught how to drop in jeeps and other supplies to enable enemy communications to be attacked over a wider area in conjunction with the D-Day landings.

In August 1944, Holland took part in 'Operation Trueform', involving 1 and 2 SAS Regiments being dropped behind enemy lines to harass the German forces and destroy their supplies. Holland was appointed to command Trueform 1, a troop of ten men from 2 SAS that was dropped into France by parachute on the night of 16/17 August. The men were designated to operate in the area north of Neubourg and were tasked with targeting German petrol supplies for their retreating motor transport, general harassment and wireless reporting on the general situation.

Shortly after arriving behind enemy lines, Holland successfully made contact with the leader of the local Resistance and they quickly assessed the most suitable locations for ambushes. On 19 August his unit captured four Germans and then a further sixteen SS soldiers, including an officer. However, later that day a firefight took place in which one of the men in the unit, Private Bintley, was killed. The following day was spent observing Tiger Tank movements and tyre busters were laid on the road, which were later heard to go off. On 21 August a truck at the front of the convoy was blown up and then shot at, while three days later Holland's unit met up with Canadian and American columns. On 28 August Holland and his team returned to Britain for a debrief, having, as well as taken prisoners and attacked marching infantry, accounted for at least four Germans killed, and four trucks and two light cars destroyed.

The *SAS War Diary 1941–1945* reveals that, on his return from Operation Trueform, Holland drew up a report on the mission that he concluded with 'General Remarks'. His assessment of both the German Army and the French Resistance was scathing, and even his SAS men came in for criticism. 'Enemy. Morale poor but no panic. Very frightened of terrorists, but not many rumours of parachutists. Like to give themselves up to the British. They seemed to have no information. Their rations were very short and they were living on the country. Their M.T. [Motor Transport] was in appalling condition and petrol was very scarce, as proved by the fact that so many trucks were in tow.' He wrote of the local Resistance: 'The French were very friendly but windy in action. They were mostly youths who had avoided service in Germany. The old sweats were good but too old and unarmed. They were generally very glad to see us. Their discipline and knowledge of arms was very poor. One, for example, shot another through carelessness.' His final remarks were on the SAS, of which he wrote: 'A severe handicap if troops have no previous battle experience owing to difficulty of contacting nervous people in the dark . . . Nuisance value. To some extent achieved, but more could have been done with an experienced stick. The conditions were ideal for S.A.S. operations.'

In April 1945, Holland took part in 'Operation Keystone' as part of an SAS patrol consisting of several jeep-mounted and airborne teams that operated in German-held territory in the central Netherlands. On his return from operations, he prepared an eight-page report on his and his men's activities from 11 April to 19 April. For the night of 11/12 April, when he and his men were parachuted into enemy-held territory, Holland wrote of an apparent meet-up with another Allied force:

> The DZ [Drop Zone] at Z 518038 was marked with white lights but as the pilot had been briefed to look for a system of coloured lights, which was the method adopted by S.F. [Special Forces], there was a slight hesitation while the pilot asked me whether I wished to jump. We dropped at 00.15 hrs, a little wide of the DZ. Four kitbag ropes broke on the way down, including my own (I suggest stouter ropes be used in future). Otherwise the drop was successful and the reception was good. We were taken to a barn at Z 519040 where we laid up for the night.

The next day Holland met up with local Resistance groups and the next night he sent three parties to carry out reconnaissance duties. On the night of 13 April he and a small group of men were involved in a small firefight with German soldiers and two other parties laid charges beside railway lines. Other regular night and day patrols followed and the SAS had one man killed, apparently because of an exchange of fire with a Dutch Resistance group that they had not realised was in the area. Holland's entry for 16 April read:

I led the whole party in daylight to a fork road at Z 483034 as Germans were reputed to be in that vicinity. We surprised and captured 8 Germans who were sitting alongside trucks in a farmyard having lunch, and about 30 others in a neighbouring farm were put to flight. I kept one of the prisoners to help us start the trucks while the other seven were marched back to our base. Unfortunately, Pct. [Parachutist] Hawe and the escort which was taking the prisoners back to base encountered a German patrol and to avoid being captured had to leave the prisoners. Nevertheless we had achieved our object of causing a disturbance to the enemy and we retired with one prisoner to the barn at Z 505054.

That night Holland and his men were involved in yet another firefight with the Germans.

His entry for 17 April stated:

I did not intend operating that night until midnight, but at 23.00 hrs we were shelled. Pct. Edwards who was on sentry duty was killed by the first shell. Our position was good and had adequate cover nearby so I decided to remain as I thought it was to be only temporary harassing fire. However, the shelling continued to be consistently near and Lieut. Wardley evacuated his stick into the woods. The map indicates the barn on the wrong side of the road and the majority of the shells fell 20 yards East where the barn was marked on the map.

During the night's fighting, a Resistance fighter was also injured and needed medical treatment.

The eight-day SAS mission ended on 19 April when Holland and his men contacted the Canadians at Barneveld. After moving on to Nijmegen and, later, Brussels, the SAS team flew back to Croydon aerodrome, south London, on 24 April after an eventful and successful mission.

It was for his courage behind enemy lines in 1944 and 1945 that Holland was decorated by two foreign governments. The

Netherlands awarded him the Bronze Lion, Officer Grade – one of only two such awards to the SAS during the war – on 7 March 1951, when his citation stated: 'As a member of the S.A.S. he distinguished himself by performing particularly courageous and tactful deeds during the battle for the liberation of the Netherlands occupied territory. In every respect setting an outstanding example in difficult circumstances.'

France awarded Holland the Croix de Guerre with Silver Star – one of only a small number of such awards to the SAS for the war – and the citation stated: 'This officer, having parachuted with a detachment of 11 men on a mission of harassment and destruction of the enemy in retreat, completed his mission despite the difficulties created by the continuous movement of enemy on the roads of the region. On 21 September 1944, with the help of three men, [he] succeeded during an ambush, to delay an important enemy convoy by 3 hours. In an extremely wide area he successfully created total insecurity for the enemy.'

Holland survived the war and, after the conflict ended, served in the Middle East. He retired in the rank of major on 28 August 1958 after exactly twenty years' military service. He died in Chichester, West Sussex, in 1977.

LANCE CORPORAL STANLEY BOLDEN
AWARD: MILITARY MEDAL (MM)
GAZETTED: 25 MARCH 1943

Stanley Bolden was born in Giffnock, Renfrewshire, Scotland, in 1920. The son of a Scottish couple, Thomas and Annie, he was brought up in Renfrewshire before joining the Cameron Highlanders, though his parent unit was the Army Air Corps. Some time after the start of the Second World War he was given an opportunity to serve with the Special Service Brigade, where he distinguished himself with his dedication and his courage.

Bolden was awarded his MM for courage during 'Operation

Cartoon', an attack on enemy forces in Norway. The once-confidential recommendation for a gallantry award was signed by 'R Laycock', the commander of the Special Service Brigade, who wrote: 'L/Cpl. Bolden was with the detachment of the Special Service Brigade which landed at Sagvaag Norway on the night 23rd/24th January, 1943. Before the actual landing took place, L/Cpl. Bolden was wounded in the side, but although in pain, he continued and carried out his duties ably and well. He personally led a party which cut the communications and was later in charge of a road block party on the Sagvaag/Fitjar road. Throughout the operation he showed that good leadership and determination upon which a small raid of this nature depends for its success.' Bolden's MM was announced on 25 March 1943.

Later in the conflict, Bolden served with 2 SAS Regiment, again distinguishing himself. Along with his comrades, he was dropped by Dakota aircraft behind enemy lines in the winter of 1944–5 in order to operate in the Tombola Valley region of Italy. By the early spring of 1945 the SAS party was keen to make a meaningful attack on the enemy. In his book *Winged Dagger*, Major Roy Farran, who was in charge of the SAS party, described how he had approaching 100 men at his disposal: 'They were a motley crowd of ruffians. In all there were thirty Russians, forty mixed Italians and twenty-four British.' Using air photographs from the partisans in Florence, Farran planned a hit-and-run strike on the headquarters of the 51st Army Korps based near Albinea. The attack, as part of 'Operation Tombola', was planned for the night of 26/27 March 1945. Farran recalled: 'Each sentence was translated first into Italian and then into Russian. We would infiltrate through the enemy positions as soon as it became dark, marching quietly in three tightly-packed columns led by me with two local guides and two British scouts . . . We would march all night until we reached our lying-up position in a farm called Casa del Lupo, ten miles from the objective. If we encountered any opposition during the march, everybody would lie still in their tracks until orders were received from the front. On no account would fire be returned unless ordered.'

In fact, the 'objective' was the German headquarters, spread over two villas each guarded by four sentries and a total of six machine-gun positions. One of the buildings was the Chief of Staff's villa, with an operations room, while the other was the residence of the corps commander. By nightfall the raiding party was in position, having avoided German patrols and a minefield. Farran takes up the story:

> The firing started first at Villa Calvi. A tremendous burst, which must have been a whole Bren magazine, was fired by someone. Tracer bullets began to fly in all directions. Although we had reason to congratulate ourselves on getting a hundred men to the target unobserved, the Germans were by no means asleep. Spandaus were soon spraying the whole area from the south. I thought at first that the Russians were firing in the wrong direction, but it was not long before I realised that at least seven German machine-guns were awake. I told Kirkpatrick [a comrade] to strike up 'Highland Laddie,' just to let the Germans know that they had the British to contend with. He had only played a few bars when the phut-phut of a Spandau picked us out. I pushed him into a slit trench and he continued to play from his cramped position.

The raiders were firing from the villa's lawn up through the top windows and several Germans were killed by bazooka and Tommy-gun fire. They had given themselves twenty minutes to take over the whole house, but realised this would not be possible. They therefore piled up furniture and other belongings in the ground-floor operations room and ignited the pyre with petrol and explosives. The wounded were carried to safety first, and the Germans held back by further fire until soon the whole villa was ablaze.

However, the attack on the second building, Villa Rossi, had not gone so well, because one of the raiders had opened fire too soon. Four sentries were killed by Tommy-gun fire and at least seven more Germans were also shot dead. Yet the raiders received casualties too, with three SAS men, including Bolden, being killed and others wounded. As the Allied casualties were removed from the building, a fire was started in the kitchen of the villa. Farran wrote: 'Rossi was beginning to burn and Villa Calvi was like an inferno. I pointed my pistol at the sky and fired a red Verey light – the signal to withdraw. There was little hope of collecting the whole party, so we moved off in twos and threes on the line of retreat due west to the River Crostollo. Somehow, the various companies collected together on the far side of the river.' Other than the three British dead, the raiders had only lost six Russians, all of whom had been captured. However, the raiders had to trek for twenty-two hours before they reached safety, where Farran slept for fully fourteen hours.

Bolden had died aged just twenty-four. He left a widow, Audrey, who lived in Havant, Hampshire. There is a memorial in honour of this decorated soldier in the Milan War Cemetery in Italy.

LANCE CORPORAL (LATER LANCE SERGEANT) CHARLES DALZIEL
AWARD: MILITARY MEDAL (MM)
GAZETTED: 21 OCTOBER 1943

By the end of 1942, Winston Churchill, the prime minister, had been totally won over to the merits of using Special Forces. So much so, in fact, that he asked the then Commanding Officer of the 1st Special Air Regiment, Lieutenant Colonel David Stirling, to give him his thoughts on tactics for the rest of the war. Stirling's ideas, incidentally, involved the SAS leadership taking overall charge of all Special Operations, something that even Churchill thought went too far in detaching it from the mainstream Army.

By the spring of 1943, however, the Allied victory in North Africa was imminent and it was decided to replace the 1st SAS Regiment with an organisation known as HQ Raiding Forces. This controlled the Special Boat Squadron (SBS) and what remained of 1st SAS Regiment, which was restyled in April 1943 to become the Special Raiding Squadron (SRS). To those involved, however, the new group soon became known simply as 'Paddy's Men' after their commander, Major Robert Blair 'Paddy' Mayne, a colourful Irishman. Mayne's men trusted and respected him, while he, as well as valuing team spirit, repeatedly told them: 'Every man has to be his own saviour and has to be totally self-sufficient.'

Paddy's Men first went into action to spearhead the invasion of Sicily in the summer of 1943. Sicily, which has an area of 10,000 square miles, is the largest island in the Mediterranean, with a coastline of 600 miles. On 1 July 1943 eighteen officers and 262 other ranks boarded their ships and set sail for the Egyptian city of Port Said, where they spent three days doing final training and making last-minute adjustments. On 5 July the squadron embarked on what would be the start of the invasion of mainland Europe, with the target of seizing the coastal batteries at Capo Murro di Porco, known affectionately as 'Cape Pig's Snout' to its attackers. Among those taking part in the raid was Lance Corporal Charles Dalziel, who had originally served with the Scots Guards and who, along with his SAS colleagues, had seen action in the North African desert.

Mayne and his men, all of them hand-picked and with experience of SAS-style operations, had been tasked with silencing the enemy guns at Capo Murro di Porco ahead of an amphibious assault by half a million men – at the time the largest such assault of the Second World War. The plan was that, if Mayne and his men failed in their task, the landings would be called off.

In the early hours of 10 July, Paddy's Men were supported by glider-borne troops who were all supposed to land further inland, with the aim of preventing Italian and German troops from reinforcing the beachhead (though, in fact, poor weather and bad navigation techniques meant many of these men ended up in the sea and almost 1,000 drowned). The SRS had been dropped from larger ships into their smaller landing craft in a Force 7 gale and in mountainous waves. One landing craft had even crashed into a British submarine that had surfaced – though, in the confusion, Paddy's Men feared they had collided with a German U-boat. However, by 3.15am the men had landed on the beach without opposition. Although they had been prepared to scale the cliff, most of them in fact found a small, steep path with steps carved into the cliff by the enemy to enable the Italian forces to reach the beach.

Once the men were in place, they had another piece of even better fortune. The first mortar round – a phosphorous/smoke round intended only as a target-marker – landed in the middle of the battery's main cordite dump. The intense heat from the marker round ignited the cordite and a massive explosion ensued. As individual SRS sections made their way into position, the skies were lit up by huge fires.

Some men had contact with the Italian defenders of the coastal battery, while others were given an alternative objective: a heavily defended farmhouse known locally as Damerio. Dalziel, an acting lance sergeant with No. 1 Troop, was part of the force tasked with attacking the battery and barracks. Lieutenant John Wiseman single-handedly charged the battery gun position, killing or capturing forty enemy, while Sergeant Reg Seekings ordered his men to fix bayonets, believing the Italians would take fright at such a sight. As Seekings led a fearsome charge against the main barracks complex and command post, the occupants fled into the night. However, No. 1 Troop then came under heavy fire from a fortified machine-gun emplacement. Private 'Nobby' Noble, armed with a light machine gun (LMG), shot his way through and eliminated the problem – an action that led to him being awarded the Military Medal (MM). At the same time, No. 3 Section succeeded in capturing the farmhouse while two enemy pill-boxes that had been missed in the initial charge were also silenced.

Mayne had expected the storming of the battery to be relatively easy and he was right. The SRS had not lost a single man and yet they had killed or wounded fifty of the enemy and taken between fifty and sixty prisoners. Furthermore, they had captured and destroyed four six-inch guns, three 20mm anti-aircraft guns, one range-finder and several heavy machine guns. With all the known enemy guns silent, Mayne signalled to the main Allied force that they could make their run to the beachheads as their path had been cleared. However, at 6am, first light, two further enemy batteries – neither of which had been identified by intelligence – opened up. Mayne at once led his men forward, knowing that to leave these batteries operational would have had disastrous consequences for the invasion force. So, as the vessels returned fire, the SRS moved forward, although they too came under enemy fire from the heavy-calibre naval shells. As Paddy's Men advanced, they mopped up farmhouses along the way where the sight of drawn bayonets often made the Italians surrender without a fight. However, after waving a white flag, an Italian opened fire on the advancing SRS, killing a corporal. Elsewhere, advancing SRS men faced sniper fire, but many of these enemy troops were stalked and eliminated.

Once Paddy's Men eventually reached the offending batteries, they were surprised by the force of the enemy fire. The SRS positions were sprayed with machine-gun fire, and mortar fire also added to their difficulties. It was decided that Seekings, Dalziel and No. 1 Troop would try to outflank the enemy machine-gun posts that were protecting the batteries. Showing a disdain for the heavy fire that they confronted, the men rushed towards the enemy positions. The Italians were overcome by the speed and ferocity of the attack: the pill-box was overrun and all the enemy soldiers manning it were killed. No. 1 Troop again stormed forwards, this time to the enemy's mortar positions. Yet again, the Italians' resistance was brushed aside and the mortars were put out of action. Dalziel's sub-section was specifically tasked with outflanking the enemy positions from the left. Despite being heavily outnumbered, they routed the enemy, with Dalziel leading from the front and personally killing several men. It was not long before the two final enemy batteries were silenced, the enemy ammunition dump blown by mortar fire and Paddy's Men were tucking into a well-deserved late breakfast.

At 4pm the same day, the SRS moved out from Alacona Farm, where they had been lying up, and advanced across Syracuse Bridge, the scene of heavy fighting by glider troops that morning. As they crossed, a single enemy aircraft spotted them and made a bombing run. With Mayne at the head of his men, they did not bother to pause for cover; the bomb, fortunately, missed them and exploded in a nearby field. In fact, the one man who broke ranks to seek cover was immediately dismissed from the SRS and returned to his parent unit, proving, perhaps harshly, that there was no place for anything but total courage for those who wanted to be called Paddy's Men.

Although Mayne usually preferred to recognise acts of great personal courage with promotion rather than gallantry awards, he made an exception and personally sought recognition for Dalziel because of his bravery and leadership. The recommendation for his MM concluded: 'With great determination he killed and routed a party of enemy many times as large as his sub-section without casualties to himself.' The award was announced on 21 October 1943. Dalziel was not alone in having his courage formally recognised: Mayne received a Bar to his Distinguished Service Order (DSO); two other officers, including the heroic John Wiseman, were awarded Military Crosses (MCs); Reg Seekings (already awarded the Distinguished

Conduct Medal for bravery in North Africa), another lance corporal in addition to Dalziel, and two privates, including Nobby Noble, were all awarded the MM.

Within a few days of their bravery at Capo Murro di Porco, Dalziel and his comrades were involved in the fierce fighting to capture Augusta, a vital harbour town. Dalziel made it through this action too and went on to see further service in Italy and north-west Europe later in the war. It is not known what happened to him after the war.

Members of the SRS went on to serve with distinction in various phases of the war. Their contribution to the war effort has not always been fully recognised, but Stewart McClean, a former Territorial Army warrant officer, splendidly rectified this in 2006 with his book *SAS: The History of the Special Raiding Squadron 'Paddy's Men'*. It is a book that fulfils the wish of some of his collaborators on the project who wanted the SRS to be given 'its rightful place in history'.

PRIVATE ALEXANDER GRANT SKINNER
AWARD: MILITARY MEDAL (MM)
GAZETTED: 21 OCTOBER 1943

Alex Skinner was awarded the MM for bravery in Sicily while serving with the Special Raiding Squadron (SRS) of 1st SAS Regiment. At the time, the SAS was employed in various operations close to, and sometimes behind, enemy lines. However, the Italian forces were aware of the presence of the SAS in the area and they deployed snipers to try to locate them and shoot them dead.

Alex Skinner was born in Newcastle-upon-Tyne but later lived in north-west London. Originally serving with the Royal Engineers, he was with 1st SAS Regiment, and under the command of the legendary 'Paddy' Mayne, in the summer of 1943. There he became involved in fighting on Capo Murro di Porco, south of Syracuse, Sicily, on 10 July 1943. An account of what happened next is contained in *SAS: The History of the Special Raiding Squadron 'Paddy's Men'*, written by Stewart McClean.

On most occasions incoming fire from enemy machine-gun positions could be fairly easy to spot and deal with, but the deadly threat to the Squadron from the sniper's rifle was increasing steadily. Private Alex Skinner had been hit and wounded in the leg and hips during the initial actions and was beginning to suffer severe pains from his wounds. However, that did not deter him as he decided to take matters into his own hands and do something about the snipers. While the rest of his comrades were involved in an attack on and capture of one of the farmhouses, called Massa Alacona, he managed to spot the concealed positions which the snipers were using as firing points. He moved out very slowly and cautiously towards them. The area of ground that he had to cross to get within rifle range was rock hard, with very sparse growth and provided little or no cover to use for protection. Despite those problems, Skinner managed to get close enough to deal with them. He waited and watched for any telltale signs, the slightest movement, smoke or a muzzle flash. Then, one by one, he got them into the cross hairs of his sights and put them permanently out of action. The long hours of target practice on the rifle range paid off and in relatively quick succession he had accounted for three snipers.

In short, Skinner had given the enemy snipers a devastating taste of their own medicine, patiently waiting, first, to discover their exact positions and, then, to 'take them out'. Having been so successful in the most trying of circumstances, Skinner might have been expected to go to get treatment for his wounds. However, as Mayne's recommendation for a gallantry award made clear, he sought no medical aid and instead went into battle again only three days later:

Pvt. Skinner was wounded by shrapnel in the leg and hip during the first hour of fighting on Cape Murro di Porco on 10th July 1943. Nevertheless he took his full share in the advance and continued to fight throughout the action which lasted 17 hours and covered over 24 miles. During the attack on the Farm House Marsa Alacena [*sic*] he himself stalked and killed three enemy snipers. On hearing that another operation was to take place shortly he did not visit the unit Medical Officer but had his wounds dressed privately. He went into action again with the Squadron on 13th July at Augusta. Only after this operation were his wounds discovered and he was then admitted to hospital. For his determination and fighting spirit and/or his disregard of his own discomfort and pain he is recommended for a M.M.

Skinner continued to serve in Italy, where, during action at Termoli as part of 'Operation Devon', he was killed on 5 October 1943, aged twenty-three. His parents, Samuel and Elsie Skinner of Ilford, Essex, were presented with their son's MM by George VI at a private audience. His parents were also visited after the war by David Stirling, the founder of the SAS, who gave the couple two photographs of their son taken overseas, one in uniform and one in 'civvies'. In 1974 Mrs Skinner, by then a widow, personally presented her son's MM as a gift to her other son, Dennis, who treasured the decoration that had been awarded to his older brother.

PRIVATE (LATER WARRANT OFFICER) RICHARD HIGHAM
AWARD: MILITARY MEDAL (MM)
GAZETTED: 13 JANUARY 1944

Richard Higham saw action with the SAS and the Special Raiding Squadron (SRS) in Africa, Italy and north-west Europe during the Second World War. He was awarded his gallantry medal for an act of supreme courage in which he saved three wounded comrades. Later in the war, Higham went missing in action after being wounded, but he survived and, years later, his gallantry in Malaya was also publicly recognised.

Higham was born in Preston, Lancashire, in 1918 and enlisted in The King's Own Royal Regiment on 23 February 1937, aged nineteen. After seeing active service with his regiment in Palestine in 1938, he served in Iraq, India and Egypt from 1939 to 1942. He qualified as a parachutist and transferred to the 1st Special Air Service on 1 October 1942, and this unit subsequently became the SRS under the leadership of Lieutenant Colonel 'Paddy' Mayne.

He served with distinction with the SRS, known affectionately as 'Paddy's Men', in North Africa. When the squadron was transferred to Italy, he took part in fighting at Bagnara, where he displayed bravery that led to him being awarded the MM. On 4 September 1943, the SRS was involved in 'Operation Baytown', a mission in which the objectives were to capture, occupy and hold Bagnara. Provided the squadron successfully landed at the small town on Italy's east coast, they were then to advance and try to prevent the retreating enemy from destroying key bridges and installations that would, in turn, delay the main Allied force that was to follow.

During the initial landing in the early hours of 4 September, there was no enemy resistance, but this soon changed and, as the men of 'B' and 'C' Sections of No. 1 Troop moved forward, they encountered a deadly machine-gun and mortar fire. Two soldiers were killed and another seven received critical wounds. As the situation became more and more serious, some men from the two sections eased forward in order to rescue their injured comrades, some of whom were lying on an open road as machine-gun fire continued to fall on them.

Stewart McClean takes up the story in his book *SAS: The History of the Special Raiding Squadron 'Paddy's Men'*:

Brave and undoubtedly committed as they were, the ferocity and accuracy of the enemy fire forced them to retreat. One man, Private Richard Higham, however, felt that he had spotted a solution to the problem when he noticed a small gutter than ran alongside the road. He knew instinctively that there was no time to waste so he decided not to wait for any help. Acting alone, he took his chance and by using the gutter as cover was able to crawl up alongside the casualties. Private Higham showed total disregard for the continuous enemy fire thrown at him and managed to bring the wounded and dead back one by one.

However, both Higham and the wounded were still in great danger. Although they were out of the line of direct fire, there was still a heavy mortar fire. At this point Captain Phil Gunn, the squadron's medical officer, who had been watching the events unfold, moved forward to treat the wounded men. Details of Higham's bravery were also recounted in a recommendation for his MM from Mayne himself: 'During operations at Bagnara on the 4th September 1943 while crossing a road which was swept by machine gun fire three men were wounded and fell in the middle of the road unable to move. Several attempts were made to reach these wounded but the heavy enemy machine gun fire drove them back. Pte. Higham however using a small gutter crawled up the road and although each time he appeared heavy fire was brought down on him he brought the wounded back one by one.'

Another senior officer, a major commanding 'D' Squadron, supported Higham's MM with more general praise for the young private: 'There are many qualities here worthy of mention. He is conscientious, hard-working, on many occasions devoting his leisure time to administrative issues; his exercise of discipline has always proved to be sensibly applied, and his fairness and counsel has been appreciated by all ranks of this Squadron, with whom he is popular and an excellent example.'

Higham's gallantry award was announced in the *London*

Gazette on 13 January 1944. In the spring of 1945 he left for an operation in north-west Europe with 1 SAS, departing on 6 April. On 1 May he was reported wounded and missing. He was later found and, although details never emerged about how he received his injuries, he was repatriated back to the UK.

After the war, Higham served with the Army Air Corps and the Parachute Regiment until August 1947, when he was transferred back to his parent unit, The King's Own. By 1951 he was back with the SAS (Malayan Scouts), serving in Malaya and taking part in 'Operation League' against the Malayan National Liberation Army, the military arm of the Malayan Communist Party. For his courage during this action, Higham was Mentioned in Despatches (MiD), after his recommendation stated: 'Throughout Operation League Squadron Sergeant Major Higham fulfilled the requirements of a Troop Commander, leading his Troop with spirit and applying the principles of success which he has developed over a period of fifteen years. On occasion there were periods of difficulty calling for endurance and the exercise of firm discipline in the Field, and over a confusing jungle country he operated with his Troop independently. The success with which his troop performed was largely due to his inspiration and the excellent spirit of the Troop was a firm reflection of his leadership.'

In 1954 Higham returned again to The King's Own, remaining with his parent regiment until he was discharged from the Army on 10 May 1960. By this point he had served for twenty-three years and thirty-six days, and his military conduct was described as 'exemplary'. He died on 2 March 1993, aged seventy-three.

TEMPORARY CAPTAIN (LATER LIEUTENANT COLONEL) JOHN ANTHONY MARSH

AWARDS: DISTINGUISHED SERVICE ORDER (DSO) AND ORDER OF THE BRITISH EMPIRE (OBE)
GAZETTED: 27 JANUARY 1944 AND 18 JUNE 1970

Tony Marsh served in the SAS for the final three years of the Second World War and during this time he was awarded an outstanding DSO for courage in Italy and was Mentioned in Despatches (MiD) on two occasions. During a distinguished Army career, he had the distinction of – almost certainly – being the first British officer into Tripoli, Libya, after it was captured by the Allies in 1943 and also of parachuting behind enemy lines to link up with the Maquis, the French Resistance, after the Normandy landings of 1944.

John Anthony 'Tony' Marsh was born in 1900 and, even as a boy, showed a great interest in the Army. He was an under officer in the Officer Training Corps (OTC) and achieved the King's Hundred at Bisley (a rifle-shooting achievement). On leaving school, he joined the Artists Rifles as a private and, at the outbreak of the war, he was commissioned into the Duke of Cornwall's Light Infantry (DCLI). At this point in his career he nearly burnt down the officers' mess, although the exact circumstances of this unfortunate accident are not known. Incidentally, this anecdote and other information about Marsh is courtesy of a splendid obituary carried by the Journal of the Light Infantry.

In 1942 Marsh was posted to 1 DCLI, but his arrival in Egypt coincided with the aftermath of the disastrous Battle of Bir-el-Harmat and he discovered there was no battalion left to join. He therefore applied to transfer to the SAS and was successful: he found himself in the Western Desert as part of 'A' Squadron, 1st SAS Regiment, of which he would later become second in command. It was during his time in North Africa that, as stated, he was almost certainly the first British officer into Tripoli in January 1943: he led a patrol into the city from the west as the main forces from the Eighth Army approached from the east.

Next, Marsh joined his comrades from 1 SAS in Italy and it was at the battle for Termoli in the autumn of 1943 that he was involved in an action, while serving with the newly formed Special Raiding Squadron (SRS), for which he was awarded the DSO. The formidable 'Paddy' Mayne, one of the SAS 'Originals' and his Commanding Officer, wrote the recommendation for his gallantry award:

Captain Marsh, with fifty six men, was holding a front of one mile on the right flank of the Sector west of Termoli. At mid-day on the 5th October 1943, his positions were subjected to very heavy and accurate shelling and mortar fire, at the height of which, his position was further weakened by the transfer of one of his sections to another sector. At this time the enemy was developing a determined counter-attack on his left flank. Despite the intensity of enemy fire he held fast and with his own fire pinned down groups of the enemy infantry which attempted to infiltrate into his position. Later in the afternoon several of his men were badly wounded, whilst some distance away on his right flank his remaining other section was being gradually forced back. Although by this time, Captain Marsh's position had become untenable, he refused to move until he was able to communicate his intention to the troops on his left. Meanwhile, with his few remaining men, he succeeded in beating off further attacks on his position by German Infantry. Striking north to join up with his right hand section he came across two wounded men. From them he learned that he was completely cut off, but pushed on, taking the wounded men with him, until finally pinned down by machine gun fire. He eventually succeeded in evacuating all the wounded men to our own lines under cover of darkness although only 150 yards from an enemy post. Throughout Captain Marsh showed great coolness and determination. His high standard of courage and complete disregard for personal safety throughout the operation played a decisive part in saving a very dangerous situation.

Marsh had won the respect of his men and his fellow officers with his calm authority and his impressive leadership, especially when he and his men, some wounded, had become cut off from the main body of the SRS. His DSO was announced on 27 January 1944 and soon he found himself back in Britain as a major. Following the formation of the Special Air Service Brigade, he took command of 'C' Squadron of the reconstituted 1st SAS Regiment. Some small groups of men from 'C' Squadron operated behind enemy lines in France, but, after the Normandy landings, Marsh took some other comrades through German lines to relieve 'A' Squadron, which had been operating in the Morvan area in central France.

During the final year of the war, Marsh operated behind enemy lines in Belgium, Holland, Germany and, finally, Norway. His final task in Norway was to help disarm some 300,000 German troops. Marsh was MiD twice – on 10 May 1945 and 6 November 1945 – for distinguished services in north-west Europe.

After the war, Marsh remained in the Army, serving as a staff captain in the South West District, based at Taunton, Somerset. Next, he joined 1 DCLI, serving with them in Cyprus and Somaliland. After a further staff appointment in Tripoli, he returned to Britain as a training major of 21 SAS, which, by this time, was affiliated to the Artists Rifles. In fact, only now was he belatedly presented with a pewter tankard that he had won, but never received, in Bisley in 1939. The war had intervened.

Marsh rejoined 1 DCLI in the West Indies in 1954, where he took over the command of 'A' Company. His duties included organising guards of honour for visiting world statesmen and military tattoos. Following a tour as adjutant and training major of 4/5th DCLI in 1957, Marsh retired but, because of the warm welcome he had received in the Caribbean, he then returned to Bermuda to work for the Trade and Development Board. Within months, he was commissioned into the Bermuda Militia Artillery, which he commanded until the amalgamation of the island forces, after which he commanded the Bermuda Regiment. He was awarded the OBE on 18 June 1970, following his retirement.

Marsh died suddenly at his home in Devonshire, Bermuda, on 14 November 1984, aged sixty-four. Derrick Harrison, a trooper who served under him, was among those who praised his military and human talents: 'Tony Marsh was not only a first class Commander, clear thinking and unruffled in action, he was an understanding and compassionate man with a fund of boyish good humour, deservedly respected and regarded with great affection. He will truly be missed by all who knew him and operated with him.'

STAFF SERGEANT (LATER WARRANT OFFICER) CHARLES A.W. MITCHELL
AWARD: MILITARY MEDAL (MM)
GAZETTED: 9 MARCH 1944

The history of the SAS is littered with tales of great heroism and men who have taken on a far superior force in battle. However, few men have, like Charles 'Mitch' Mitchell, taken on an enemy patrol of up to fifty men with a far smaller force and lived to tell the tale. This action came only six days after he had attacked a German parachute battalion, killing several of their number, capturing their sergeant major and seizing important papers.

Mitchell, who was brought up in Romford, Essex, enlisted in the Queen's Regiment after the outbreak of the Second World War. After volunteering to serve in the Commandos, he was posted to North Africa. Early in 1943 he volunteered for the Special Air Service and was posted to serve with 'D' Squadron, 2nd SAS Regiment, under Major Roy Farran. In September

1943 Mitchell was a member of a composite squadron from 2 SAS that landed at the Italian port of Taranto with orders to conduct reconnaissance patrols and attack, as and when the opportunity arose, targets ahead of the Allied advance. The SAS was suspicious of the surrendering Italians' intentions when their ship arrived in the port, but no opposition was met and the town was taken.

During this deployment, Farran's men used jeeps, but it was dark before the vehicles had been unloaded. Soon he and his men were pushing forward along the main road. Fearing Germans were located inland from the port, the convoy of jeeps stopped at regular intervals so that Farran could listen, thereby using his maxim that 'good reconnaissance is done by the eyes in daylight and by the ears at night'. After several miles, the convoy stopped and Farran beckoned forward his second in command. A number of armed figures could be seen standing around a bridge a short distance ahead.

In his book *Winged Dagger*, Farran described what happened next:

> As we were peering into the half-light, an Italian sentry shouted a challenge. I called back that we were 'Inglesi' and began to walk towards them, telling Sergeant-Major Mitchell, my gunner, to cover me with his Bren. I had just reached the bridge, on which stood an excited little group of men in green uniform, when a sentry rushed towards me with a brandished rifle and fired a round through my legs at under five yards' range. The Sergeant-Major filled him with a whole magazine of Bren bullets. And then there were profound apologies on both sides when we had established our identity. An officer produced a bottle of wine from which he insisted that we drank a toast to our new alliance. Ignored by his friends, the dead sentry lay crumpled in the dust – an innocent victim of an accident of war. Before we moved on the officer gave me his address in Rome, but all his hospitality could not make me forget the body of a dead Neapolitan, lying unmourned

on the bridge with his life blood running in the gutter, killed after the armistice.

It was the first, but not the last, time that Mitchell saved the life of Farran.

On 18 September 1943 Mitchell was patrolling up to the German-held village of Grottole, south-west of Matera, when he decided to mount a surprise attack. He killed several enemy soldiers and knocked out three trucks, even returning with the truck of the German parachute battalion, a prisoner of war (the German orderly-room sergeant major) and many important papers. Farran later wrote in his book: 'Mitchell, who was justifiably proud of his success, had driven halfway into Grassano before he had realised that it was occupied. He killed several Germans in the street in a brief fight before he made off with his valuable trophy.'

Days later, Farran and his men were ordered to Bari, which had shortly beforehand been taken by 'Popski's Private Army', as the Eighth Army's No. 1 Demolition Squadron, under Major Vladimir Peniakoff, was known. From Bari, they had to push inland on a long-range patrol to Melfi and report on the progress of a Canadian column, which was advancing on a parallel axis. The two columns, in fact, met up, but – had it not been for Mitchell's quick thinking – there could have been a major disaster on 24 September.

In his book, Farran wrote:

Some minutes later we were coffee-housing with French Canadians in the streets of Rovreto. In the excitement of this meeting, I had foolishly neglected to post look-outs. Only the prompt action of Sergeant-Major Mitchell saved us from disaster when about fifty Germans entered the village from the other side. The first notion of danger that I received was a sudden burst of Bren from the tail of the column. Rallying the crew of the last jeeps, who had all dismounted to talk to the civilians, Mitchell seized a Bren and charged the German platoon. Firing from the hip, he drove them out of the village and down the hill on the other side. His party pursued the enemy until they were pinned in a river bed by his fire from above. Four wounded Germans were captured in the streets.

The recommendation for Mitchell's MM, awarded for the two actions in September, told a similar story: 'With great initiative and gallantry, Squadron Sergeant-Major Mitchell led the four members of his two jeep crews on foot against the enemy with accurate Bren and Tommy Gun fire from the hip . . .' The recommendation concluded: 'In these engagements, SSM Mitchell's dash and courage were outstanding and his example stimulated all those under his command to the highest degree.' His MM was announced on 9 March 1944.

'D' Squadron returned to Taranto and, on 3 October, Farran, with a detachment of twenty men, including Mitchell, embarked on a seaborne landing to the town of Termoli. The raid involved several SAS units, including the 1st Special Air Service Regiment, which had recently been renamed the 1st Special Raiding Squadron (SRS). The aim was to create a base for future raids behind enemy lines, but, in the face of stiff Axis resistance, the situation became stalemated. At one point Farran and his men joined the rest of 1 SRS in repelling a fierce German counter-attack, supported by armour. Positioned on a ridge with six Bren guns, a light mortar and several six-pounder anti-tank guns, they held their position in the face of a major enemy onslaught.

Mitchell was also involved in 'Operation Archway', under the command of Lieutenant Colonel Brian Franks and involving two squadrons from the 1st and 2nd SAS Regiments. During this time, Mitchell carried out single and double jeep ambushes on German transport and other targets, all deep behind enemy lines. In one action, he was noted to have fought a courageous rear-guard action with a Bren. In the final months of the war Operation Archway supported British armoured divisions during their advance into Germany. In an unarmoured jeep, Mitchell and a comrade joined in the attacks of the Guards Armoured Division, which received return fire from the formidable German 88mm anti-tank guns. Furthermore, he was present during the Liberation of Norway, for which he received a diploma of thanks from the Norwegian government. He can be seen in many of the photographs of the Victory parade that survive to this day.

Mitchell had many admirers among his SAS comrades, including his CO, Major Roy Farran, who wrote an open reference for him when Mitchell was leaving the Army at the end of the Second World War:

Of all the people I have met in this war, I think that Sergeant Major Mitchell is the nicest. I first met him as a Sergeant in my Squadron, early in 1943, when he came to us from the Commandos.

In a very short space of time I made him Squadron Sergeant Major and never regretted it. He is the sort of man who finds it easy to enforce discipline, because the men always respect him and, in my squadron, they looked up to him as a sort of hero. Although he was quiet and unassuming, there was nothing a soldier is called upon to do that he could not do better than anybody else. He is smart in appearance, a wonderful pistol shot, good at games and has a tremendous fund of common-sense.

In Italy, S.S.M. Mitchell won a very good Military Medal, when he drove off an enemy patrol with a one man counter attack with a Bren gun. He again distinguished himself in France and Germany. He was finally made Regimental Sergeant Major of the regiment, which itself is a token of his efficiency. Mitchell is a thoroughly nice young man and will succeed in what ever job he is called upon to do, because he will try with all his heart and soul.

Mitchell died on 29 November 1984. After his death, Farran wrote to Mitchell's widow telling her: 'I admired him enormously. He was always cool and clear-headed, a gentle, understanding sort of Sergeant-Major, much loved by his men and he saved my life at least once . . . I don't know what to say in consolation except to say that none of us expected him to live so long [because he was so brave]. He was a fine man. God bless you.'

Mitchell's death was announced in *Mars & Minerva*, the SAS journal, in which Harold 'Tanky' Challenor, an SAS legend and fellow MM recipient, wrote: 'He was a man among men at a time when Officers, NCOs and men relied heavily upon each other and there was little distinction. He never let us down. "Mitch" was a big, strong man, quiet of voice and possessing a lovely dry humour. A simple, kindly man, he was always willing to listen to any of our troubles. He always got instant co-operation and compliance because we loved him.'

SERGEANT RUDOLF FRIEDLANDER (ALSO KNOWN AS ROBERT LODGE)
AWARD: DISTINGUISHED CONDUCT MEDAL (DCM)
GAZETTED: 29 MARCH 1945

In a letter to his father written towards the end of the war, Rudolf Friedlander wrote: 'Our sacrifices will not be futile if the survivors have learned the lessons of this disastrous war.' His words provide a fascinating insight into the motivation for Friedlander's monumental contribution to the war effort: a German Jew, he fought with the SAS under the alias of 'Robert Lodge'. He took part in amphibious and overland raids with Lieutenant Colonel Bill Stirling before he (Friedlander) was captured during the Sicily landings of May 1943. However, he escaped from a German prisoner-of-war camp and made his way back to Britain. Eventually, he was parachuted behind enemy lines in order to take part in 'Operation Loyton' in the eastern Vosges region of France in August 1944. The story of his extraordinary wartime exploits can be told in such vivid detail because he kept a diary.

Friedlander was born in Munich, southern Germany, on 15 August 1908. He was the third child of Max Friedlaender, a successful Jewish lawyer, and his wife Bella (although his father's surname was 'Friedlaender', Rudolf and some of his siblings later chose to drop the second 'e'). Rudi, as he was always affectionately known by his family and friends, witnessed the First World War and then the economic and political turmoil in Weimar Germany and the rise of the Nazi Party. As a young child he was nervous and sickly, and he hated thunderstorms. However, in his late teens he became bolder and was a good skier and mountaineer. Friedlander studied law and economics and between 1930 and 1933 he worked in a lawyer's office and judge's chambers. However, due to the persecution of Jews in his homeland, he left Germany in September 1933 to enrol at the University of Lyon in France, but stayed there for only one semester. After briefly returning to Germany in April 1934, he left again, this time for Holland to learn a trade: carpentry. When his course ended, he came to Britain in February 1936, where he remained for the next three years until the outbreak of war. Meanwhile, the other members of his family all managed to escape from Germany (shortly after his mother's death from cancer in October 1937, his father moved to Switzerland and then to Britain – where he eventually died in 1956).

From the moment the Second World War broke out in September 1939, Friedlander was determined to serve in the British Armed Forces – despite 'aliens' initially being restricted to serving in the rank of warrant officer or below and not being allowed a combat role. Friedlander wanted to defeat what he saw as the evil forces of Nazism and fascism. On 10 April 1940 he joined one of the 'Alien Pioneer Companies' of the Auxiliary Military Pioneer Corps at Hanley, Staffordshire. He was employed as a tradesman, carrying tools rather than a weapon, and was involved in clearing bomb debris from London during the Blitz. However, he wanted to be a combatant and, in November 1942, he volunteered and was finally accepted for military service.

After serving with the Royal Army Ordnance Corps (RAOC) and Royal Electrical and Mechanical Engineers (REME), Friedlander was posted for 'special duty' to No. 62 Training School, Warwick, where he underwent fitness, unarmed combat, map reading and other training needed to be a Commando soldier. He was attached to the headquarters of the Special Service Brigade and arrived in North Africa in March 1943. He joined No. 1 Small Scale Raiding Force, commanded by Lieutenant Colonel Bill Stirling, and took part in amphibious and overland raids in connection with operations in Tunisia. He was posted to the 2nd SAS Regiment on 13 May 1943, where he was given a new name – 'Robert Lodge' – for protection in case he was captured by the Germans. Friedlander chose 'Lodge' because it was the surname of his British fiancée, Win. Around this time, he wrote in his diary: 'I was happy and proud to be in A Squadron and to be chosen for the dragon team. We were then training for a special job, the landing behind the enemy line by sea, to walk by night with heavy packs toward our operational area and there to do a special work of sabotage against the Germans in the Bizerte sector.'

In July 1943 Lodge was parachuted into Sicily as part of 'Operation Husky' – the Allied invasion of the island. However, he and four other soldiers became separated from the main group and were captured by Italian soldiers as they hid behind a wall. Friedlander's diary entry read: 'We heard voices and saw plenty [of] farm people moving – something was astir. And after half an hour suddenly behind us came the call to surrender in Italian. Looking up we saw about five Carabinieri with rifles pointed at us. The Captain gave the order to give up. We obviously could not get away, and to shoot a few Carabinieri with our pistols would not have been worth the lives of the five of us.'

Friedlander and his comrades were imprisoned and interrogated – at one point, he was threatened with execution as a spy. However, he and three others managed to escape while being held at a train station – only to be recaptured soon afterwards when they tried to make off in a small boat. The men were taken to Capua, Camp 66, close to Naples, where they were held in the transit camp for a month. In the late summer of 1943 Friedlander and others were switched to another Italian prison, Camp 73. Later, the Germans moved them on again and, after a long march, Friedlander and a fellow prisoner managed to escape as they were paraded through an Italian town. They were able to dodge into a hostelry without being seen by their guards, and soon they discovered where eight other British PoWs, who had also escaped, were already being shielded by friendly Italians. Friedlander wrote in his diary:

> The tension of those next minutes is difficult to describe. We were excited and flushed with joy. Free at last! But the fear of losing this new freedom gripped our hearts. Would the Germans search the house on their way back? . . . I shuddered at the thought of what would happen if the Germans should find us here. All those brave and kind people in the house would pay with their lives for their good deed. How terribly that would weigh on our conscience.
>
> But the minutes passed and nothing happened. Men and women came to and fro, whispering, giving hints and asking questions. The women were beyond praise. One old woman specially, with tears in her eyes, embraced and kissed us, then she brought food and drink – eggs that made our mouths water. Then we gave them some of our tinned food.

Next, the Italians gave the British some civilian clothes, some money and directions out of the town. For the next five weeks they walked southwards, never staying more than one night in the same place and keeping away from Rome and other cities on the grounds that these would be the German and fascist strongholds. At one point, towards the end of their journey and with fierce fighting nearby, Friedlander and the Briton with whom he had initially escaped spent more than a month holed up in a cave. They were joined by some local Italians, but eventually Friedlander made it alone through the enemy lines to safety, setting out on the evening of 2 December 1943 and finding safety early on 4 December. In his diary he wrote:

> I resolved to wait till I heard the first British word spoken. The wind was against me and I could not make out the shouting. Then during a lull in the storm I heard distinctly the command 'Heave, heave and one more.'
>
> The next minute I acted like a madman, I am ashamed to say. I just jumped up and ran forward, crying something like 'yes, heave boys, heave away.' A wonder they did not shoot me. Instead they carried on with their job, fixing the guns to their trucks for transport back to the base. Only a few came up, looked at me and tried quietly to understand what I wanted, what I said and where I came from. Then they grasped it; they had found many escaped POWs before me and they efficiently did the right thing, called the officer, handed me over, and gave me some encouraging words.

Military records show that Friedlander officially reached Allied lines on 23 December 1943. Once back in the UK, he was hospitalised and treated for dysentery and jaundice. However, he was released on 9 May 1944 and allowed to return to the 2nd SAS Regiment. On 4 May, four days before his release from hospital, Friedlander wrote an extraordinary and lengthy letter to his father outlining his philosophy of life, his political and economic beliefs and his hopes for the future, both personal and worldwide. Although he said it was not intended to be a 'last letter', he clearly feared that he might not survive his next SAS assignment. In a delightful, self-deprecating style, he wrote:

> Whatever may happen to me, mine is a better cause and a great aim and I have the satisfaction that I could use my life several times over to the same end. If I am lucky and come back I shall have the right after the war to hold my head high and to live, think, fight and write in my own way for those principles of freedom and justice which now are inextricably bound to allied victory. Then I shall write a book ... But if this is not granted to me you must act once more as biographer. Don't think I am so conceited to attribute to my life any great importance. I know only too well how little I have actually accomplished in spite of an excellent education and a very happy and sheltered childhood, a cultured, harmonious home, and moral guidance.

He ended his letter: 'I am happy to be able to fight for my principles and for Britain, the nation which now champions these principles and has become a second home to me. If I survive there will be only one ambition left: to be able to continue the fight for freedom and peace as a British Citizen.'

On 14 May Friedlander turned up at his father's flat in Twickenham, south-west London, and, despite his long ordeal, was in good spirits. On 15 June 1944, under his pseudonym of Lodge, he was Mentioned in Despatches (MiD) for his earlier gallantry.

Next, Friedlander was assigned to an SAS operation where, after the D-Day landings, the Special Forces had been involved in missions against enemy troops. 'Sergeant Lodge', as he was then known, was detailed to take part in 'Operation Loyton', in the Vosges region of north-eastern France close to the German border. In 1944 it was sparsely populated and consisted of wood-covered hills, valley pastures and small isolated villages. In short, it was an ideal area for a small mobile raiding force to operate. In late 1944 it was also the area towards which General

George Patton's Third Army was heading but, outrunning their supplies, they had stopped at Nancy. To counter the American advance, the Germans had moved reinforcements, including the 17th SS Panzergrenadier Division Götz von Berlichingen, into the area.

On 12 August Friedlander and his four-man reconnaissance party landed by parachute into the eastern Vosges Mountains. The drop zone was in a deeply wooded mountainous area, forty miles west of Strasbourg. The advance party's objective was to contact the local French Resistance, carry out a reconnaissance of the area, identify targets for an attack and locate a suitable dropping zone for the main force. However, the Germans quickly became aware of their presence and conducted operations to destroy the SAS team.

On 18 August Friedlander's detachment of four found itself surrounded by a large force of the enemy, who gradually closed in on them. In the face of intense automatic and small arms fire, he stood up and emptied a Bren magazine into the enemy at a range of about thirty yards. This allowed the rest of the detachment to escape to temporary safety and inflicted a considerable number of casualties on the enemy.

Later that day, the same situation arose and one of the SAS troopers was killed. Friedlander repeated the same courageous act of earlier in the day, and the remainder of the small party was extricated. However, he became separated from his men and was not seen alive again. His fate was one of the many suspicious deaths investigated after the war by the War Crimes investigation team.

Documents held at the Public Records Office state that the body of Sergeant Lodge, missing on Operation Loyton, was brought to Moussey for internment on 20 August 1944 by the Germans, who told the curé, Père Gassmann, that he had committed suicide before capture. The curé's brother, Abbé Gassmann, examined the body, on which he found a wound on the back of the head and bayonet marks to the stomach. On his uniform he found 2nd SAS shoulder badges and a Parachute badge on the left breast. He identified Friedlander from a photograph and documents contained in a pocket. The official finding was that Friedlander had been murdered by the Germans near Moussey on, or about, 18 August 1944. He was buried in Moussey Cemetery on 21 August 1944.

Friedlander was posthumously decorated when he was awarded the DCM on 29 March 1945, under his pseudonym. The once-confidential recommendation for his award concluded: 'Both on this occasion [the day he was captured] and on past operations, which once included an escape from an enemy POW camp, this NCO has continually shown complete disregard for his personal safety, a fine offensive spirit and gifts of leadership much above the average. His work on every occasion has been in the highest tradition of the British Army.'

The story of Friedlander's remarkable life is superbly told in a book written jointly by Gerhart Friedlander, his younger brother, and Keith Turner, a writer. Called *Rudi's Story: The Diary and Wartime Experiences of Rudolf Friedlaender*, the 144-page book is largely based on his wartime diary, which he sent to his father before embarking on his final campaign in 1944.

In 2003, at the initiative of Turner, the Commonwealth War Graves Commission replaced the headstone on Friedlander's grave with one bearing his real name rather than his assumed one. The new headstone also carries the inscription of a quotation from one of Friedlander's last letters to his father: 'Our Sacrifices Will not be Futile if the Survivors have Learned the Lessons of this Disastrous War.'

CAPTAIN HERBERT VINCENT HOEY
AWARD: MILITARY CROSS (MC)
GAZETTED: 9 AUGUST 1945

Vincent Hoey was decorated for his persistent and outstanding bravery while serving with the Raiding Support Regiment

(RSR) in German-occupied Greece. As the citation for his MC makes abundantly clear, he displayed great initiative and leadership during a relentless and highly dangerous ten-week period during the summer and early autumn of 1944.

Hoey was born in Pinner, then Middlesex (and now north-west London), on 17 February 1915. He was the middle of three children – with an older and younger sister – and his father was a senior banker: at one time the general manager of the Standard Bank, which was based in Cape Town, South Africa. After being brought up in Edenbridge, Kent, Hoey attended Sherborne School, the independent boys' school in Dorset. Prior to the outbreak of the Second World War he worked as a chartered accountant in London. At the start of the conflict Hoey was despatched from England to the South African Army, where he trained with the Rand Light Infantry. As part of the Eighth Army, he was involved in the 'behind-the-lines' operations in the Desert Campaign against General Erwin Rommel.

The RSR was formed in 1943, one of the many different special service units created during the Second World War. Initially intended to operate in Palestine and North Africa, it was an offshoot of the SAS and its senior officers had experience of, or knowledge of, the Long Range Desert Group (LRDG). A major purpose of the regiment was to provide partisan elements with support, including military know-how and equipment, so that the enemy could be harassed. In its early days the regiment was used mainly as raiding forces at the time of desert warfare. However, its real history as an independent unit started after the Allied Armies had landed in Italy. The RSR's members wore chocolate (later changed to beige) berets, SAS wings and a badge with the regimental motto – a quote from the Bible – of 'Quit you like men'. The regiment consisted of four squadrons and the headquarters were later established in Bari, southern Italy. Its members were volunteers and included a large number of British, South African and Rhodesian personnel. After the end of the war, it was disbanded in late 1945 and its remaining soldiers were returned to their original units.

From 1943 to 1944 many members of the RSR were involved in training operations in preparation for their role in Europe. Six men – consisting of three teams of an officer and a Non Commissioned Officer (NCO) – were chosen for roles in Greece, in support of partisans. In his memoir *Greek Adventure*, published in 1950, Jack Gage recounted their mission to Greece, in which the country was divided into three and a team assigned to each. Each two-man team had to prepare for the arrival of further Allied troops and to command them once they had arrived. Captain Gage was responsible for the southern area and Captains Hoey and Dick Gammon were in charge of the two other areas. Gage was fond of both his fellow officers and wrote of Hoey:

I had first met Hoey at the Staff College, Pretoria, when he had been one of my pupils. We were both Captains in those days. On the day of his wedding in Pretoria which I attended, I reverted to the rank of Lieut. On transfer to the 6th Division, we flew back to Egypt together, and when I decided to second to the British Army in October, Hoey was sorely tempted to do likewise, but decided to hang on for another couple of months. Eventually, like me, he couldn't resist the temptation to move off to what appeared to be more exciting work. On joining the R.S.R., Hoey reverted to Lieut., by which time I was once more a Captain. Later in Greece he got his Captaincy back, and I got ahead once again when I got my Majority. Vincent finished up on top, however, for on my return to the Union I reverted once more to the rank of Lieut. And he is still a Captain. As amateur soldiers we got a lot of amusement out of our various changes in seniority.

The final briefings for the three teams took place in Cairo, Egypt, in April and nothing was left to chance. Gage wrote: 'We spent ten busy days absorbing the very latest intelligence reports from Greece; being lectured on the Greek political set-up; the Greek character; and generally what to expect when we arrived in the country. Finally, we were each specially briefed by an expert in our own particular area. By the time this was over, we knew pretty well all there was to know about modern Greece, the German dispositions, and the general features of the country to which we had each been assigned.'

The three teams were told they must not even let their wives know anything about their mission. Gage wrote:

We were to live on the land, and our diet was to consist mainly of beans and black bread. Our medical supplies were very limited. We were to be given golden sovereigns – our only means of currency. We would, if necessary, purchase our own mules for transport purposes. We would walk or ride wherever we went in the country. Only on very rare occasions could we expect parachute drops of food. We were to be entirely self-sufficient. The British liaison officers already in the country would help us as much as possible. Until the last moment we did not know where we were going, and had, of course, no time to learn the language. We were to take the minimum of clothes, only as much as we could carry. We could expect to be cut off for at least six months.

It was a prospect which thrilled us all, for we would be able to fight the Hun just when and how it suited us. The only point we viewed with slight misgiving was how and when our troops would reach us . . . Our initial role was to harass the enemy to the greatest possible extent, disorganise his communications, blow up bridges, attack strong points, and generally keep him jumpy. All this we were to do in conjunction with the Greek guerrillas, to whom we were, in theory, to lend moral and heavy weapon support. Finally on the signal 'Noah's Ark' we were all three to attack three selected targets on a day when the High Command decided that the Germans had commenced their final withdrawal from Greece. We would be in constant wireless communication with the war station in Cairo, through the British liaison officers in the country.

In fact, Hoey, Gage and Gammon all survived their dangerous roles and all were awarded the MC on 9 August 1945. Hoey's once-confidential recommendation read:

Captain Hoey served in Greece during the operations of August to October 1944 as Officer in charge of a Machine-Gun Section Regiment troops. During that time he was outstanding for his personal initiative and leadership. His section was in action almost continuously from their arrival on 7th August 1944 until the Germans finally left the area on 19th October 1944.

In particular the following actions in which this officer took part are deserving of notice. On 22nd September 1944 he took his section forward to an exposed position north of Dhomokos and there engaged an enemy convoy of approximately one battalion strength. His section successfully held up this convoy when the failing light made accurate shooting impossible. During the 23rd–29th September 1944 when the enemy had seized high ground on the road from Lamia to Dhomokos and was making strenuous efforts to pass his convoys through, Captain Hoey's section three times penetrated the German positions and inflicted heavy casualties on the enemy convoys.

One night, 15th/16th October 1944, Captain Hoey with one other rank entered the town of Lamia which was then strongly held by the enemy, killed a sentry, fired with a Bren gun into two loaded truck-loads of troops and while withdrawing from the town, stopped to attack with hand grenades a billet occupied by German officers.

The known results of this patrol were the destruction of two trucks and five Germans certainly killed. The officer then went north with a force commanded by Colonel Jellicoe and while in command of two sections of Machine-Guns he showed the greatest coolness and courage in action near Kozani on 27th October 1944 when his sections moved in under heavy fire and covered the withdrawal of a company of the 4th Parachute Battalion.

Hoey met his wife, Prudence, when she was a bridesmaid and he was the best man at the wedding of a school friend. They were married during the war in Pretoria, on 31 July 1943. Throughout the war, Prudence was working with the Foreign Office in South Africa and was employed on a number of different projects. Later she worked in various European stations and in England, including using her language expertise in Bletchley Park. The couple had a long and happy marriage that produced five sons.

At the end of the war, Hoey opted for a dramatic career-switch and took up farming. He trained in agriculture – dairy-cattle husbandry and grass production, in particular – in Hatch Warren, near Basingstoke, Hampshire. From there, he went to a farm at Minterne Parva, Dorset. He was asked by an uncle in Kenya to run his farm and stud there, but instead, in July 1948, he bought a farm in Devon which he farmed for forty-three years. He lived in South Brent, a small town on the edge of Dartmoor, for most of his remaining years and his wife predeceased him. At the time of his death, in Ivybridge, Devon, on 17 July 2003, he had nine grandsons and three granddaughters.

During his time in Devon, Hoey put in years of work in several official capacities for the Royal British Legion. In the church community he was respected both for his work at his local church in Avonwick and also for his appointment as deanery treasurer. A family spokesman said of Vincent Hoey: 'He is remembered for his contribution to the world as an accountant, a soldier, a farmer, a father and grandfather, and as a stalwart in the community.'

4

SBS HEROES

The Special Boat Service (SBS) was formed by Roger 'Jumbo' Courtney, a Commando officer, in July 1940. Courtney had initially been unsuccessful in his attempts to convince British military leaders of the merits of an amphibious Special Forces unit. However, he then decided to infiltrate HMS Glengyle, an infantry landing ship anchored in the River Clyde. After paddling to the ship, he climbed aboard undetected, wrote his initials on the door to the captain's cabin and stole a deck-gun cover. After Courtney presented the cover to a group of high-ranking Royal Navy officers, his antics swayed them. He was promoted to captain and given command of twelve men, the first Special Boat Service.

For the first few months of its existence, it was known as the Folbot Troop, the name deriving from the 'folbots', or 'folboats' – folding boats or kayaks – used on its missions. The SBS was tasked with carrying out similar roles to the SAS, but with a stronger focus on amphibious operations. It was, however, a smaller unit, never comprising more than 100 men during the Second World War, even when the SAS had grown to more than 1,000 strong. As such, the SBS was Britain's most exclusive force and, arguably, its most ruthless.

As happened with the SAS's first operation, bad weather meant that the SBS's initial mission got off to a troubled start. German operations off the Dutch coast had been the intended target: the men were taken there on motor torpedo boats (MTBs), but their folbots could not be launched. Eventually the mission had to be aborted, but not before Courtney had learnt a lesson: as carriers, submarines were preferable to MTBs. The SBS was renamed No. 1

Special Boat Section in early 1941 and it made its mark for the remainder of the war, including when, in February 1941, it sailed with No. 8 Commando for the Middle East. The SBS later carried out successful work on the Greek islands, undertaking beach reconnaissance on Rhodes and evacuating Allied troops from Crete.

Courtney formed No. 2 SBS in December 1941, while No. 1 SBS became attached to the SAS as the Folbot Section. In June 1942 the SBS took part in a raid on Crete airfields and, two months later, it carried out 'Operation Anglo', a raid on two airfields on Rhodes. However, only two men returned from the mission, which had destroyed three aircraft, a fuel dump and numerous buildings; the survivors had to hide in the countryside for four days before they could be picked up by a submarine. Afterwards the SBS men were absorbed into the SAS.

Under a reorganisation in April 1943, 1st SAS was divided into two, with half being commanded by 'Paddy' Mayne as the Special Raiding Squadron (SRS) and the other half forming the Special Boat Squadron under the command of Major Lord Jellicoe. The SBS moved to Haifa, now part of modern-day Israel, and trained for operations on the Aegean. As well as taking part in the Dodecanese Campaign, it was involved in the Battle of Leros and the Battle of Kos. In July 1944 the SBS was involved in a successful raid on the island of Symi, working with the Greek Sacred Band. Further operations followed with Long Range Desert Group (LRDG) in the Adriatic, on the Peloponnese, in Albania and Istria.

On 4 September 1945 Commander Anders Lassen became the only Special Forces operative in history to be awarded the Victoria Cross (VC): a posthumous decoration for his outstanding gallantry at Lake Comacchio on the night of 8/9 April 1945 during the final weeks of the Italian Campaign. Lassen, aged just twenty-four, was mortally wounded as he led his men in battle.

The SBS performed with distinction until the end of the war. In 1946 it was disbanded, but the functional title was adopted by the Royal Marines. It became part of the School of Combined Operations, active in the Middle East and, later, in the Korean

War. The Special Boat Section officially became the Special Boat Squadron in 1977 and, in turn, the Special Boat Service in 1987. The SBS continues to be drawn mostly from the ranks of the Royal Marines and is part of the Naval Service. Its wide-ranging tasks include intelligence-gathering, counter-terrorism operations (surveillance or offensive action), sabotage and the disruption of enemy infrastructure, capture of specific individuals, close protection of senior politicians and military personnel, plus reconnaissance and combat action on foreign territory.

The SBS today – motto 'By Strength and Guile' – is a highly respected fighting force and it has taken part in operations all over the world, including the First Gulf War, when it liberated the British Embassy in Kuwait. The SBS is under the operational command of the Director Special Forces.

PRIVATE STANLEY RAYMOND HUGHES
AWARD: MILITARY MEDAL (MM)
GAZETTED: 23 MARCH 1944

Prior to embarking on the daring raid on the north side of Lake Comacchio in enemy-held Italy, the legendary Major Anders Lassen of the SBS issued a coded order to his men: 'Every reasonable risk must – repeat MUST – be taken.' The sixteen men on the mission followed their leader's instructions to the letter and suffered terrible casualties as a result of one of the most courageous assaults by a Special Forces unit of the entire Second World War.

Private Stanley 'Wally' Hughes enlisted in the Royal Irish Fusiliers before transferring to the SBS some time after it was founded in July 1940. Little is known of his early military career, but he was awarded his MM for his part in taking the town of St Vito in Italy during the Italian Campaign. His decoration was announced on 23 March 1944, after his recommendation stated:

At approximately 04:00 hours, 2nd December 1943, Corporal Hughes entered St Vito as second in command of a patrol led by Lieutenant Day.

The main German positions were five miles to the south and the town itself was strongly held by Germans. As the patrol fought their way into the town, two Germans pounced on the Bren gunner, these Corporal Hughes promptly killed with his Tommy-Gun. He then took charge of one section of the patrol and advancing boldly down the main street, he took eight German prisoners and killed three German motorcyclists. By this time, the town was in uproar and finding that Lieutenant Day had been badly wounded by the fire from German Armoured Cars, he collected the patrol and cleverly hid them in houses until the town was taken by the 6th Inniskilling Fusiliers twelve hours later.

It is considered that his spirited entry into the town and the havoc wrought by this N.C.O. and his men must have seriously embarrassed the main German forces holding the river to the south. Reports from the men in the patrol prove that Corporal Hughes is a fearless and outstanding leader.

The wording of such praise from comrades in the final sentence of the citation is extremely rare and gives an indication of just how courageous he was. In fact, Hughes was originally recommended for a Distinguished Conduct Medal (DCM), but received the MM instead.

The night-time raid on the north shore of Lake Comacchio took place in early April 1945 when Lassen and his men, including Stanley Hughes, pitted themselves against eight Spandau machine guns in a terrifying assault. What happened to them is best described in the citation for Lassen's posthumous VC, published in the *London Gazette* on 4 September 1945:

In Italy, on the night of 8th/9th April, 1945, Major Lassen was ordered to take out a patrol of one officer and seventeen other ranks to raid the north shore of Lake Comacchio.

His tasks were to cause as many casualties and as much confusion as possible, to give the impression of a major landing, and to capture prisoners. No previous reconnaissance was possible, and the party found itself on a narrow road flanked on both sides by water.

Preceded by two scouts, Major Lassen led his men along the road towards the town. They were challenged after approximately 500 yards from a position on the side of the road. An attempt to allay suspicion by answering that they were fishermen returning home failed, for when moving forward again to overpower the sentry, machine-gun fire started from the position, and also from two other blockhouses to the rear.

Major Lassen himself then attacked with grenades, and annihilated the first position containing four Germans and two machine-guns. Ignoring the hail of bullets sweeping the road from three enemy positions, an additional one having come into action from 300 yards down the road, he raced forward to engage the second position under covering fire from the remainder of the force. Throwing in more grenades he silenced this position which was then overrun by his patrol. Two enemy were killed, two captured and two more machine-guns silenced.

By this time the force had suffered casualties and its fire power was very considerably reduced. Still under a heavy cone of fire Major Lassen rallied and reorganised his force and brought his fire to bear on the third position. Moving forward himself he flung in more grenades which produced a cry of 'Kamerad'. He then went forward to within three or four yards of the position to order the enemy outside, and to take their surrender.

Whilst shouting to them to come out he was hit by a burst of spandau fire from the left of the position and he fell mortally wounded, but even whilst falling he flung a grenade, wounding some of the occupants, and enabling his patrol to dash in and capture this final position.

Major Lassen refused to be evacuated as he said it would impede the withdrawal and endanger further lives, and as ammunition was nearly exhausted the force had to withdraw.

By his magnificent leadership and complete disregard for his personal safety, Major Lassen had, in the face of overwhelming superiority, achieved his objects. Three positions were wiped out, accounting for six machine guns, killing eight and wounding others of the enemy, and two prisoners were taken. The high sense of devotion to duty and the esteem in which he was held by the men he led, added to his own magnificent courage, enabled Major Lassen to carry out all the tasks he had been given with complete success.

Lassen was aged twenty-four when he was killed. He had already been awarded the Military Cross (MC) and two Bars, and now he was awarded a posthumous VC for his courage. He remains the only SAS/SBS recipient of Britain and the Commonwealth's most prestigious award for gallantry in the face of the enemy.

Hughes was one of three SBS men also killed in action that day. Lassen and Hughes are buried in adjoining graves at the Argenta Gap War Cemetery in Italy.

CAPTAIN (LATER MAJOR) HAROLD VERE HOLDEN-WHITE
AWARD: MILITARY CROSS (MC)
GAZETTED: 27 APRIL 1944

The attack on the harbour of Oran, Morocco, was the first British-American combined operation of the Second World War. It was later described by Winston Churchill, the wartime prime minister, as 'the finest British naval engagement since Trafalgar'. The action led to the award of a posthumous VC for Acting Captain Frederick Peters, the Canadian captain of HMS *Walney*, who, although he survived the assault on Vichy France-held Oran on 8 November 1943, tragically died in an aircraft crash off Plymouth, Devon, only five days later. Harry Holden-White was awarded the MC for his courage during the same attack on Oran, the result of being summoned weeks earlier to something that was 'hush-hush'.

Born in London in 1917, Holden-White was educated at Stowe School in Buckinghamshire and, later, in Switzerland. He was commissioned as a 2nd lieutenant into The King's Own Yorkshire Light Infantry on 25 September 1937 and transferred into the Royal Sussex Regiment on 21 December 1940. In 1942 Holden-White volunteered for Special Duties and was accepted. In his book *SBS: The Inside Story of the Special Boat Service*, John Parker wrote:

> Before he knew what was happening, he was on his way to Scotland, where Jumbo Courtney was hastily assembling a contingent who would form 2 SBS, now that 1 SBS was under so much pressure at the eastern end of the Mediterranean. The new section would include some returned members of the original section, with new recruits such as Holden-White and the merging of 101 Troop, 8 Commando, the latter hand-picked by its commanding officer, Captain Gerald Montanaro . . . Their billet was a private hotel in a suburb of Ardrossan, and soon Holden-White was being initiated into the gospel according to Jumbo.

At Ardrossan, Holden-White and his comrades primarily learnt about sabotage, coastline reconnaissance, how to land agents behind enemy lines and how to live off the land. In the second week of October 1942, Holden-White, by now a captain, was summoned to Lord Mountbatten's Combined Operations Headquarters in Whitehall, central London. It was here, where Courtney had an office, that he learnt that something big – something 'hush-hush' – was being planned.

The mission – codenamed 'Operation Reservist' – was to be Holden-White's first operational sortie with his new unit. Operation Reservist, in turn, was to be a subsidiary of 'Operation Torch', the planned mass invasion of North Africa scheduled for November 1942. Operation Reservist was an amphibious landing against an enemy force that was well protected by shore batteries and numerous ships.

As the detailed planning was finalised, Holden-White selected five pairs of canoeists and the men loaded their stores, weapons and canoes on board two American Coastguard cutters, by then both under a Royal Navy flag: HMS *Walney* and HMS *Hartland*. Three pairs of canoeists went with Holden-White in *Walney*, while the two other pairs went with Lieutenant E.J.A. Lunn in *Hartland*. The intention was that once they reached Gibraltar they would join a large convoy that would have submarines and destroyers for protection. At Gibraltar, they would pick up 400 American troops, who would mount a seaborne assault on Oran and then, if all went well, hold it until reinforcements arrived from inland. The SBS's role was to go in first, blowing up shipping with their experimental torpedoes. Each pair of canoeists was to be given two mini-torpedoes in Gibraltar, with the aim of releasing them at suitable targets in the harbour at the earliest opportunity. The innovative weapons, measuring just twenty-one inches in length, had been designed by Sir Donald Campbell, famed for his land and water speed records.

However, after arriving in Gibraltar, Holden-White and his men encountered the first of many problems. In his unpublished memoirs he explained:

When we got to Gib, there was no bloody officer to explain it all, no bloody instructions, and the baby torpedoes were in bits. Luckily, I had Sergeant-Major J. Embelin with us, who was a demolition expert, and he was able to assemble them. But we still had only a vague idea about range and so on, and a greater surprise was to come on that score much later. Another problem for us was launching the canoes from ships. Normally, SBS crews are floated off submarines or lowered from MTBs [motor torpedo boats]. These cutters gave us a drop of eight to ten feet and our flimsy folbots could have been damaged. So on the way out we decided to practise and unpacked the canoes we had brought aboard in kitbags to assemble them, staggering about the heaving deck like some mad ballet. Fortunately the *Walney*'s shipwright designed a sling to lower our boats into the water.

Holden-White's concerns for what lay ahead were picked up by those more senior to him:

In the evenings, amid the buzz of conversation and the clink of glasses of the pre-dinner get-together in the Wardroom, my gloom about the future of the operation would return, and, although I tried to hide it as much as possible, must, at times, have been apparent. Certainly, Captain Peters R.N., who was in overall command of *Walney* and *Hartland*, noticed it. I can see him now, as, coming into the Wardroom for a drink and a chat with the assembled officers, he catches sight of my face as he passes the table where I am sitting. 'Don't look so worried, Harry, it's going to be all right,' and he gives me an encouraging slap on the back.

It was in the early hours of 8 November 1942 that British and American forces entered the area. In his memoirs, Holden-White gave a detailed description of what happened next:

As we sailed into Oran, it was evident that the harbour was a death-trap for a seaborne assault. Although the overall length of the harbour straddled the coast for about a mile, the opening to it was protected by a boom, which we knew about, of course. Once inside, there was no escape. *Walney* was supposed to ram the boom and, if that failed, Sergeant-Major Embelin, the demolition expert, was to break open the boom with explosives. Sadly, he was subsequently killed by French machine-gun fire from the shore.

Anyhow, as soon as we sailed in, the Vichy-French shore batteries started firing. The three SBS pairs on board *Walney* were virtually thrown overboard and started paddling towards the docks. Frankly, I was so bloody glad to be away from it. Soon that feeling turned to guilt as I and my number two, Corporal Ellis, paddled off to find suitable targets for our mini-torpedoes. We had not travelled far when there was a huge explosion. We looked back. *Walney* had been hit by shore batteries and was already sinking. Then *Hartland* was hit; they were being shot to pieces and eventually we learned that around half the men on board were lost. Sally [nickname] Lunn had been unable to launch his pair of canoes because they were damaged by shells. They joined escaping US troops on Carley life rafts.

Ellis and I paddled on. We had lost sight of our other chaps. We hid behind a barge to get our bearing, and as we did a ship loomed up out of the darkness coming towards us, a bloody great ship, absolutely enormous. Anyway . . . a suitable target, I thought. I fired one of my mini-torpedoes. There was no big bang, although the ship slowed down for a moment. Whether we hit it or not I don't know. She was eventually sunk outside the harbour by one of our subs. Then a submarine came out and I fired my second mini-torpedo at the sub.

Unfortunately, my arm was jolted as I put it in the water, so that one went astray. We watched it go, streaking through the water, but at least it made a bang. It hit the harbour wall just below the lighthouse, which was not, of course, lit . . . After that there was nothing we could do but go on.

The original plan, in the event of failure, was to paddle back out to sea and get aboard one of the many Allied ships outside the harbour. This was now impossible. *Walney* and *Hartland*, still ablaze and listing, blocked our route. There was no alternative but to go on to the harbour and try to make our escape there and link up with the troops coming inland.

The harbour was swarming with Vichy French troops who captured them straight away. Because they were not in uniform, they were warned they might be shot as spies, but the two men were eventually taken to a makeshift PoW camp on the edge of the town, where they were reunited with other SBS men and survivors from the two cutters. After being captured, Lunn, one of the SBS men, had been horrified to see a mini-torpedo floating in the water near the quay. Within five days, the PoWs had been freed by advancing US troops. Amid the confusion of war, Holden-White eventually managed to get a flight back to Gibraltar before hitching a second lift on a flight to Cornwall. After landing, the men, in strange clothes and without papers, were arrested. They were finally taken under escort to London, where their identities were confirmed and they were able to report back on the operation in general, and the trials of the mini-torpedoes in particular.

Lord Mountbatten summoned Holden-White and Lunn to his office, where he confessed to the two men his disappointment at the performance of the mini-torpedoes. Holden-White was unable to hide his anger at what he saw as the 'shameful waste of life at Oran', pushing his dissatisfaction as far as he could in the presence of such a senior officer. Mountbatten wanted both men to be interviewed for the BBC, as it was the first operation of its kind involving British and American troops working together. Mountbatten was keen to capitalise, for propaganda purposes, on the success of the operation as a whole, even if the initial assault on Oran had been chaotic. Despite huge pressure to carry out Mountbatten's wishes, Holden-White refused, saying it would be a betrayal of those who had lost their lives in the raid. Despite Holden-White's stubborn opposition, Mountbatten never held it against him – personally approving Holden-White's MC and, later, recruiting him for his new enterprise in south-east Asia.

Furthermore, in April 1944, Mountbatten established the Small Operations Group (SOG) – approved of by Holden-White – which brought together the skills of the several units involved in amphibious raiding, sabotage work and reconnaissance behind enemy lines. In the same month – 27 April 1944 – Holden-White's MC was announced, after his recommendation stated: 'Capt. Holden-White was in command of the Special

Boat Section Unit, which was detailed to carry out dangerous and delicate operations in conjunction with the assault on the port of Oran. He was in charge of the party operating from H.M.S. *Walney* in folbots and displayed courage and initiative of a high order in attacking with small torpedoes a French destroyer which was leaving the port, and it is believed that one hit on the vessel was obtained.'

From 1944 to 1945 Holden-White, by now a major, was Commanding Officer of 'A' Group, SBS. His role was to run operations against the Japanese on the Arakan coast of Burma and his was one of three SBS units seconded to the SOG, along with Detachment 385 from the Royal Marines Commando assault troops, four Sea Reconnaissance Units (SRUs) and four parties from Combined Operations Pilotage Parties (COPPs). After training in Ceylon (now Sri Lanka) and Pakistan, 'A' Group moved to the Arakan front from 16 October to 14 December 1944 and during this time they used motor launches (MLs) and paddled Mark 1 canoes. Holden-White was involved in a substantial amount of reconnaissance work and was Mentioned in Despatches (MiD) for his exploits on and off the Arakan coast.

In January 1945 Lunn, who had accompanied Holden-White on the Oran raid, took over command of 'A' Group. Holden-White himself had been ill due to the appalling jungle conditions and required a lengthy period of treatment in a naval hospital in Colombo, Ceylon. Once recovered, he took up the position as SOG liaison officer at the Headquarters of South East Asia Command in Kandy, also in Ceylon. He initially found it hard to settle into the new role, but eventually embraced all 'opportunities'.

At the end of the war Holden-White stayed in Ceylon, working as garrison adjutant before becoming Troop Commander with 3 Commando based in Hong Kong. After being demobilised, he pursued his passion, studying painting at the Chelsea School of Art and in Paris. After a time living and painting in the south of France, he moved to Scotland, where he did a great deal of fishing. In his later years Holden-White devoted a substantial amount of his time to his memoirs and to preserving the history of the SBS. He died in 1999, aged eighty-two.

COMPANY SERGEANT MAJOR (LATER CAPTAIN) GEORGE BARNES
AWARDS: MILITARY MEDAL (MM) AND BAR
GAZETTED: 24 FEBRUARY 1942 AND 4 NOVEMBER 1942

George Barnes was one of the original nine members of the 1st Special Boat Section (later the Special Boat Service), founded in July 1940. He was twice awarded the MM for his part in equally daring SBS raids almost exactly a year apart, in June 1941 and June 1942. He also took part in the ill-fated attack on General Erwin Rommel's suspected headquarters.

Barnes was originally enlisted into the Grenadier Guards, before transferring to, first, No. 8 Commando and, then, the SBS, where he served in North Africa and southern Europe. His first MM was awarded when he was a company sergeant major and it was for a daring seaborne raid on the Libyan coast. His decoration was announced in the *London Gazette* on 24 February 1942, after his once-confidential recommendation stated: 'On 11th June 1941 this NCO displayed great coolness and courage under fire during a seaborne raid of a dangerous nature into enemy territory, and by great presence of mind ensured not only the success of the operation but also the safe withdrawal of the raiding party.'

An account of the same raid – but given as four days earlier than in the above recommendation – was given by Major Roger Courtney, who wrote:

On June 7th, 1941, I and Sergeant Major Barnes of the Grenadier Guards landed at the fort of el Brega on the Libyan coast in bright moonlight. When going towards the fort we were severely shot up by native Italian levies and from this we learned the lesson that native levies, who in ordinary times are accustomed to herd sheep, make very good coast watchers. Though the range was very short neither I nor Sergeant Major Barnes were hit and made good our escape on the submarine, Taku, which had put us ashore. The submarine put a 4 inch shell into the camp of the native levies and shattered it.

In November 1941 he took part, in a supporting role, in the raid led by Lieutenant Colonel Geoffrey Keyes to try to assassinate Rommel deep behind enemy lines at his supposed headquarters in Libya. However, the mission was a hopeless failure and eventually led to the death of Keyes and many of his comrades. Keyes was awarded a posthumous VC for his bravery, but by any standards the raid was wasteful of Allied resources and lives.

In the summer of 1942 Barnes was part of a highly successful raid on German-occupied Crete. He was awarded a Bar to his MM on 5 November 1942, after his recommendation stated:

The above named, together with another NCO of the Special Boat Section, and an officer in charge, carried out an attack on Kastelli Aerodrome, Crete, on the night of 9th–10th June 1942. They left their hide-out on the beach at 19.00 on the 6th June and returned at 05.30 on the 13th June after a difficult and hazardous march through enemy occupied territory and a successful attack on the objective. Their bag amounted to seven aircraft, 219-60 Gallon drums of petrol, six transport vehicles, three bomb dumps and one large oil fuel dump, fires and explosions are also believed to have caused 70 casualties to German personnel on the aerodrome. The success of the attack was due to the good leadership of the officer in charge and the courage and skill of C.S.M. Barnes.

It is not known what happened to Barnes after he left the military.

SERGEANT HAROLD WHITTLE
AWARD: GEORGE MEDAL (GM)
GAZETTED: 2 MARCH 1944

Members of the SAS and other Special Forces units are rarely put in a position where they can carry out acts of bravery that entitle them to be awarded the George Cross (GC) or George Medal (GM). Special Forces men operate behind enemy lines or in hit-and-run raids directly confronting the enemy, whereas both the GC and GM are awarded for gallantry not in the face of the enemy, often for bomb disposal work. In fact, during the entire Second World War only two George Medals (and no George Crosses) were awarded to the Special Forces units. The only GM awarded to a Briton during the conflict was to Sergeant Harold Whittle of 'X' Detachment, Special Boat Squadron (SBS), 1 Special Air Service Regiment. The other GM, for the same action, was awarded to Private Jarrell Porter, an 'X' Detachment medic who was an American serving with the SBS.

In civilian life, Whittle worked as a miner but, after the outbreak of the war, he enlisted into the Royal Artillery. He joined the SBS in 1942 and was assigned to the so-called 'Irish Patrol' commanded by Captain Anders Lassen, the legendary Danish officer who was later awarded a posthumous VC for his courage during the Lake Comacchio operation in Italy on 9 April 1945. To this day, Lassen is the only SAS/SBS member to be awarded Britain and the Commonwealth's most prestigious gallantry decoration.

After the Italian Armistice of September 1943, the SBS occupied Kastellorizo, the easternmost of the Dodecanese Islands. Whittle's patrol moved on and was involved in the seizure of Symi, a small Greek island close to Rhodes. Both

Lassen and Whittle played a prominent part not just in this action but also in repelling German efforts to recapture the island. Days later, the Germans subjected Symi's inhabitants and the SBS to a heavy and prolonged attack by Stuka dive bombers. At around 1pm on 8 October 1943, the neighbouring buildings that formed the new temporary headquarters of the SBS were blown apart and two of the unit's numbers were trapped under the rubble.

Whittle's relentless bravery over the next day and a bit is described in a recommendation, marked 'Secret', that was submitted by Colonel D. Turnbull, of Commanding Raiding Force:

> This NCO displayed gallantry, leadership and initiative of the highest order during operations by X Detachment, S.B.S. in the Dodecanese, 13 Sept 1943 to 18 Oct 1943, at 1300 British HQ which received a direct hit during a Stuka raid. Two ORS [other ranks] were trapped alive under the debris. Whittle supervised rescue operations, working like a man possessed himself. He worked for a period of 27 hours without rest, exposing himself to extreme personal risk. He continued work throughout two further raids when a bomb falling anywhere in the slightest vicinity would have brought the remnants of the building upon him. He was a source of inspiration to all workers and the credit that the two were released alive (unfortunately both died later) and it was almost entirely due to his direction, initiative, in making do with the crude tools at his disposal, and his entire disregard of personal risk. He himself made and shored up a passage under debris to one man.

Jarrell, the American medic, had spent much of the same twenty-seven hours working close to Whittle and gave medical attention to the two badly injured men. The recommendation for Jarrell's GM stated that 'with Sergeant Whittle, [Jarrell] shares the credit for the two men being rescued alive. He entirely disregarded his own risk, crawling along perilous tunnels through the debris to administer morphia, feed and cheer [up] the trapped men; the next minute working feverishly to clear the debris. Owing to the RAF doctor having an injured wrist, under the doctor's supervision in appalling conditions, by candlelight, on his back, he did most of the leg amputation necessary to release one man. His movement was restricted by the likelihood of the shored up debris falling in on himself and the trapped men.'

After this double GM action, the squadron moved back to the island of Leros. When this fell to the Germans, they escaped to Turkey and then travelled overland back to their base in Palestine. In 1944, Whittle took part in a number of raids mounted from secret bases in Turkey on German garrisons in the Aegean.

Whittle was demobilised shortly after the end of the war and died in 1967.

SERGEANT ROBERT ARTHUR LEVER SUMMERS
AWARD: MILITARY MEDAL (MM)
GAZETTED: 4 JANUARY 1945

Robert Summers was decorated for exceptional leadership and courage during a raid on the German-occupied Greek island of Crete. Initially, he carried out a reconnaissance of the situation in the summer of 1944 and, two weeks later, led a patrol on a raid to blow up a petrol dump. The reconnaissance was particularly risky because he was wearing plain clothes for his mission – this meant that, if caught, he could have been arrested as a spy and executed. The mission itself was extremely difficult because the patrol was spotted by the enemy and fired upon.

Summers initially served with the King's Royal Rifle Corps, but at some point, almost certainly after volunteering, became attached to the Special Boat Squadron (later the Special Boat Service). Little else is known about his military career, but details of his action have emerged in a once-confidential recommendation for an immediate MM. It stated:

> This NCO was ordered to carry out a reconnaissance and make an attack on a petrol dump at Dhrasi [Drasi] in the island of Crete. He did a daring and successful reconnaissance in civilian clothes on 6th and 7th July [1944]. Having collected his patrol he attacked the dump on the night 22nd–23rd July, cutting his way through considerable wire defences. By cool leadership and courage he directed the laying of all the bombs carried by his patrol and remained in the dump for about half an hour. Although discovered and fired upon he kept his patrol together and withdrew them through the wire without casualties. In spite of the fact that he was without an interpreter, and that one of his men was suffering from malaria, he succeeding [sic] in leading his patrol from the Kastellion area to the target, and back to the beach over exceptionally difficult country for a period of eight days. On this and many similar occasions this NCO has shown exceptional qualities as a leader and his courage and devotion to duty have been of a high standard.

Summers MM was announced on 4 January 1945. He died in Sefton North, Lancashire, in late 1988.

CORPORAL RONALD GEORGE JOHNS (ALSO SPELT JOHN)
AWARD: MILITARY MEDAL (MM)
GAZETTED: 22 MARCH 1945

Ronald Johns (whose surname in some records is spelt 'John') was decorated for his gallantry during 'Operation Infatuate' – the Flushing landings of November 1944 close to the Belgian city of Antwerp. During the assault, many members of his 'Tarbrush' section were killed or wounded. Despite being injured himself and remaining under sustained fire, he saved the lives of his SBS team by crawling into the engine room of his landing craft assault (LCA) and starting the engines.

At the time of the incident, Johns was serving with the SBS, 4th Special Service Brigade, a crack Commando-style unit led by Brigadier B.W. 'Jumbo' Leicester. Johns, a native of the Yorkshire town of Doncaster, was a qualified mechanic in 'dories', special craft used by the SBS for clandestine coastal-reconnaissance operations in enemy-occupied territory.

'Operation Infatuate' was the code name given to the attempted opening of the port of Antwerp to shipping: the city had been captured in September 1944 by the British Second Army but the Germans still controlled the port's approaches. Operation Infatuate was part of the wider Battle of the Scheldt in northern Belgium and south-west Holland that was spearheaded by the Canadian 1st Army.

As a member of the SBS's 'Keep Force', charged with finding a suitable landing place for No. 4 Commando, Johns saved several lives in LCA 957 on 1 November 1944, when, their task completed, the SBS section prepared for the return trip to Breskens, less than two miles across the water. In his book *SBS: The Invisible Raiders*, James Ladd takes up the story: 'The "Tarbrush" party – now in an LCA – sailed for Breskens, but near the breakwater they were hotly engaged by German machine-guns. One "Tarbrush" officer was killed, as was the craft's engineer in the unarmoured space aft. She drifted on the current, her ramp still down, bullets "beating a tattoo on the armoured sides of her well" as she slowly swung towards the gun. Seeing the danger, Corporal Jones [*sic* – Johns], the party's dory mechanic, dragged the dead engineer from the aft compartment and restarted her engines before more damage was done . . .'

In fact, as confirmed by official Admiralty records, LCA 957 had earlier received '5 hits from shore batteries which damaged one engine, the steering and the telegraphs'. This strike, combined with the machine-gun fire, resulted in seven Army personnel being killed, and Corporal Johns and two ratings being wounded.

Johns' MM was announced in the *London Gazette* on 22 March 1945, after his once-confidential recommendation stated:

> On 1 November 1944, this N.C.O. was a member of the team in the leading L.C.A. detailed to make a passage through beach obstacles into Flushing. The officer in command of the team was killed and only two of the team remained unwounded, of which Corporal Johns was one. During the withdrawal on completion of the task, an enemy machine-gun got on to the L.C.A., directing its fire through the open ramp, killing two of the occupants. The rest took cover forward and close in to the sides. Corporal Johns realised that the engines were not running and that the L.C.A. was turning with the tide, so that the occupants would soon be exposed and raked with machine-gun fire. With complete disregard for his own personal safety, he ran through the tracer to get to the engine room. He fell, hit with a burst through the leg. Although he could have taken the cover he had just left, he continued to the engine room by crawling, and was hit again. Despite this he got in and started the engines before collapsing through loss of blood. But for his gallantry, there is little doubt most of the occupants of the L.C.A. would have become casualties.

No further information is available on Johns' later career. However, he died in Southend-on-Sea, Essex, in mid-1995.

BOMBARDIER ARTHUR MORGAN
AWARD: MILITARY MEDAL (MM)
GAZETTED: 2 AUGUST 1945

Bombardier Arthur Morgan was awarded the MM for an act of outstanding gallantry during a remarkable action while he was serving with the SBS. He took part in the unit's raid on Villa Punta on the Yugoslav island of Lussino (Lošinj today, off the coast of Croatia) in the Adriatic Sea. It was such a daring operation that it was later described by a military author as 'verging on the suicidal'.

Morgan had originally enlisted into the Royal Artillery, but long before the end of the Second World War he had become attached to the SBS. A detailed account of the attack on Villa Punta on 8 March 1945 is contained in James Ladd's book, *SBS: The Invisible Raiders*. Villa Punta was a large fortified house overlooking a beach. The property had substantial gardens and several outbuildings, and the Germans had apparently strengthened the cellar to provide greater protection against an air attack. At any one time, some forty-five German soldiers occupied the villa.

The initial plan by Ambrose McGonigal – an SBS officer later destined to be knighted and become a senior judge – was to seize the building by drawing the Germans to the back (seaward) side of the house. At that point, the main body of raiders – a total of only seventeen men – would storm the front of the villa. However, things did not go according to plan. One of the three lieutenants in the party led his men along the beach, where they encountered thick barbed wire. As they apparently tried to deal with this obstacle, the soldiers were heard by a German sentry, who fired on them. At this point, the Germans did not wait to see how the attack would unfold: instead they sent out a small fighting patrol to attack the intruders. However, as these men ran out of the building, they were met by a salvo from SBS Bren gunners, including Morgan, who were positioned at the back of the villa on walls and other vantage points. This fire drove the German fighting patrol back into the village.

McGonigal then led his men into the attack, storming the front of the house while Bren gunners kept up a steady fire to try to prevent the Germans from shooting down or dropping hand grenades on the raiders. Once inside the villa, the SBS worked in pairs to clear the passages and rooms one by one, and then tackled the outbuildings. Ladd wrote of this phase of the operation: 'At night, with a scratch plan of action, the job was verging on the suicidal. Lieutenants Jimmy Lees, Thomason and Jones-Parry got into the building, but the difficulties for the Bren gunners in identifying friend from foe led to some confusion. The dark of the passages was lit by the occasional flash of a grenade, while the sudden noise of firing – the ripping burst of a Schmeiser's rapid fire, answered by the slower staccato of Sten or tommy-gun – seemed to reverberate from all directions.'

At times, there were spells of sudden fire followed by long silences: it was not a place for the faint-hearted. Lees, one of the three lieutenants, reached the last room along one of the passages. As he entered a large lounge, he fired his sub-machine gun, only to be shot by a German hiding behind a sofa. Lees was not found by his comrades and died the next day in a German dressing station.

At one point, Jones-Parry, another of the lieutenants, got a message to the Bren gunners not to fire on the north side of the house. Jones-Parry saw two or three of the enemy in a corridor and threw a grenade at them that failed to explode. He followed up with a phosphorous bomb and then a round of fire before advancing, with Marine Kitchingham, through the thick white smoke. As he moved tentatively into one room, he opened fire, but the room was apparently empty. As the two men advanced to another door, Jones-Parry again opened fire before leaping into the darkened room. 'Are you all right, sir?' asked Kitchingham. 'Yes,' replied the officer. However, he had spoken too soon: a German, hiding in the darkness, opened fire, shattering the lieutenant's arm and leaving a bullet lodged in his spleen. Still he managed to re-load his sub-machine gun and spray the room with bullets. This time there was no return fire, only groans. As Jones-Parry, bloodied and wounded, crawled from the room, he saw that Kitchingham had been shot dead and was slumped in the doorway.

Ladd concluded his account of the mission: 'As Jones-Parry staggered from the building, Thomason's team were also working their way from room to room, but they had to send messages to the Bren gunners that their fire was hindering the house clearance. But now, with the villa on fire, there seemed little likelihood of many of the garrison escaping. As McGonigal had only eleven more or less fit men, the rest being seriously wounded, Lees dying and Kitchingham dead, he withdrew the patrols.' It had been a successful operation, but the SBS had also paid a heavy price.

The precise role that Morgan played in the attack is detailed in the once-confidential recommendation for his MM, which stated:

On the night of 8th March 1945, Bombardier Morgan was a member of a force attacking 'Villa Punta' on the island of Lussino in the Dalmatian group. In the first phase of the operation Bombardier Morgan was acting as a Bren gunner in an exposed position, directing fire into the windows of the villa. The enemy returned intense and accurate fire, wounding him seriously in the back. He, however, refused to leave his position and continued firing the Bren gun. In the second phase of the attack he entered the house with the Bren and engaged the enemy in the ground floor rooms. At this stage he received further wounds in the right leg. On the completion of the attack he walked back unaided to the boats, a distance of some four miles over a range of hills. Although suffering from intense pain from his first wounds Bombardier Morgan insisted on carrying on to the objective and completing his task. His complete disregard for his own safety and his persistence in carrying out his duty was an inspiration to all ranks.

It is not known what happened to Morgan after the war.

5

Commando Heroes

In the wake of the evacuation from Dunkirk from 27 May to 4 June 1940, Winston Churchill, who had recently been appointed prime minister, started increasingly to appreciate the merits of the Special Forces. Simultaneously, Lieutenant Colonel Dudley Clarke, who at the time was serving as Military Assistant to General Sir John Dill, the Chief of the Imperial General Staff (CIGS), came up with the format for a new force. Clarke, who had admired some of the guerrilla tactics of the Boer Commando units fighting the British during the Boer War of 1899–1902, started using the word 'Commando' and Churchill warmed to this term too. So in June 1940 the Commandos were born, with the intention of carrying out hit-and-run raids on the enemy until, at least, Britain and its Allies were in a position to launch a major new offensive against Germany.

Remarkably, No. 11 Commando – a wholly made-up name, often given as No. 11 (Scottish) Commando because it was formed in Scotland – was created within three weeks of Clarke's desire to establish such a raiding force. Commandos were initially drawn from within the British Army from men who volunteered for the Special Service Brigade. They were trained in physical fitness, survival, orienteering, close-quarter combat, silent killing, signalling, amphibious and cliff assault, vehicle operation, weapons and demolition.

On the night of 23/24 June 1940 the first Commando raid of the war took place, when 120 men from No. 11 Commando/ Independent Company took part in an offensive reconnaissance manoeuvre on the French coast south of Boulogne-sur-Mer and

Le Touquet. Hilary St George Saunders, author of The Green Beret: The Story of the Commandos *(first published in 1947),* wrote: '*Two factors limited the numbers who could take part in this first raid: the quantity of boats, and the quantity of Tommy guns available. Both were scarce.*' *The mission led to a skirmish in which two German soldiers were killed.*

At their inception, each Commando unit was intended to consist of a headquarters plus ten troops of fifty men but, as the war progressed, the size of the units varied. Some commanders resented losing their best men to the Commando units, but in general the system worked well. Much of the early training, including the use of fast landing craft, took place in Inverary, in Argyll in Scotland, but not all the volunteers for the Commandos made the grade.

John Durnford-Slater, who had observed the Commandos' first raid, was placed in command of No. 3 Commando, the organisation's first unit in the field. Soon, too, he was put in charge of expanding the force. Over the summer of 1940 six more Commando units were formed: Nos 4, 5, 6, 7, 8 and 9. Late 1940 and early 1941 saw some short-lived restructuring of the units, but by the spring of 1941 they had been re-formed and expanded to create eleven Commando units (numbered from 1 to 12 with No. 10 missing).

In North Africa, a key area of the early fighting in the Second World War, General Erwin Rommel, the 'Desert Fox', and his Afrika Korps soon came up against a British unit called Layforce, commanded by Colonel (later Brigadier) Robert Laycock. This was a 2,000-strong Commando brigade consisting of 7, 8 and 11 Commandos. During his time with 8 Commando, David Stirling, a lieutenant serving in the Scots Guards, had started to appreciate the merits of hit-and-run attacks behind enemy lines. And so, from these modest origins, the SAS was born.

The Commandos reached a wartime strength of more than thirty units and four assault brigades, serving in numerous theatres of the war, from the Arctic Circle to Europe, and from the Middle East to the Mediterranean. Commandos took part in a range of operations, *from small groups of men landing by sea to a brigade of assault troops spearheading the Allied invasion of Europe. Initially, Commandos had been drawn only from the Army, but later they were recruited from other services, notably the Royal Marines, resulting in the formation of Royal Marine Commandos.*

The end of the war led to most Commando units being disbanded, leaving just the Royal Marines 3 Commando Brigade. Nevertheless, the present-day British Royal Marine Commandos, Parachute Regiment, SAS and SBS can all trace their origins to the original Commandos. Hilary St George Saunders concludes his book by writing: 'When in course of time the present generation of Commando soldiers grows old and dies, the memory of great deeds greatly performed will remain with the glory, and that same sun which gilded the bayonets of [Lord] Lovat's men as they charged the guns at Vasterival, will shine upon a new generation as strong, as all-compelling as their fathers. For a tradition has been created.'

2ND LIEUTENANT (LATER LIEUTENANT AND FLIGHT LIEUTENANT) ERIC FRANCIS GARLAND

AWARDS: MILITARY CROSS (MC) AND BAR, AND ORDER OF THE BRITISH EMPIRE (MBE)
GAZETTED: 20 DECEMBER 1940, 21 OCTOBER 1941 AND 7 JANUARY 1947

Even in a book crammed full of remarkable achievements by extraordinary men, the daring and wide-ranging actions of Eric Garland take some beating. He was initially decorated for rescuing three men during the retreat to Dunkirk in 1940, only to have his courage publicly recognised again less than a year later for his part in the famous Litani River Raid. During this action, Garland fought a 'duel' with a sniper and was the first man to cross the river. Not content with his efforts on land, he joined the RAF to satisfy his desire to be a fighter pilot, but his Spitfire was shot down in May 1944. For lesser men, being a prisoner of war (PoW) would have been a respectable end to their part in the conflict, but Garland simply saw it as a new challenge: he escaped from a hospital train bound for Germany, evaded capture, fought with the partisans in Italy and, eventually, secretly returned to Allied lines in January 1945. Finally, more than a year after the war ended, he was awarded his third and final decoration: an MBE.

Garland was born in London in 1920 and was educated at Whitgift School in South Croydon. In September 1939 he joined 163 Officer Cadet Training Unit (OCTU), initially serving in the Artists Rifles. In November of the same year, Garland was commissioned as a 2nd lieutenant into the 6th Battalion, York and Lancaster Regiment. He served with the regiment as part of the 138th Infantry Brigade, 46th Infantry Division, British Expeditionary Force (BEF) in France.

Garland was present during the retreat to Dunkirk and on 27 May 1940 he distinguished himself at Wormhoudt, on the Dunkirk to Cassel road, and again at Watou the next day when he rescued three men, including one who was seriously wounded, from a house that was being used as an ammunition store. His MC was announced on 20 December 1940 after his recommendation stated:

At Watou on May 28 1940 during a very intense bombing raid [Garland] showed conspicuous bravery by entering a bombed and burning house while the raid was at its height and carried out 4750206 Private Nicholson to a place of safety. He at once returned and rescued two military policemen who had been wounded, and bound up their wounds. Private Nicholson died shortly afterwards. Heavy bombing was taking place while Second Lieutenant Garland was engaged in this rescue work.

The previous day this same officer carried out a reconnaissance under machine gun fire on a motor cycle at Wormhoudt and was able to guide his unit transport on a safe route.

During his final three full days on French soil before being evacuated, Garland showed still further courage. On 31 May, the 6th Battalion was tasked with holding three bridges over the Canal des Moëres at Téteghem and 2nd Lieutenants Garland, Nelson and Milne were each given a bridge to defend with the orders that they were to 'be held at all costs'. In fact, Garland held his position until late into the evening of 2 June, when his position became hopeless. At this point he retreated with his men to the beaches of Dunkirk and was one of the last to be evacuated on the *Medway Queen*, a paddle steamer, on 3 June. In fact, one of her ship's paddles broke during the voyage and it took fully seven hours to reach Ramsgate, Kent.

Ever eager to embark on a new adventure, Garland volunteered for service with the newly formed No. 11 (Scottish) Commando. This involved rigorous training in the Scottish Highlands under the command of Dick Pedder. On 31 May 1941, a year to the day after Garland had been in the thick of the fighting during the retreat to Dunkirk, Pedder and two other officers from the unit received urgent orders to fly to Palestine. On 5 June Pedder rejoined his men at Port Said, north-east Egypt, having received orders to take part in the invasion of Vichy-controlled Syria and Lebanon: No. 11 (Scottish) Commando formed up with the 21st Australian Infantry Brigade for this role.

At this point, the enemy was known to be holding the line of the Litani River, which runs south through Lebanon before turning west into the Mediterranean. The Allies' plan was for the Commandos, including Garland, to coordinate with the 21st Brigade's attack on the river position by carrying out an amphibious assault landing from the sea near the mouth of the river. Once ashore, the Commandos were tasked with securing the north and south banks of the Litani, and then preventing the demolition of the Qasmiye Bridge that crossed it, thereby allowing the Australian 21st Infantry Brigade to advance towards Beirut, engaging the enemy in the process.

The advancing forces were to be supported by gunfire from naval vessels offshore, as well as air support.

On 6 June, the Commando embarked on HMS *Glengyle* and set sail with escort from Port Said the following day. A reconnaissance of the coast was required and it showed that heavy surf was running at an average distance of 300 yards from the beach as a result of ground swell. Experts concluded that during the following two days any landing would result in a considerable loss of men. Despite the concerns, however, it was decided to make an attempt the following morning, 8 June. In fact, the predicted heavy seas that morning caused a false start, in spite of amphibious landing craft being lowered into the water, and the attack was postponed by some twenty-four hours until dawn on 9 June.

The plan was for the Commando to land from the *Glengyle* at dawn and attack the enemy position from the flank. Three parties were formed to carry out the task: 'X' Party consisted of the forward troops, comprising Nos 2, 3 (of which Garland was a member) and 9 Troops under the command of Major Geoffrey Keyes. The landing by 'X' Party was unopposed, but as the advanced troops reached the river bank at about 5.10am, the entire beach came under heavy and sustained fire from 75mm guns, mortars and heavy machine guns. In his book *Litani River*, Ian McHarg wrote:

> As heavy fire rained down on the party they were pinned to the ground, and several casualties were taken, mainly by accurate sniper fire from a knoll on the opposite bank and from enemy positions to the north. A Section of No. 3 Troop under Captain George Highland and Lieutenant Eric Garland succeeded in working forward on the right of No. 2 Troop before getting held up again. The area on the approach to the river from the south side was flat and open ground which offered very little cover for the advancing commandos making progress not only slow but extremely treacherous . . .

In his diary, Keyes described a similar scene, adding that Highland and Garland were 'as cool as cucumbers'.

When the Commandos' progress ground to a halt, some comrades brought a boat forward to the south bank for them to use for the river crossing. However, Keyes took over thirty minutes to advance by a mixture of crawling and sprinting to reach Highland and Garland. On arriving at their position, Keyes – according to McHarg – found 'the two men engaged in a high risk method of drawing the sniper's fire, which was inflicting many casualties. Garland, exposing himself to the sniper, drew his fire, and once located, shot him with his Bren gun . . .' With the sniper taken care of, Garland and some other men climbed into the boat that had been brought for them, which was positioned out of the line of sight of the redoubt. Two men then ferried the Commandos across the river, which was approximately thirty to forty yards wide and fast flowing, enabling Garland, six of his men and two Australians to get to the opposite bank at around 10am. Within three hours, Garland's and Highland's men had cleared the enemy position on the north side. In the process of seizing the redoubt, six enemy soldiers were killed and thirty-five prisoners were taken, but the efforts to capture the enemy position had resulted in considerable casualties for the attacking party too.

The Commando set sail for Cyprus at 6.50pm on 14 June, arriving in Famagusta at 7am the following morning. Of the 456 men who had assembled on the same quay eleven days earlier, 130 had been killed or wounded in just over twenty-nine hours of fighting. However, despite suffering heavy casualties – including Pedder, the Commanding Officer, who was killed leading his men – the Commando had achieved its overall objective of seizing and holding the enemy position long enough for the Australian Brigade to cross the river and pass on through.

Garland's Bar to his MC was announced on 21 October 1941, after the recommendation for his decoration – originally intended as the Distinguished Service Order (DSO) and written by Colonel Robert Laycock – stated:

> Litani River (Syria) 9–10 June 1941. Lieutenant Garland displayed throughout the action cool and clear-headed leadership and complete disregard for his own personal safety. He was the first individual to cross the river and personally led the party which cut out the enemy wire on the far side under heavy fire. On one occasion by deliberately exposing himself he personally drew the fire of a sniper who was causing severe casualties and, on locating the enemy position, Lieutenant Garland manned one of his Bren Guns and shot the sniper. Lieutenant Garland also put out of action a 75 Gun, which was covering the river, by accurate fire from a captured anti Tank Gun.

After the Litani River Raid, the 11th (Scottish) Commando returned to Cyprus, but both Keyes and Laycock asked Garland to allow them to stay on to take part in the proposed Rommel Raid which, as previously stated, would cost Keyes his life and lead to the award of a posthumous VC. However, in the meantime, Garland had determined to become a fighter pilot. He applied to join the RAF, and when his papers came through he transferred for training.

In March 1942 Garland was posted for pilot training to No. 26 Elementary FTS (Flying Training School), Southern Rhodesia. At this time he trained with Ian Smith, who would later become the prime minister of Rhodesia. After undertaking further training, Garland gained his 'wings' in August 1942. In February 1943 he was posted for conversion to Hurricanes to No. 74 OTU (Officer Training Unit) in Aqir, Palestine. Next, in April of the same year, he was posted for operational flying to 237 (Rhodesia) Squadron (Hurricanes), which carried out operations over the Western Desert, primarily shipping patrols and interceptions. However, within the first week of flying, on 12 April 1943 he had to carry out a forced landing because of engine failure. He was posted to 208 Squadron (Hurricanes) in Iraq in June of that year, where he flew on tactical reconnaissance sorties throughout the desert fighting.

Garland was promoted to flight lieutenant in November 1943 and, two months later, 208 Squadron was re-equipped with Spitfires. In March 1944 he moved with it to Italy, where, for two months, he carried out sweeps and tactical reconnaissances. However, on 4 May 1944, when flying over Italy during the four-month Battle of Monte Cassino, Garland was shot down. He received an injury to his left leg, a splintered tibia, and burns to his hands and face, none of which prevented him from undertaking what he saw as his obligation: escaping from his PoW camp. Following three unsuccessful bids, he jumped from a hospital train near Verona in the summer of 1944. After walking for two or three days, he reached Lake Garda, where he spent time with some friendly Italians. In August he attempted to get back to the Allied lines by walking from Lake Garda to Cremona, but the wound in his injured leg became infected and he had to abort the plan, again finding refuge with a group of Italians. In April 1945 he joined the partisans and took part in one action at Vasto di Sotto in which seventy-seven German soldiers were killed or captured, whereas the partisans had only three killed and two wounded.

After Garland had been shot down in May 1944, his Commanding Officer wrote to his parents saying:

> Your son had to bale out, and it is established by the evidence of the pilot who was flying another aircraft with him that your son's parachute opened successfully, and was seen descending slowly, unfortunately behind enemy lines.
>
> Your son had just taken over a Flight and I had the fullest confidence in him as a Flight Commander and as a pilot. His steadiness, professional ability, unassuming leadership and courage were a great asset to me, and to the whole Squadron. His fine

Army record is one of which, with you, we are all very proud. There is no more popular member of the Mess than your son, and each one of us shares in some respect at least in your anxiety. It is my earnest hope that such anxiety will be speedily allayed, and again I assure you that anything learned will be notified to you in the quickest possible manner.

However, after the allotted period of time without hearing any information with regard to Garland, the Air Ministry informed his father that he was to be declared dead. However, Garland himself had other ideas and penned the following on 9 August 1944:

Dear Mother & Father,

Here is a brief account of what has happened during the past three months. I was brought down by anti-aircraft fire on the Cassino front just before the push on May 4th. A 20mm shell hit some part of the fuel system and the plane caught fire immediately and I had to bale out some 40 miles over the line.

My hands were burnt and my left leg hit by a splinter making a fairly large flesh wound on my left shin. I was taken prisoner immediately on reaching the ground and spent 7 weeks in hospital at Mantover. I made three unsuccessful attempts to escape from there, but finally managed to escape from the hospital train to Germany on June 17th by jumping out of the window at night, the sentry was dozing. From then until now I have been hiding in the Verona area near Lake di Garda waiting for my leg to heal, my hands are quite ok. I have lived most of the time in the open; the Italian people have been extremely kind and helpful in providing food, civilian clothing, etc., and a Doctor has attended me in spite of the [threat of the] death penalty.

I change to the present tense now. Tonight I am setting out across the Po Valley to Parma and from there I shall make my way through the mountains towards the front and when the line breaks I shall get through somehow. The front at the moment is the line of the Arno River, Pisa, Florence, Arezzo. Switzerland is out and I am in an exposed position here.

In case I have the misfortune to be recaptured I am writing this letter so that you will know my movements. An Italian is going to bury it in a bottle to give to an Allied Soldier when they arrive. I am also giving letters addressed to AMGOT [Allied Military Government for Occupied Territories] to the people who helped me so it should be possible to keep track of me. If you don't hear from me for some time don't worry, I shall be giving the Jerries a pain in the neck wherever I am.

Your loving son,

Eric

Remarkably, this letter found its way into the hands of Captain J.H. Bevan, 8/22nd Battery, Royal Artillery some eight months later, and he duly forwarded it to Garland's parents with the following accompanying letter:

Dear Mr. & Mrs. Garland,

We have just arrived in this area and one of the local Italians gave me this letter. He also gave me one which your son wrote to the AMGOT authorities saying how well treated and cared for he had been whilst staying with this Italian family. I don't suppose we shall be staying here long as the chase is still on, and it's quite exciting but I shall ensure that this letter reaches AMGOT.

True to his word, Garland fought his way through and reached American lines at Solarolo in January 1945, reporting back to his unit on 2 May 1945. His family was informed of his reappearance eight days later and Garland eventually returned to the UK. After the war, he remained in the RAF for a further two years.

Garland's MBE was announced in the *London Gazette* on 7 January 1947, after his recommendation stated:

Flight Lieutenant Garland's aircraft was shot down over Frosinone in Italy on 4th May, 1944. He was immediately captured and sent to a hospital at Acre. In spite of his wounds, this officer made three attempts to escape from a hospital at Mantova in May, 1944. He collected a store of medical materials and retrieved his battledress. Twice he was caught by sentries while climbing through a window. The third time, after sliding down a laundry chute, he was captured while trying to saw through a door. In June, 1944, Flight Lieutenant Garland jumped from a hospital train near Verona. After two days he made contact with some friendly Italians, with whom he stayed for two months. In August, 1944, he set out with the intention of joining some Italian partizans. He walked for three days, but owing to a leg injury he was forced to take refuge with another Italian family. In January, 1945, Flight Lieutenant Garland left these people, his leg having finally healed, and reached the American lines at Solarolo in the Po Valley.

After leaving the RAF, Garland joined British European Airways (BEA) as a commercial pilot. However, he moved to Kenya in 1948 and was based there at the start of the Mau Mau Rebellion in 1952. He immediately joined the Air Wing of the Police Force, flying Rapide, Messenger and Bonanza aircraft. Later, he became a pilot for Manx Airlines before retiring in 1985, aged sixty-five. It is not known what happened to Garland after his retirement.

MAJOR JOHN HYNDFORD CARMICHAEL
AWARD: MILITARY CROSS (MC)
GAZETTED: 9 SEPTEMBER 1942

Johnny Carmichael, a veteran of the Great War, was awarded the MC largely for his bravery on the Bardia Raid in North Africa in April 1941. At the time, he was leading the Commandos of 'A' Battalion, Layforce, commanded by the intrepid Colonel

Robert Laycock. Carmichael's part in the successful raid was so notable that he was known afterwards as the 'Uncrowned King of Bardia'.

Carmichael was born in Coldstream, Berwickshire, Scotland, in 1889. He was educated at Edinburgh Academy and the Royal Military Academy, Sandhurst, before being commissioned into the Argyll and Sutherland Highlanders. He served in France and Belgium with the regiment's 2nd Battalion until he was wounded in April 1918.

In 1920 he was appointed aide-de-camp (ADC) to the Governor of Bombay, a role he fulfilled until the end of 1923. He subsequently served in the West Indies and in northern China, where he was posted to the British Legation Guard in Peking. In 1933 Carmichael returned to the UK, and was appointed adjutant of the 7th Battalion of the Argyll and Sutherland Highlands in January 1934. He first retired in 1935, but he was recalled to the Army in general, and his regiment in particular, after the outbreak of the Second World War in September 1939.

Carmichael was posted to the 1st Battalion in Palestine, and with that unit he took part in the Battle of Sidi Barrani in December 1940 and in the Crete Expedition of May 1941. It was because of his knowledge of the town of Bardia and its nearby beaches that he was chosen to play a leading role in the Bardia Raid. The operation was an amphibious landing at the coastal town on the night of 19/20 April 1941. It was carried out by 'A' Battalion, Layforce, consisting of men from No. 7 Commando, commanded by Colonel Laycock, together with a small detachment from the Royal Tank Regiment supported by five Navy ships and a submarine. Carmichael landed with the Commandos on the night of 19 April and in the ensuing hours they destroyed an Italian supply dump and an Italian coastal artillery battery before returning to their waiting landing craft to re-embark in the early hours of the following day. The raid was a considerable strategic success; alarmed by it, the Germans diverted the greater part of an armoured brigade from Sollum, on the Egyptian/Libyan border, where it was beginning to exert heavy pressure on the Western Desert Force, and kept it for some time in the rear areas.

Carmichael's MC was announced on 9 September 1942, when his citation read:

> Major Carmichael was appointed 2nd in Command of the 1st Battalion in October 1940 and except for a brief period, Feb–May 1941, he retained the appointment until wounded at Gondar [Ethiopia] 27th November 1941.
>
> Major Carmichael has been through all the operations in which the Battalion has taken part and has rendered conspicuously meritorious service on each occasion i.e. The Battle of Sidi Barrani and the operations that followed in the Western Desert until 16th February 1941; the operations in Crete and the Operations at Gondar.
>
> In addition Major Carmichael accompanied the Commandos in their raid on Bardia in April 1941 where his previous knowledge of the beaches and the Bardia area enabled him to give valuable advice and assistance to those taking part in the operations.
>
> Throughout these operations, Major Carmichael has thrown his whole heart and soul into his work, he has always remained cheerful, he has on all occasions shown grit and determination in action, and he has always been able to meet every emergency. By his own personal example he has inspired all ranks and kept them in good heart.

Carmichael's last active engagement was in Abyssinia (later Ethiopia). On 25 November 1941 he took part in the attack on Gondar that resulted in its capture. Carmichael dictated the surrender terms but, when returning to the HQ with a number of Italian prisoners, his truck struck an enemy mine. He was severely hurt and the major injuries to both his ankles not only ended his war, but incapacitated him for the remainder of his

vate Bill Morris, a founder
mber of 'L' Detachment, SAS
gade, was awarded the MM for
avery after escaping as a PoW
d then linking up to fight with
e Italian and Yugoslav Partisans
ainst the Fascists.

low left: The appropriately named
vid Danger was awarded his
M for bravery as a corporal while
rving with the SAS. One of the
AS Originals', he eventually retired
th the rank of lieutenant-colonel
ving been awarded the MBE.

low right: Captain (later Major)
chard Holland was awarded the
C for repeated courage during
e Dunkirk evacuations in 1940.
ter joining the SAS, he took part
daring missions behind enemy
es in the Netherlands and in
ance in 1944.

Sergeant Rudolf Friedlander was a German Jew who left his homeland to fight with the SAS under the pseudonym 'Robert Lodge'. He kept a vivid diary of his exploits as a PoW and later escaped to fight against the Nazis. He was awarded a posthumous DCM.

Private Alex Skinner (both images) was awarded the MM for bravery in Sicily, Italy, while serving in 1943 with the Special Raiding Squadron (SRS) of 1 SAS Regiment. Despite being wounded, he risked his life to 'take out' enemy snipers.

Captain (later Lieutenant-Colonel) Tony Marsh was awarded the DSO for courage in Italy in 1943 and, the following year, parachuted behind enemy lines to link up with the French Resistance after the D-Day landings. After a distinguished war-time career, Tony Marsh pursued an equally formidable peace-time career in the Army. He was awarded the CBE in June 1970, shortly after his retirement.

Captain (later Lieutenant-Colonel) Tony Marsh is photographed with his Army comrades and local civilians after apparently capturing a previously German-held, but unspecified, town. Marsh can be seen on the extreme left, sporting a beret.

Captain (later Major) Harry Holden-White was awarded the MC for his courage during the raid on Oran, Morocco, in November 1943. Just weeks earlier, he had been summoned to be briefed on a 'hush hush' operation, later codenamed 'Operation Reservist'.

Company Sergeant Major (later Captain) George Barnes was one of the original nine members of the 1st Special Boat Section (SBS) founded in July 1940. He was twice awarded the MM for his part in daring SBS raids in June 1941 and June 1942.

Trooper Alfred Amesbury was awarded the MM for gallantry during the Salerno Landings in Italy in September 1943. At a crucial point in the battle he showed conspicuous courage to knock out two enemy mortar posts, sniping with his rifle.

Corporal Ernest 'Knocker' White (left) is pictured with a comrade, Roy Herbert, during their investiture at Buckingham Palace. White received one of only two DCMs awarded for Commando amphibious operations against enemy-occupied Vaagso and Maaloy, Norway.

life. In fact, some twenty-six years after Carmichael was injured, he had to have one of his feet amputated.

Carmichael died in 1968, aged seventy-nine.

CORPORAL ERNEST GEORGE WHITE
AWARD: DISTINGUISHED CONDUCT MEDAL (DCM)
GAZETTED: 3 APRIL 1942

Ernest 'Knocker' White was a colourful character, one of those soldiers who is easier for his superiors to handle in war than in peacetime. With an enemy to concentrate on, such soldiers can be less of a handful than when they have too much time to spare. During the Second World War, particularly during his time serving in Norway, White was certainly a handful for the Germans, receiving one of only two DCMs awarded for Commando amphibious operations against enemy-occupied Vaagso and Maaloy (also spelt Malloy).

White had enlisted in the Royal West Kent Regiment, but by 1941 was serving with 3 Commando, which became involved in operations in Scandinavia. From the very start of the war in 1939, Britain was aware of the strategic advantage of the Scandinavian peninsula and its offshore islands. For example, Lofoten and Vaagso produced large quantities of fish and fish oil, while Norway had endless useful ports for military ships. When the Norwegian Nazis failed to mount a political coup, Hitler invaded Norway and Denmark on 9 April 1940.

On 4 March 1941, a 500-strong force, consisting of members of 3 and 4 Commandos, supported by the Royal Engineers and Norwegian soldiers, launched a major raid on the Lofoten Islands, some 110 miles west of Narvik. Five Royal Navy destroyers escorted the two troopships because it was feared they would be attacked either en route to the islands or as they landed. The raid was highly successful: 800,000 gallons of oil, eleven fish plants, an electric plant, 18,000 tons of shipping and a fish factory ship were destroyed. Furthermore, 225 Germans were taken prisoner and 300 Norwegians volunteered for service with the British forces. On Boxing Day 1941 a force of 300 men, including 223 men from No. 12 Commando, carried out a second raid on the Lofoten Islands, receiving even more naval protection than the March force. The Commandos, who wore white as camouflage in the snow, encountered little or no resistance: two wireless stations were blown up, twenty-nine Germans were taken prisoner and 260 Norwegian volunteers came forward.

However, it was the raids on Vaagso and Maaloy on the same date – 26 December 1941 – that concerned White and his comrades from 3 Commando. Indeed, 600 men from 2 and 3 Commandos were designated to target coastal defence guns, oil tanks, fish factories, a power station and an ammunitions store. They were supported by the likes of the Royal Engineers (No. 6 Commando), the Royal Army Medical Corps (No. 4 Commando) and the Royal Norwegian Army. Also on hand were ten RAF bomber and fighter aircraft to attack nearby enemy-controlled airfields, while the cruiser HMS *Kenya* with four destroyers were designated to escort the troop carriers and also to shell shore installations in advance of the landings. The submarine *Tuna* was tasked with being the marker ship (in an amphibious operation, a marker ship takes accurate station on a designated control point).

The force arrived off Maaloy at 7am on Boxing Day and soon a ten-minute bombardment was under way. More than 100 men from Troops 5 and 6 of 3 Commando came ashore and the German Commanding Officer and thirty of his men were soon captured. After a bombardment from HMS *Kenya* that silenced all but one of the enemy's coastal guns, Maaloy was secured.

Group 1, which landed on Vaagso, swiftly seized the villages on the south of the islands. However, Group 2, which landed on South Vaagso, took part in fierce hand-to-hand fighting to achieve its objectives. Their task was made easier when they were reinforced by Group 3, deployed from Maaloy, and Group 4, the reserve unit. Several enemy snipers caused casualties until they were hunted down and killed: one sniper found in a house refused to surrender and was burnt to death after the building was set on fire. Among the British to be killed was Captain Forrester, of 4 Commando: already wounded, he fell on a grenade that he was about to throw and received fatal injuries. However, the fighting was over by early afternoon and the British forces had destroyed four coastal guns, all fish-oil factories, barracks and the wireless station, as well as setting many other buildings on fire.

George A. Brown, in his book *Commando Gallantry Awards of World War II*, concluded his account of the day's fighting by saying: 'Probably the most important gain was the capture of the German Naval Code which enabled the navy to "read" the German mail for many months. Casualties, considering the ferocity of the defence, were surprisingly low – five killed and 23 wounded. Valuable intelligence was acquired, German morale suffered a severe blow and those who had fought on the day gained valuable experience for their next assignment.'

White's DCM for his courage in Norway was announced on 3 April 1942, after the once-confidential recommendation for his award stated:

Throughout the operations at Vaagso in South Norway on 27th December 1941, Cpl White displayed leadership of a very high order coupled with a remarkable spirit. When his Troop Commander had been shot, the other officers in his troop put out of action and the Troop Sgt.-Major delayed, Cpl White took command of the remnants of the troop. He carried out a series of assaults and proceeded in destroying a hotel which was manned as a strong point and continued in charge until the end of the operation. He personally accounted for some fourteen of the enemy. His gallantry and leadership were of a high order, and had a direct bearing on the allotted tasks being carried out, within the time limit which had been laid down.

In his book *The Vaagso Raid*, Joseph H. Devins Jr wrote:

> Napoleon once remarked that every soldier carries a Field-Marshal's baton in his knapsack. Now as 4 Troop lay stunned and leaderless the baton [emerged] from an unlikely knapsack indeed – Corporal "Knocker" White, one of those soldiers who give their superiors ulcers in peacetime but are a joy to command in action when the enemy is at hand, watched the attack lose its momentum and gradually peter out as the officers fell before the German positions. Not even a sergeant was left on his feet within White's range of vision and the hated Germans seemed to be getting the best of the encounter. Taking a deep breath, White stood up and began giving orders – tentatively at first, then with growing assurance as he saw them obeyed. The transformation was amazing; the surviving members of 4 Troop reloaded their weapons, grouped around White, and then went at the Germans with renewed fury. At this critical moment Sergeant Ramsey appeared with the 1 Troop mortar detachment and lobbed ten rounds through the roof of the hotel. White and his men, accompanied by two vengeful *Kompani Linge* [British Second World War unit consisting of Norwegian volunteers] soldiers who had seen their captain die, threw a shower of grenades into exposed doors and windows and charged. 4 Troop's attack overran the blazing building at last.

White's bravery on other occasions was also noted and, in particular, he later showed great courage when 3 Commando held the bridge at Ponte dei Malati, in Italy, having been ordered to do so by Field Marshal Montgomery. In his book *Storm from the Sea*, Brigadier General Peter Young described how White, who by this time was sergeant major of 4 Troop, helped seize the Italian headquarters, a former hotel, near the beach, despite it being heavily defended and the British forces receiving many casualties.

It is not known what happened to White after the war.

GUNNER THOMAS MCDONOUGH
AWARD: MILITARY MEDAL (MM)
GAZETTED: 2 OCTOBER 1942

Thomas McDonough displayed both bravery and stamina during the Dieppe Raid of August 1942. The attack on a key port in German-occupied France led to heavy Allied casualties, but McDonough's unit, Lord Lovat's No. 4 Commando, got off relatively lightly despite being involved in heavy fighting. As a result of the gallantry displayed by 4 Commando, the unit was awarded seven MMs. Furthermore, it was the only unit involved in the day's fighting that succeeded in capturing all its objectives.

McDonough was born and brought up in Liverpool, Merseyside. As a member of 4 Commando for the Combined Operations raid on Dieppe, he found himself tasked with taking and destroying 'Hess' Battery, also known as 813 Battery. The target was three and a half miles west of Dieppe and 1,100 yards from the sea, at which point there were steep cliffs. The target was a formidable battery, consisting of six 150mm guns situated behind the village of Varengeville. Each of the six guns was mounted on a concrete platform and behind the position there was an anti-aircraft gun or flak tower. Furthermore, barbed wire surrounded the battery on three sides.

The detailed planning of 4 Commando's mission was left to Lovat and he opted to divide his men into two groups for the attack on 19 August 1942, which was due to start at 5am. The first group, under the command of Major D. Mills-Roberts, was eighty-eight men strong and it consisted of a headquarters, 'C' Troop (including McDonough), a fighting patrol of 'A' Troop, a mortar detachment and a signalling section. Mills-Roberts and his men were instructed to land at 'Orange 1' beach, which was located at a point where two high-sided gullies led to woods which, in turn, ran to within 300 yards of the battery. Mills-Roberts was ordered to ensure that his men climbed the cliffs, formed a bridgehead and opened up on the enemy position with small arms and mortar fire. However, they were warned not to close in on the battery until it had been overrun by the second group. The second group's instructions were more straightforward: to encircle the battery and attack it from the rear.

There were also strict orders relating to how Lovat's men should reach the French coast. The men of 4 Commando were to be taken by HMS *Prince Albert*, an infantry assault ship, to some ten miles from the coast, before going ashore in landing craft assault (LCAs). In fact, when the men arrived on the beach, the routes up to the woods were blocked by wire and other objects. However, two Bangalore torpedoes were used to blast away an entrance and the explosions were not heard by the enemy because of sounds of heavy fighting further down the coast and because of overhead aircraft. 'C' Troop, including McDonough, scrambled up the cliff and, after searching some houses and moving through the wood, took up a position from where they could attack the battery. Indeed, three snipers from 'C' Troop and three Bren gunners caused heavy casualties from their positions between 150 and 250 yards from their target. In all, three enemy machine-gun positions were silenced and McDonough was able to fire a remarkable sixty rounds from his anti-tank rifle.

Mills-Roberts, who had reached the battery just as it began firing at the British fleet, later gave a vivid account of what happened next:

Suddenly a 20-millimetre gun starting firing from a high flak tower on stilts. It possessed an all-round traverse. One could see the streams of phosphorescent shells as they raked the edge of the wood and [hear] the noise as they exploded against the tree trunks.

Fortunately this fire tended to go high . . . Suddenly over from some farm buildings on the extreme left of the battery came the phut, phut, phut of German mortars and soon all round us resounded the crash of mortar fire . . . Two of our other detachments were now ready and joined the fray – the anti-tank rifle, a ponderous but powerful weapon with great penetrating power, and the handy little 2-inch mortar. The anti-tank rifle was to pierce the steel-plated armour with which we knew the enemy perimeter defences were protected. Bren-gun and rifle fire was no use alone against such armour. Gunner McDonough was firing this gun, with Pte Davis as his No. 2, and he operated against the flak tower with great effect. It ceased to revolve and gave the appearance of a roundabout checked in full flight. Then he devoted his attention to the German machine guns, ably assisted by the Brens . . .

Then our 2-inch mortar detachment started to shoot from some yards to the left of the barn. Their first round fell midway between the barn and the target, but their next round was a good one and landed in a stack of cordite, behind No. 1 gun, which ignited with a stupendous crash, followed by shouts and yells of pain. We could see the Germans as they rushed forward with buckets and fire extinguishers, and every thing [weapon] we had got was directed on to this area. The fire grew, and meanwhile the big guns remained silent. I sent a report of the situation back by Corporal Smith to the signallers – they were close up but out of sight in rear.

However, at this stage the German firing improved, and retaliation followed. Several Commandos were wounded: one had all his equipment and half his clothes blown off by a mortar. Soon the flak tower opened up again, this time more accurately.

Mills-Roberts again takes up the story:

So far so good. But I was desperately anxious to know how Lovat's main assault force were getting on in their wide detour round the flank. We had been unable to get them on the air and did not even know if they had got ashore all right. Otherwise it would be our task also to carry out the assault on the battery at 6.30am after the cannon fighters had raked it with their guns at 6.28am.

The German mortar fire was becoming heavier, and the forward position more precarious, when I received a signal that we were in touch with Lovat's party. They were now actually in their forming-up position behind the battery . . . By this time our 3-inch mortar communications had got going and the mortar came into action with a heartening crash.

At 6.25am. we deluged the whole battery area with smoke and saw the cannon fighters roar in for their two-minute strike at 6.28am.

Lovat fired three Verey Lights into the air at 6.30am, thereby signalling to Mills-Roberts and his men that the ground assault on the battery was about to begin. As soon as he sounded his hunting horn, the Commandos rushed 250 yards across open ground with fixed bayonets. They overcame heavy enemy machine-gun fire and tore into the Germans, leaving 100 dead or seriously wounded. Other enemy soldiers ran off, while just four prisoners were taken. The Commandos suffered forty-five casualties, including two officers. Elsewhere, the Allied soldiers had fared far worse: out of a total force of some 6,000 British and Canadian troops, 4,131 had been killed, wounded or captured in the space of just six hours. Indeed, no other Allied operation of the war is thought to have lost so many men in such a short space of time.

McDonough's MM was announced on 2 October 1942 after his recommendation stated: 'Gunner McDonough fired no less than 60 rounds with the Anti-Tank Rifle at the Flak Towers (Pincer and Pieface). Each time he fired the Anti-Tank Rifle, heavy fire was immediately brought to bear on the flash from the muzzle of the rifle. McDonough repeatedly changed his position and continued to engage the enemy, each time incurring heavy enemy fire. He scored a great number of hits and his endurance was quite phenomenal.'

McDonough's MM was presented to him by George VI at an investiture at Buckingham Palace on 27 October 1942. McDonough survived the war and, in his later years, lived on Merseyside until his death in 1980.

TROOPER ALFRED EDMUND AMESBURY
AWARD: MILITARY MEDAL (MM)
GAZETTED: 27 JANUARY 1944

Alfred Amesbury was decorated for bravery during the Salerno landings in Italy, which took place in September 1943. At a crucial point in the battle, he showed conspicuous courage and coolness in knocking out two enemy mortar posts, sniping with his rifle. During a period of two weeks, nearly 190,000 Allied troops eventually landed on the Italian coast and some of the fighting was both prolonged and intense. Indeed, at the end of six days of bitter fighting, which were later seen as a turning point in the battle, Colonel 'Mad' Jack Churchill displayed such bravery during 'Operation Avalanche' that he was recommended for the VC. In fact, Churchill was awarded the first of his two Distinguished Service Orders (DSOs) for this gallantry, and was later awarded the Military Cross (MC) and Bar for further bravery in the Second World War.

The Allied invasion of Italy began on 3 September 1943 and lasted until 16 September. It involved General Harold Alexander's Fifteenth Army Group, consisting of Lieutenant Mark Clark's US Fifth Army and General Bernard Montgomery's British Eighth Army. The main invasion force landed at Salerno on Italy's western coast from 9 September in Operation Avalanche, with supporting operations in Calabria ('Operation Baytown') and Taranto ('Operation Slapstick').

Once ashore on 9 September, the British Commandos, led by Brigadier Robert 'Lucky' Laycock, consisting of men from

No. 2 Commando (Special Service Brigade) and No. 41 (Royal Marine) Commando, secured the high ground on each side of the road through the Molina Pass, important because it was the main route between Salerno and Naples. Next, 2 Commando advanced towards Salerno and pushed back tanks and armoured cars from the 16th Panzer Reconnaissance Battalion. At the same time, Special Forces advanced north across the Sorrento Peninsula, from where they had a good position high above the Plain of Naples. German reinforcements arrived over the next three days, but so too did reinforcements on the Allied side. The Germans were determined to halt the advance and, on 13 September, they launched their counter-offensive, which, in turn, led to the fiercest fighting seen since the initial Allied landings. The thrust of the enemy attack was from the town of Battipaglia towards the sea.

It is the recommendation for 'Mad' Jack Churchill's proposed VC that gives a wonderful insight into the bravery of members of 2 Commando, as well as emphasising how uncertain the eventual outcome of the battle was at this stage. It stated:

> On the night of 15th–16th September Lt-Col Churchill organised the advance of his Commando up the Piegolette Valley, personally directing the advance by leading the right hand troop which had only one newly-joined subaltern left. On reaching the objective he went forward with one man into the village in which the enemy were sniping and throwing hand grenades. Although the bright moonlight made movement in the streets dangerous, his disregard of danger resulted in the capture of over 100 prisoners.
>
> Subsequently the captured position was heavily attacked under cover of intense machine-gun and mortar fire. Lt-Col Churchill at once left his headquarters and visited each troop post in turn proceeding alone in order not to endanger the lives of others. Throughout the day Lt-Col Churchill supervised our successful efforts to hold the determined onslaught on the enemy continually visiting our exposed positions.

All through the following night he remained on duty directing artillery and mortar fire onto the enemy patrols which were seeking to turn our position by the wooded valleys.

When dawn broke Lt-Col Churchill had again had no sleep for 36 hours, had personally led two long and heavily opposed attacks and had inspired our troops to beat off all attempts by the enemy to penetrate the positions.

It is beyond any doubt that Lt-Col Churchill's gallantry tilted the scales of battle on more than one occasion.

The magnetic power of his personal leadership frequently rallied his exhausted troops when they could scarcely move forward. His powers of endurance and the cool unflinching manner in which he exposed himself to danger so that he seemed to bear a charmed life were unquestionably a brilliant inspiration ranking with the highest traditions of the British Army.

One of the many men to gain inspiration from Churchill's own courage was Trooper Amesbury, originally from York, who, as a pre-war soldier, had served with the East Yorkshire Regiment in Palestine. Following the outbreak of war, Amesbury served in Egypt and in October and November 1942 was present at the Battle of El Alamein, at which the 'Desert Rats' received heavy casualties. After volunteering for the Commandos, he was selected and posted to No. 2 Commando and it was for this reason that he was part of Operation Avalanche.

His MM was announced on 27 January 1944, after the recommendation stated:

On 16th September 1943, Trooper Amesbury was one of the crew of an anti-tank gun in a position south-west of Battipaglia.

During the morning a strong enemy attack preceded by mortar and artillery concentrations, was made on this position. The gun position was heavily fired on by enemy machine guns and mortars at close range, but Trooper Amesbury displayed great coolness and succeeded in knocking out two enemy mortar posts by sniping with his rifle and subsequently helped to carry ammunition to forward section posts under heavy enemy fire.

During the whole of this engagement Trooper Amesbury showed conspicuous courage and coolness.

This single battle cost 2 Commando twenty-eight dead and fifty-one wounded. However, after a day's rest, the unit moved to Mercatello, some three miles east of Salerno. At this point, 2 Commando and 41 (Royal Marine) Commando were tasked to 'sweep the area and clean out the German forces'. After carrying out this role, they returned with 150 captured Germans. As Churchill led the men and prisoners back, and the wounded were transported on carts pushed by the prisoners, he famously commented that it was 'an image from the Napoleonic Wars'.

Next, the two Commando units were instructed to occupy the area known as the 'pimple' and, over the next few days, Commando losses grew, and they included the then Duke of Wellington. The Commandos were finally relieved on 18 September, when they withdrew to Sicily. During the entire Salerno operations, the Commandos suffered fifty per cent casualties, dead and wounded. The whole Italian invasion had resulted in more than 12,000 Allied soldiers being killed, wounded or missing in the first two weeks of the fighting. Before the Allied invasion of Italy, Winston Churchill had called it 'the soft underbelly of the Axis'. Yet, after the invasion, General Mark Clark, an American, described it as 'one tough gut'.

After the Italian Campaign, Amesbury served in north-west Europe with the Special Service Brigade. He was released from the Army soon after the end of the hostilities in 1945. It is not known what happened to him after the war.

CAPTAIN (LATER MAJOR) LESLIE STUART CALLF

AWARDS: MILITARY CROSS (MC) AND BAR
GAZETTED: 20 JULY 1944 AND 21 SEPTEMBER 1944

Leslie 'Iron Man' Callf was decorated with the MC twice within three months during 1944. His first award was for his bravery when leading 5 Troop in a determined assault against German forces at Anzio beachhead in March 1944, where his men killed or captured twice their own number. The Bar to his MC was awarded largely for earlier gallantry behind enemy lines at Garigliano, including the attack on Monte Faita. Later still in the war, Callf participated in 'Operation Roast', the amphibious assault across Lake Comacchio in April 1945, and, immediately after the war ended, he served with 'Foxforce', clearing enemy resistance in the Greek islands. He combined being a fine, determined soldier with being an astute, inspirational leader of men.

Callf was born in Seaford, Sussex, in December 1915 and was educated at Glendale College, Westcliff-on-Sea, Essex, where he excelled as an all-round athlete, establishing a college record for the 440 yards and keeping wicket for Essex Schools. After completing his education, he stayed on for two years at Glendale as a junior master. He left teaching to work in insurance before, along with a friend, setting up a business called Westcliff Physical Culture Club.

Shortly after the outbreak of the war in September 1939 he volunteered for the Army and, in 1940, he was commissioned in the Royal West Kent Regiment. Within months he had volunteered to join the newly formed Commandos and was accepted. After completing his training, he eventually joined 9 Commando, where he first saw active service in November 1943 during 'Operation Partridge', the amphibious landing and diversionary raid on the Garigliano River. Later he wrote that 'the action was successful, we caught the Germans napping'.

Next came 'Operation Shingle', the spearhead of the Anzio landings, and then to the peaks around Cassino, a period that Callf would later refer to as 'our mauling in the mountains of Ornito and Faito, where we suffered 50% casualties'.

It was for his experiences in battle on 2/3 March 1944, in the encircled Anzio beachhead – which he described as his 'proudest and most thrilling' moment – that he was awarded the MC on the recommendation of his charismatic CO, Lieutenant Colonel 'Ronnie' Tod. The recommendation for an immediate MC stated:

On 2 March 1944, the Troop under command of Captain Callf was ordered to clear a wadi [dry gully] which had been occupied by the Boche, and which threatened the maintenance of the forward positions of the unit which occupied this particular part of the line.

Although the enemy held this wadi in considerable strength, particularly the surrounding high ground which dominated the whole area, Captain Callf led his Troop into a most determined assault which finally drove the Boche completely out of his positions, thereby closing a dangerous gap in our own lines. As a result of this action it was officially reported that the enemy casualties were 23 P.O.Ws and 25 killed, these figures being approximately twice the strength of the whole of Captain Callf's Troop.

It is considered that the success of this action was almost entirely due to this officer's most courageous and determined leadership, as the action was carried out approximately six hours after the unit had disembarked in the Anzio beach-head and before he had any opportunity to carry out a reconnaissance under normal conditions. What reconnaissance Captain Callf was able to do was done under heavy enemy fire, and it was chiefly due to his personal courage and disregard for his own safety whilst doing the reconnaissance, and to his outstanding leadership and determination during the attack, that his Troop was able to carry out a difficult task on ground which it had never seen or operated on before.

Throughout the action, this officer's gallant and courageous conduct was an example and inspiration to his men, and he displayed the finest qualities of a first class officer.

Callf later wrote his own account of that memorable action:

Immediately on landing I was given orders to take my Troop up to the front line and deal with a Troop of German Paratroopers who had infiltrated the Royal Fusiliers' lines. A one Troop action was very much to my liking – decisions could be made quickly, control was reasonably simple and action taken immediately.

This was a rush job, without any recce, and the orders were, 'Find them and destroy them.' So at 0430 hours on 3 March we made all speed to arrive at the area of infiltration before first light at 0545.

The time was important because we were quite expert at night attack and over-running the enemy before he could see us properly. In full daylight an attack needed a different and usually a more difficult technique.

Dressed in light assault order, wearing vibram [Italian rubber] boots that made little noise and with darkened faces, we arrived at the forward Troops area, where I set about trying to find information as to the enemy's position.

Corporal Searle, later to win the D.C.M., hearing whimpering, found a young lad, deeply distressed in a dug-out. He said he was 16 years old and had arrived in Italy that day, having been immediately sent to the front. Searle told him 'You've little to worry about especially while we are around, and as soon as possible you must disclose your correct age to your superiors.'

The troops in the Anzio Beachhead, contained in a small perimeter, had been subjected to heavy 24 hour bombardment from artillery, mortar and the dreaded S.P. [Self-Propelled] gun fire. Fighting in the wadis [dry gullies] had been fierce with heavy casualties. It was just too much for a 16-year-old lad to be thrust into this. However, many a lad of spirit put a few years on his age to join up.

The Royal Fusiliers, like all other front line troops, were understandably battle weary and it took me some time to find the Company Commander in whose sector the enemy had infiltrated. By this time it was daylight; so much for our night attack!

The Company Commander came out of his dug-out waving a piece of paper. I asked the Captain 'Where are these German Paras, and how many?'

'I've just been made a Major,' he replied. 'They are over there somewhere, about fifty of them,' he went on.

Corporal Bostock, the assault team leader, and I turned and studied the area in question. When we turned round to the Captain for further information, we found he had disappeared down his dug-out. So we got on with the job we had come to do.

The wadis were deep ravines more than 30 ft. in depth, with stunted growth, shattered trees and shrubs, usually very muddy with water at the bottom. This was the only cover. So we used it.

I sent on a Bren gun team to the other side of the wadi to give any covering fire, and to watch for gun flashes. The other Bren covered the top nearside.

To find the Boches we had to draw their fire and this important and dangerous task was given to Corporal Bostock's team of Hopkins, Belasco and McGill. They went ahead moving from cover to cover, followed by Troop H.Q. and the remainder. The mortar team set up their position ready to give smoke or explosive at very short notice.

Corporal Bostock engaged the enemy quicker than we had expected. The Sturm Paras were well sited on the high piece of ground bordering the top of the wadi and much closer to the Royal Fusiliers lines than we were led to believe. They could cover all the open ground and also most of the wadi.

Bostock had his trigger finger and part of another shot off while returning automatic fire and, covered by Belasco and

Hopkins, he reported back to me, marching back as if on parade, standing rigidly to attention before me, asking permission to fall out as his arm was useless. All this while heavy automatic fire was causing casualties throughout the Troop. The Bren gunner had eight bullet wounds in his two legs. Corporal Searle replied with the 2-inch Mortar while I regrouped the Troop in the 'dead' ground just outside the wadi.

Quigley, the Medical Orderly, attended the wounded. The walking wounded helped with the more serious casualties. All other fit bodies, including the mortar team, were needed for a bayonet charge.

Sergeant Frank Walsh was a tower of strength as we organised a two wave attack up the slope. As we were getting into position, Fusilier Storey, a giant of a man, immediately behind me, was hit and killed instantly.

Each man was armed with two No. 36 H.E. [high explosive] grenades and two No. 77 Smoke grenades. It could be said that we carried our own smoke screen and mini artillery. Riflemen fixed bayonets, Tommy gunners reloaded. Our remaining Bren gun gave covering fire from the flank.

In broad daylight across rising ground, without any cover, we were ready to bayonet charge the enemy, who were well sited, and well dug in, about 60 to 80 metres away. I had no doubt at all in our ability to deal with anything or anybody.

At this moment each man's world was the little bit of ground in front of him.

I looked to the right and then the left and to Sergeant Walsh next to me, face flushed with excitement, and I shouted 'throw' and the smoke grenades were hurled ahead. As the smoke thickened I shouted 'charge' and in we went, racing and shouting, enough to put the fear of God into anyone; through the smoke and into the Sturm Paras. I think we looked a fearsome bunch as we came out of the smoke.

Sergeant Walsh was injured but bayoneted his assailant. I had emptied my Colt 45 magazine and the grey uniform in front of me had done likewise. As he turned to pick up another magazine, I was on him and lashed out with my boot, catching him in the hip. As he staggered away he put up his hands.

It was fairly quickly over. The German N.C.O.s were good and brave fighters, but once their leadership was broken the younger ones soon put up their hands. Our second wave immediately behind the first were dealing with other positions who had surrendered, and for several minutes things were chaotic. I knew only too well that there may be other positions covering this one, ready to mortar any new occupants. So leaving C.S.M. Mann and Medical Orderly Quigley to organise the walking wounded and prisoners, I carried on with about half my force and covered our front, digging in fresh weapon pits.

After the danger and excitement it now seemed an anti-climax but there was plenty to do. Reloading and checking weapons and ammo. Reporting our success, numbers of dead and wounded prisoners. Patrols to send out. Lookouts posted. Men rested and fed if possible. Above all vigilance in case of a counter-attack. Other bodies were found and we had yet to search the wadi.

Our casualties were three dead and nine wounded, and in my immediate small sector we killed four and took nine P.O.W.s. The total official enemy casualties for that day were 25 killed and 23 P.O.W.s. or nearly twice our attacking strength.

Within three months of his first gallantry award, Callf received a Bar to his MC after the recommendation for the award stated:

Captain Callf has served with this unit during the whole period it has operated in Italy since November 1943 and has taken part in all actions which the unit has fought. Throughout all actions this officer has shown outstanding powers of leadership and fighting ability, and his personal courage and disregard for danger have always been of the highest order.

During the landing carried out by the unit behind enemy lines on the Garigliano on 29–30 December 1943, Captain Callf led his Troop through a minefield to reconnoitre advanced positions from which the remainder of the unit could subsequently advance. Although it was night and mines could not be detected and lifted, Captain Callf personally selected an area by means of trial and error, in which the unit could form up.

During an attack on Monte Faita on the night of 2–3 February 1944, Captain Callf commanded the leading Troop and although 50% casualties of all ranks were suffered from enemy artillery and mortar fire, he continued to lead his Troop in the attack until the final objective was captured. During the subsequent withdrawal this officer organised an effective rearguard which prevented the considerably depleted main force from being overwhelmed by a counter-attack.

During operations in the Anzio beach-head from 2–26 March 1944, Captain Callf at all times led his Troop in a succession of actions, the success of which were [was] almost entirely due to his outstanding leadership, courage and determination. Captain Callf's military character is of the highest order, his gallant, efficient and courageous conduct in action has at all times been an inspiration and example to the men under his command, and he has always displayed the finest qualities of a first class officer.

Callf and his troop remained actively employed in Italy up until VE-Day, including participation in 'Operation Roast', action at Lake Comacchio in April 1945, where the so-called 'special boats' intended to convey the Commando got stuck in the mud and 'had almost to be carried themselves by the troops'. Nonetheless, the operation was deemed a success. Since landing in Italy in November 1943, No. 9 had sustained total casualties of ten officers and sixty other ranks killed, and eighteen officers and 271 other ranks wounded.

After the end of the war, Callf was deployed in the Greek islands as part of 'Foxforce', with elements of the Special Boat Squadron (SBS) and Long Range Desert Group (LRDG). Callf and his men found themselves employed in policing the tense situation between nationalists and ELAS (Greek People's Liberation Army) on mainland Greece. Next he was re-embarked for Italy and then, in the New Year, for the UK. He was released from military service in April 1946.

Throughout his time in the Commandos, Callf had been a superb athlete and was known as 'Iron Man'. When the war ended, his sporting prowess continued and he won numerous tennis trophies in singles and doubles tournaments. After the war he returned to Seaford and, following training with the Royal Horticultural Society, opened his own nursery. Callf had married in 1943 and went on to have a son and a daughter. In later life he became a keen sailor and qualified for his Certificate of Competence as Yachtmaster (Ocean) in September 1981. After his day job, he taught navigation at Newhaven College of Further Education, in Sussex, for nineteen years, instructing more than 1,000 students. For many years, too, Callf enthusiastically attended Commando reunions and, in 1987, he was appointed president of the Commando Association. He used his role to collect wartime memories from old comrades, which, together with his own formidable archive of maps, photographs, correspondence, reports and nominal rolls, formed the basis of a definitive unit history.

Callf died in 1994, aged seventy-eight. His obituary in the *Daily Telegraph* stated: 'Leslie Callf was full of energy and initiative and for most of his life combined two or even three jobs which others might have thought were each full-time. He was inventive and would turn his hand to anything. Though possessed of steely determination, he was patient and sociable, and always behaved with great courtesy. His success at teaching, as in soldiering, lay in his ability to instil confidence.'

DRIVER FRITZ SIGMUND HAUSMANN (ALSO KNOWN AS FRED STANLEY HOUSEMAN)
AWARD: DISTINGUISHED CONDUCT MEDAL (DCM)
GAZETTED: 20 JULY 1944

Fritz Hausmann was a German Jew who escaped from Nazi Germany shortly after the outbreak of hostilities in September 1939. Initially, he joined the 'Palestine Brigade', whose members openly wore Star of David uniform insignia and were, accordingly, executed on the spot if captured by the Nazis. However, after developing links with the British, he was recruited into the Special Operations Executive (SOE), where he changed his name to 'Fred Stanley Houseman' and adopted a cover story that he was British and from Manchester. Posted to Lieutenant Colonel 'Mad' Jack Churchill's No. 2 Commando, he proved to be bold and aggressive in the face of the enemy, personally killing one and capturing six others during the raid on Brac Island, the largest island in Dalmatia (and now part of Croatia). Later, during the assault on Šolta Island, he personally took out a machine gunner who was holding up the Commando advance. Hausmann's write-up could easily have gone into Chapter 6 on SOE members, but, especially as he was awarded his DCM for his service with 2 Commando, I feel it sits more comfortably in this chapter.

Fritz Sigmund Hausmann was born in Germany on 27 April 1921, the son of a Wehrmacht officer. His mother was Jewish and, soon after the outbreak of the war, she was arrested by the Gestapo and met an early death in a Nazi concentration camp. Hausmann managed to escape from Germany and made his way to Palestine, where he joined the Haganah organisation that guarded Jewish settlements against the Arabs. A well-educated man, fluent in English, German, Italian and Yiddish, he enlisted in No. 650 Company, Royal Army Service Corps (RASC), a component of the Palestine Brigade, around the time of its formation in November 1942.

Having served in North Africa, and survived the sinking of his troopship, he went on to participate in the Salerno landings and then transferred to No. 2 Commando, a unit of Force 133, charged with holding the island of Vis in the Adriatic and with mounting regular raids against neighbouring islands off the coast of Yugoslavia.

Hausmann was awarded the DCM on 20 July 1944, after the once-confidential recommendation submitted by the formidable 'Mad' Jack Churchill stated:

In the Commando raid on Brac Island on the night of 5 March 1944, Driver Hausmann was the leading scout of the section which carried out this raid. The section was seen approaching and two sentries opened fire with Schmeiser automatics which pinned them to the ground. Driver Hausmann dashed forward firing his T.S.M.G. [Thompson sub-machine gun] and killed one sentry, but the other ran into the house. Hausmann followed, kicked open the door and threw in a hand grenade. When it exploded, he dashed in shouting to the Germans to surrender, and having killed one and wounded two more, the remaining five men gave themselves up.

On the morning of 19 March during the Commando attack on Solta Island, the behaviour of this man was exemplary. In the forefront of the final assault on the village, he led a small group of men in house-clearing in an area where the German garrison was holding out, and during this operation severely wounded a German who was holding up the advance with a Spandau M.G. [machine gun] which was mounted in an upper window.

Driver Hausmann is a Palestinian of German origin serving in the Commando. He has taken part in three Commando raids in these islands during the last six weeks, and in each of these his behaviour has been outstandingly bold and aggressive. He insists on being the leading scout on all approaches by day or night and is not content to await his turn for this duty. He has set a magnificent example and his conduct under fire is in the highest traditions of the Army.

On 11 January 1945, Hausmann was Mentioned in Despatches (MiD) for gallant and distinguished services in Italy. Jack Churchill had recently been recommended for the VC in the Sicily operations, and a good summary of the events surrounding the raid on Šolta Island on 19 March 1944, in which Hausmann excelled himself again in 'house-clearance duties', is to be found in the recommendation for the Bar to Churchill's Distinguished Service Order (DSO):

On 19 March 1944, Lieutenant-Colonel Churchill, who commands No. 2 Commando, led a combined force of Commandos and U.S. Operation Groups in an attack on the German Garrison of Solta Island. The sea approach was made in darkness and disembarkation was completed by 0200 hours. Lieutenant-Colonel Churchill led his heavily laden H.Q. in its rendezvous overlooking the town of Grohote where the enemy garrison was known to be located. The advance was difficult and slow, over rocky ground intersected by walls and piles of stones, and the guides called many halts because of suspected enemy machine-gun posts on the route. Whenever necessary, Lieutenant-Colonel Churchill went forward alone to investigate and when necessary to pick an alternative route. Enemy fire was opened at 0530 hours, by which time the Commandos had surrounded the town. An air bombing attack had been arranged at 0630 hours and the Commandos assault on the town was to follow this bombing . . . At 0630 hours the bombing attack by aircraft was carried out, and immediately it was completed the Colonel gave the order to fix bayonets and enter the town. He himself led the advance and directed the house to house searches and street clearance in the face of enemy automatic fire and hand grenades which were thrown from windows and doors. The entire German garrison, consisting of an officer and 108 ranks, was either killed or captured, the Commando party led by the Colonel himself capturing 34 Germans including the Garrison Commander.

On operations with 2 Commando in Yugoslavia during April 1944, Hausmann was wounded by a Spandau bullet, and on operations in Albania during August 1944 he sustained injuries caused by shell and grenade fragments. He returned to duty with the Palestine Brigade later that month and was discharged in Italy after the war.

Hausmann lived in America for many years and died in Stamford, Connecticut, on 25 April 2006, two days before his eighty-fifth birthday.

ACTING SERGEANT JAMES DONALD
AWARD: DISTINGUISHED CONDUCT MEDAL (DCM)
GAZETTED: 31 AUGUST 1944

James Donald was awarded the DCM for bravery fighting with the Chindits against the Japanese. Having landed by glider deep behind enemy lines in Burma during 'Operation Thursday', Donald led his platoon with distinction and was decorated for the defence of Colonel Mike Calvert's jungle stronghold of 'Clydeside'. In fact, after seventeen relentless days of fighting, Clydeside had to be abandoned following the arrival of the heavy monsoon rains. However, Donald, having been ordered to make a counter-attack on the final day of the fighting and been wounded early in the engagement, rallied his men and succeeded in destroying one heavy machine gun and killing between twenty and thirty Japanese soldiers. I should point out that Donald did not serve with the Commandos, but I feel his write-up sits more comfortably in this chapter than any other, since he and his fellow Chindits carried out Commando-style raids.

The Chindits were a British India 'Special Force' that served in Burma and India in 1943 and 1944 during the Burma Campaign. They were formed on the suggestion of Brigadier Orde Wingate, who at the time was serving under General Archibald Wavell, the commander-in-chief of India Command. They were named after a corrupted form of 'Chinthé' or 'Chinthay', statues that guarded Buddhist temples. The Chindits were formed to put into effect Wingate's newly developed guerrilla-warfare tactics of long-range penetration and they usually operated deep behind Japanese lines, often after prolonged marches. The troops were under-fed and weakened by diseases such as malaria and dysentery. They often faced monsoon weather conditions and suffered from high casualty rates: during two years of warfare, 1,396 were killed and 2,434 wounded. Furthermore, their tactics were controversial because of the debatable military value of their achievements. However, the Chindits were undoubtedly brave, with four of their members being decorated with the VC.

Operation Thursday was the code name given to the aerial invasion phase of the Burma Campaign. The intention was to fly a force of men, mules, equipment and supplies into clearings in the heart of Burma behind enemy lines, a type of operation that had never been attempted before. Three sites were selected for the initial landing grounds and were given the code names 'Piccadilly', 'Broadway' and 'Chowringhee', after famous roads in London, New York and Calcutta. These landing sites had been chosen in inaccessible areas to avoid contact with Japanese ground troops and all sorties were to be flown at night to avoid Japanese aircraft. The plan was for a first wave of gliders to land troops to secure the site. A second wave would land more troops and American engineers with their equipment to construct an airstrip so that C47 Dakotas could bring in the remaining troops and equipment.

Operation Thursday began on 5 March 1944 but, just before the launch, a reconnaissance aircraft returned with photographs showing that Piccadilly had been blocked with tree trunks covering the landing area. It was feared – incorrectly, as it turned out – that the Japanese had learnt about the plans and sabotaged the area, so Piccadilly was withdrawn from the plans and it was decided that the initial landings would be at Broadway and Chowringhee only.

Brigadier Michael Calvert, the commander of 77th Brigade, flew with gliders into Broadway. Furthermore, shortly after the glider landings, a larger runway was cleared, allowing Dakota sorties to fly in, and over the next six days they successfully brought in men from the 77th and 111th Brigades. The site at Chowringhee was, however, abandoned soon after the glider landings because it was found to be vulnerable to ground and air attack.

Wingate now had three brigades in Burma and all enemy attacks had been repulsed. Operation Thursday was successfully over and Churchill sent Wingate a telegram congratulating both him and the Chindits on their outstanding success in what was the largest airborne operation of the war prior to the D-Day landings. Operation Thursday was undoubtedly one of Wingate's greatest triumphs, but tragedy followed just days later when, on 24 March, the aircraft carrying him crashed, killing him, at the age of forty-one, and several other men.

In April 1944 the main body of 111 Brigade west of the Irrawaddy, by now commanded by John Masters, was ordered to move north and build a new stronghold, codenamed Clydeside, which would block the railway and main road at Hopin, some thirty miles south of Mogaung. Masters' force established Clydeside on 8 May and was almost immediately engaged in fierce fighting. Situated close to the Japanese northern front, they were attacked by Japanese troops with heavy artillery support. One sustained attack on Clydeside was repulsed on 17 May, but a second attack on 24 May captured vital positions inside the defences. It was for this action, the culmination of seventeen days of bitter fighting, and for a successful ambush some days earlier, that Sergeant Donald was awarded the DCM. His decoration was announced on 31 August 1944, after his once-confidential recommendation stated:

> This N.C.O. was in command of No. 7 Platoon 26 Column. He was ordered to counter attack a position in 'Clydeside' on the evening of 24 May against a position strongly held by the enemy. He led the attack with dash and determination, and although wounded early in the engagement in the back and the arm, continued to rally his men. By his display of personal courage, the attack succeeded in destroying one heavy machine gun, one LMG [light machine gun] and 20–30 Japanese.
>
> On the morning of 19th April 1944 at Pt. SC 235311 whilst the Column was engaged in blocking the road Pinlebu–Pinbon, after the Column had made a most successful ambush on an MT [military transport] convoy, the enemy attacked the Column and blocked the selected line of withdrawal for the columns. Sgt. Donald's platoon attacked this position and by his example and complete disregard for his personal danger, enabled the column to make an entirely successful withdrawal, suffering no casualties.
>
> Apart from this incident, Sgt. Donald has time without number been an inspiration to all in the column by his steadiness and cheerfulness under fire. He has commanded a rifle platoon since the commencement of operations and set a standard of military efficiency and leadership equalled only by few officers.
>
> Recommended for the D.C.M. for conspicuous gallantry and outstanding leadership in the field.

By now, the monsoon had broken and heavy rain made movement in the jungle difficult, with the result that reinforcements could not reach Masters to help him defend his position. He was finally forced to abandon Clydeside on 25 May, because the men were exhausted after seventeen days of continual combat.

It is not known what happened to Donald after the war.

GUNNER JOHN GILZEAN
AWARDS: MILITARY MEDAL (MM) AND BAR
GAZETTED: 28 JUNE 1945 AND 5 JULY 1945

John Gilzean displayed such great gallantry in Italy towards the end of the Second World War that he was awarded the MM and Bar, both decorations being 'gazetted' in the space of a week in the summer of 1945. His first award was for gallantry with the Royal Artillery at Mondaino Castle, near Rimini in Italy, in August 1944 and his second was for courage, despite being wounded, at Lake Comacchio in April 1945. On the latter occasion, Gilzean was in good company: on the same day and in this same action, Lance Corporal Tom Hunter, also of the Commandos, gained the award of his posthumous Victoria Cross (VC) and, just a few days later, Anders Lassen, of the SAS, was similarly decorated.

Glizean, from Stanley, Perthshire, was a specialist forward observation post signaller and wireless operator serving with 142 Royal Devonshire Yeomanry Field Regiment and No. 2 Commando, Special Service Brigade. Because of its key role on, or close to, the front line, the position of observation post signaller was notoriously perilous. Gilzean, however, fulfilled the role with distinction throughout the Italian Campaign.

His initial MM was announced in the *London Gazette* on 28 June 1945 after his once-confidential recommendation stated:

Gunner Gilzean, on 31 August 1944, was detailed for O.P. [observation post] duty with Captain Edgar in support of 46 Reconnaissance Regiment who were protecting the left flank of 46 Division. That day Mondaino was captured and Captain Edgar occupied an O.P. in the castle. He worked with remote control from his Dingo [armoured military vehicle] which was parked outside.

The following night the castle and surrounds came under heavy fire from 150mm. guns. The remote control was twice cut by splinters, and each time Gunner Gilzean volunteered to go out to repair it, which he succeeded in doing. When the wireless failed a third time, Gunner Gilzean again went out to repair it, this time finding that part of a tombstone had been thrown into the Dingo, breaking the steering wheel and damaging the wireless set. He removed the set, repaired and replaced it, again under shell fire.

Gunner Gilzean has acted as O.P. Signaller for over a year. He has invariably proved himself to be exceptionally calm and courageous under shell fire, and most efficient at his job.

It was the costly offensive launched against the Argenta Gap, east of Bologna, in early April 1945, that resulted in Gilzean's second MM, in an action linked to the strategically important spit of land that separated Lake Comacchio from the Adriatic. The Bar to his original decoration was announced on 5 July 1945 after the recommendation stated:

During No. 2 Commando Brigade's operation of 2–4 April 1945, on the spit east of Lake Comacchio, Gunner Gilzean was Wireless Operator to one of the Forward Observation Officers with No. 2 Commando.

During particularly heavy mortar and shell fire on 2 April, Gilzean was wounded, but continued to maintain a first class communication, and as a direct result quick fire was brought down on an enemy counter attack which developed on the evening of 2 April 1945, and which was successfully broken up.

Shortly after this, while weak from loss of blood and in some pain, he was confronted by a German Officer whom he promptly took prisoner. He continued at duty until ordered to the rear on the morning of 3 April by his Troop Commander.

Gunner Gilzean's standard of coolness, courage and efficiency was of the highest order and he was an inspiration to those around him.

Gilzean recovered from his wounds, but it is not known what happened to him after the war.

LIEUTENANT ROY ROYSTON COOKE
AWARD: MILITARY CROSS (MC)
GAZETTED: 13 SEPTEMBER 1945

Roy Cooke took part in one of the most daring and, with the benefit of hindsight, foolish Special Forces missions of the entire Second World War: the attempt to kill General (later Field Marshal) Erwin Rommel at his suspected headquarters deep behind enemy lines. Cooke was captured during the ill-fated raid of November 1941 and later, as a prisoner of war (PoW), was shot and wounded following a failed escape bid in a shameful incident in which his fellow officer was killed.

Before the war, Cooke was a talented and prominent sportsman, including being a top rugby player. At the outbreak of the war he volunteered for military service and was enlisted into the Queen's Westminster Rifles. After being selected for a commission, he was appointed a lieutenant in the Queen's Royal West Kent Regiment and was posted to the Middle East. By now a captain, he became interested in the Special Forces and, on a whim, walked into the headquarters of 11 Commando and enquired if he could join. The unit was undergoing significant changes at the time and, although he had never undertaken Commando training, he had the advantage of speaking fluent Italian and was allowed to join.

On 9 November 1941, 11 Commando received orders to participate in 'Operation Flipper', the attack on Rommel's suspected headquarters and other specific objectives in the area. In the case of Rommel, the plan, devised by Lieutenant Colonel Geoffrey Keyes, was to destroy the headquarters some 250 miles behind enemy lines at Beda Littoria, Libya, and capture Rommel. The Commandos learnt that for the mission they would be transported in two submarines and dropped behind enemy lines. Cooke was berthed with Keyes, who was leading the mission, on the submarine HMS *Torbay*. The operation got off to a bad start when the disembarkation took much longer than anticipated because the submarines drifted from their intended spot. Then the freezing conditions, driving rain and heavy equipment also slowed down Keyes and his men.

After lying up during the day, the raiders finally reached Rommel's suspected headquarters. Cooke was ordered to trek ten miles away to blow up the cable mast at the Cyrene Crossroads, while Keyes and his group headed towards the villa they believed Rommel was using. Cooke, who was in charge of six other men, was presented with a series of mishaps. His first necessity was to cut telephone wires, but there were no wire cutters, just pliers, amongst the equipment. However, the men succeeded in completing this task, then set off for the crossroads where they decided to capture the first car that approached. When headlights were seen, Cooke moved into the middle of the road with a torch in order to wave down the driver. However, as the car approached him, it sped up and narrowly missed him. The Commandos sprayed the vehicle with machine-gun fire and it careered off the road. As the Italian officer and his driver ran into the night unharmed, the Commandos tried to start the car, but without success. Instead, they advanced towards the crossroads on foot, but one of the party had lost a plimsoll and, with a bare foot on rocky ground, was finding the trek hard going. When Cooke ordered the struggling man back to the pick-up point accompanied by another man, the party was down to five men, carrying heavy explosives intended for seven men, and now, once again, the party was facing driving rain.

The five men eventually reached the cable mast but, with the explosives set, they discovered that their fuses had been ruined by water that had seeped through the oilskin pouches as a result of sixteen hours of relentless rain. Their matches were equally useless and, with the situation now becoming desperate, a grenade was placed under the charge. Cook removed the pin and ran as fast as he could from the scene, but the grenade misfired. A second attempt saw only a small, rather pathetic explosion. Finally, one of the party remembered scrounging a self-igniting thermite incendiary and this device, with the explosives, caused a blast that brought down the cable along with three of the four poles.

Cooke, in fact, later gave a good description of this incident to Elizabeth Keyes when she wrote a biography of her brother, *Geoffrey Keyes V.C. of the Rommel Raid*. In September 1945, Cooke wrote to her:

We pushed on and hit the communications pylon about dawn. Unfortunately all matches, etc. for setting off the charges were soaked, even inside the oilskin pouches – It had rained for some sixteen hours – Very worrying, because it was getting light and there were one or two posts around us.

I tried a grenade under the charge and then running like hell and falling flat – and felt very foolish when it turned out a blind [faulty] – the second one went off, but the charge didn't. I returned to the boys nearly frantic with wind up and frustration and nerves, cursing pretty profusely.

Then one – bless his heart – who had been watching me running about with grenades, trying to strike matches that wouldn't [light] and so on, sort of metaphorically took the straw out of his mouth and said: 'I suppose a self-igniting incendiary wouldn't be any good, sir, would it?'

Of course, it was just the answer to our prayer. We set it off, touched off by the fuse, and up she went in fine style.

With their task finally achieved, the party made off back to their rendezvous point. They hid in a crypt in a graveyard during the day and trekked across the country at night. When they were only five miles from the rendezvous point, and with a day in hand, they came across some pro-British Arabs who led them to a safe cave. All now seemed to be going smoothly, but an Italian patrol, apparently on the look out for the raiders following the explosion at the crossroads, came across their hide-out. When two Italians entered the cave Cooke opened fire on them with his revolver, mortally wounding one of them. However, the other was unhurt and ran out of the cave to alert his comrades. Some twenty hand grenades were thrown into the cave and Cooke rightly concluded that a shoot-out would have resulted in a futile waste of British lives. Instead, he informed his men that he was going to surrender, instructing them: 'If they shoot me, you'd better dash out, get as many [enemy] as you can and go down fighting.' However, the Italians took the surrender, which was just as well for the Commandos, because they saw that the opening of the cave had been covered by two Breda machine guns.

Once again, Cooke described the scene on the run from the Italians in one of his two letters to Elizabeth Keyes:

We lay up in an old tomb that day; very cold and wet we were. Pushed off next night to try and get back to the ship. We went very hard and got back to within five miles of the place, but at about 8.30 that morning had to rest, which we did in a cave with some Arabs. We didn't know it, but we had sat down in front of two battalions that were beating the scrub for us and looking in all the caves.

The Arabs managed to slip out before we got the troops right on top of us, and tried to divert attention from the cave, by a little shooting on their own account, but no go. Two blokes [enemy soldiers] came down into the cave and we shot them, then they threw down so much stuff at us that the fumes nearly suffocated us, so we called it a day . . .

Meanwhile, at Rommel's suspected villa, the raid had turned into a fiasco, with Keyes and many of his comrades being killed. All but two of the Commandos taking part in Operation Flipper were killed or captured. With Cooke now a PoW belonging to the Italians, it was not long before he was planning to escape. Along with Captain Playne, of the Royal Gloucester Hussars, he succeeded, but the two men were caught and returned to their camp. Divisional Commander General Nicolo Bellomo then ordered them to show him how they had escaped. As the two men re-created their actions, Bellomo ordered his men to open fire on the two officers, with the result that Playne was killed and Cooke was injured.

However, he recovered from his wounds and the crime was not forgotten: Bellomo was the first officer from the Mediterranean to be tried as a war criminal. He was found guilty of the execution of Playne and was shot by a firing squad in 1945.

Cooke spent some time in hospital after the war but then served in the Commando Depot. The award of his MC was announced on 13 September 1945.

It is not known what Cooke did for a living after the war or where he lived. However, he died from polio in the 1950s.

6

SOE HEROES

The Special Operations Executive (SOE) was formed, following Cabinet approval, on 22 July 1940 as a British Second World War organisation. It was set up by Hugh Dalton, the minister of economic warfare, to conduct espionage, sabotage and reconnaissance in Occupied Europe, working both against the Axis Powers and in support of local resistance groups.

The SOE was highly secretive and was brought about by effectively merging three existing intelligence departments that were no more than two years old: Department EH (after Electra House, its headquarters), Section 'D' of the Secret Intelligence Service (SIS, also known as MI6) and GS (R) which had been set up by the War Office. In fact, GS (R) was renamed MI R in early 1939. The work of these three departments had overlapped and, although there was some cooperation between them, there was also competition and duplication. Once it was decided to form a new organisation, the SOE was ordered by the prime minister, Winston Churchill, to 'set Europe ablaze'. However, one department remained separate from the SOE: a department of MI R called MI R (C), which was involved in the development of weapons for irregular warfare and became an independent body codenamed MD1.

To insiders, the SOE was often known as 'the Baker Street Irregulars' after the location of its London headquarters and the group of ragamuffins of that name employed by Sherlock Holmes, Baker Street's famous literary inhabitant, to help bring him information. Others dubbed it 'Churchill's Secret Army' or the 'Ministry of Ungentlemanly Warfare', while the organisation and its branches were also given dull, fake names such as 'Joint Technical Board'. The SOE was also involved in the formation of the Auxiliary

Units, a secretive 'stay-behind' organisation that would have been activated in the event of a German invasion of the British mainland. The director of the SOE was usually known by the initials 'CD' (standing for Chief of 'D' Section) and the first man to fill the position was Sir Frank Nelson, an international businessman and Conservative MP.

The SOE controlled or employed some 13,000 people, including 3,200 women (three of whom were eventually awarded the George Cross, Britain and the Commonwealth's most prestigious gallantry award for bravery not in the face of the enemy). The SOE operated in all countries or former countries occupied by, or attacked by, the Axis forces, except where demarcation lines were agreed with Britain's principal allies, notably the United States and the Soviet Union. The SOE also made use of neutral territory on occasions, or made preparations in case neutral countries were attacked by the Axis.

According to estimates, the SOE supported or supplied a million operatives worldwide, including in France, Poland, Germany, the Netherlands, Belgium, Italy, Yugoslavia, Hungary, Greece, Albania, Czechoslovakia, Norway, Denmark and Romania. Because of its geographical closeness, the SOE was particularly effective in France, where it worked with the French Resistance to attack the German war machine. No fewer than ninety-one men and thirteen women from the SOE gave their lives for France's freedom.

After the war ended, the SOE was disbanded on 15 January 1946. A memorial to its agents was unveiled in London in October 2009 and is situated on the Albert Embankment, beside Lambeth Palace.

MAJOR JOHN HENDERSON
AWARDS: MILITARY CROSS (MC) AND ORDER OF THE BRITISH EMPIRE (MBE)
GAZETTED: 19 APRIL 1945 AND 1 JANUARY 1948

John Henderson was parachuted behind enemy lines into Italy in the summer of 1944 and thereafter coordinated the activities of the Italian partisans with the Allied forces. Despite being in constant danger of capture, he planned attacks with coolness and skill. Once his mission was completed, Henderson, who was the first British officer to appear in uniform alongside the partisans, made the hazardous journey back to the Allied forces through enemy lines – only to be parachuted back to Italy the following year to resume his clandestine work.

Henderson was born in Edinburgh on 17 July 1905 and, before the outbreak of the Second World War, was employed as a company secretary. He joined the Army as a driver with the Royal Army Service Corps on 16 September 1939, soon transferring to the Corps of Military Police. Next, he served as a sergeant with the Intelligence Corps, operating in France from January to May 1940. After being commissioned into the Intelligence Corps on 1 November 1941, Henderson went on to serve with the Persia and Iraq Command (PAIC).

Henderson was a formidable linguist, speaking fluent French and Italian, and with a working knowledge of German and some Spanish and Serbo-Croat. His background made him an ideal candidate for the SOE and, during November and December 1943, he undertook the Paramilitary Course, after which he joined Force 133, SOE. On 24 May 1944 he transferred to No. 1 Special Force (Ops Pool) and on 13 June of that year was parachuted into northern Italy to coordinate highly secretive operations with the partisans.

Henderson's MC was announced on 19 April 1945 and his once-confidential recommendation stated:

On 13 June 1944 Major J. Henderson was dropped by parachute behind enemy lines in the Ancona area. His object was to co-ordinate the activities of a clandestine patriot organisation, which had been created in that area by Italian officers operating in civilian clothes, with the activities of the Allied Armies.

As the first British officer to appear in uniform among the local patriots, he succeeded in conveying the directives of the Allied H.Q. to the patriot leaders and in directing the successful sabotage and guerilla activities which followed, and which have been recognised as having considerably assisted the advance of Allied Armies on Ancona.

Once this task had been accomplished and before the Allied troops finally over-ran the area, Major Henderson made his way back through the lines to report.

During the whole of the mission, Major Henderson was in constant danger owing to enemy reprisals on the patriots, as a result of which his H.Q. was continually on the move.

His presence and his cool example were a source of constant encouragement to the patriots, and were largely responsible for the courage and skill with which they executed all the tasks assigned to them.

However, by the time that his MC was made public, Henderson had already embarked on his second stint behind enemy lines. This had commenced on 6 March 1945, when he was again infiltrated into northern Italy, to coordinate partisan activities until the end of hostilities in Europe. In fact, German forces surrendered in Italy on 29 April 1945, while the total and unconditional surrender was signed on 7 May.

In June 1945, Henderson, by this point a highly respected figure in the former Italian Resistance movement, was posted to the Venezia Giulia Police Force to aid in its restructure and reorganisation, a task he performed with distinction for nearly three years. Shortly before his retirement, his services were recognised with the announcement of his MBE on New Year's Day 1948, after his recommendation stated:

> This officer has been with the Venezia Giulia Police Force since its inception in June 1945. He was the founder of the VGF Training School and at the present time is Commandant of the establishment through which all of the candidates must pass before entering into service. Also at this school he is responsible for the specialised education of aspirants to such police branches as Criminal Investigation, Fiscal, Mounted etc.
>
> Today, the Force is within approximately 200 of its ceiling of 6,000 all ranks and the return of law and order to Zone 'A' Venezia Giulia – where no Civil Police existed in 1945 – is proof of its effectiveness. This highly satisfactory state is due primarily to the masterly handling of indigenous police students by this officer whose devotion to duty has been outstanding at all times.
>
> In energy, resourcefulness, leadership and organising ability he is unsurpassed and these commendable qualities have gained him respect and confidence of all sections of general public and all police recruits, irrespective of nationality and creed, who have passed through his hands.

It is not known what happened to Henderson after he left Italy in 1948.

TEMPORARY MAJOR (LATER LIEUTENANT COLONEL) PATRICK JOHN FENTON WINGATE
AWARD: MILITARY CROSS (MC)
GAZETTED: 9 AUGUST 1945

Patrick Wingate was a demolitions and sabotage expert who, working closely with the Greek resistance, caused mayhem in repeated strikes against the German forces. In conjunction with ELAS, the Greek People's Liberation Army, he and the guerrilla force successfully targeted bridges, railway lines, stations and the like. Time and again, he combined coolness and technical ability to strike at chosen objectives over a period of several months.

Wingate was born in late 1914 and was a talented artist as a young boy. He attended Newton College, Newton Abbot, Devon, where he was a member of the Officer Training Corps. On 30 August 1934 he was commissioned as a 2nd lieutenant into the Royal Engineers, but he also found time to graduate with a BA from Cambridge University in July 1936. At the outbreak of war he was promoted to lieutenant before being advanced to war substantive captain on 3 April 1942. Shortly after this, he gained a further promotion and served as a temporary major for the remainder of the war.

Britain first parachuted a small Special Forces party into Greece in September 1942 in order to target a major bridge on the Athens–Salonika railway. After blowing a big gap in the Gorgopotamos Bridge, just south of Lamia, the main body withdrew to the west coast to be evacuated by submarine, with the intention of leaving an officer and a wireless operator behind. However, there was then a change of plan and they were all ordered to stay and organise the Greek Resistance. This party was first known as the British Military Mission, then later the Allied Military Mission and, finally, the title of 'Force 133' was adopted.

Everyone serving with Force 133 was given basic training in demolition equipment and technique, while the officers, including Wingate, were given more expert training. Greece was divided into areas in accordance with the guerrilla order of battle and Wingate, together with four sapper officers and two Greek officers, worked in the South Thessaly–Roumeli area from the spring of 1943 onwards. His specialist area was target reconnaissance, but he was also involved in planting the explosives. The British forces, along with their Greek allies, had supplies, including gelignite, parachuted to them and then transported by mule. A policy was adopted that every operation should be carried out at night and only with the guerillas' involvement, so as to avoid the accusation that possible reprisals were an Anglo-American responsibility.

Wingate's MC was awarded on 9 August 1945, after his once-confidential recommendation stated:

> Major Wingate dropped by parachute into Greece in May 1943 and has taken a prominent part in the two principal operational phases since that time. He was personally responsible for all reconnaissances of demolition and sabotage targets in South Thessaly and North Roumeli, as well as for the technical training of all ranks taking part in operations in these areas.
>
> Between April and September 1944 he personally took part in at least 12 operations against the railway lines in this area, which resulted in the derailment of six trains in addition to other damage to bridges, railway lines and stations. He was also responsible for demolitions carried out at various times in opposition to German drives [advances]. On every occasion he has shown not only the greatest technical ability but outstanding coolness under fire, which has played a considerable part in maintaining rebel morale and ensuring the successful completion of operations.

The operations cited included three attacks on trains in April 1944, two on the Thessaly Plain and one south of Lamia. Furthermore, Wingate oversaw the derailment of the train north of Lamia and subsequent attacks on it by the Cavalry Squadron of ELAS guerrillas. In June 1944 he also took part in the unsuccessful attempt to destroy the Kaissa railway station in order to prevent vital shipments being transported to Germany. However, this setback was followed by three successful attacks on locomotives, the derailing of a train in a tunnel north of Lamia and an effective mortar attack on the Athens express north of Lamia.

The king was unable to attend Wingate's investiture, but he

did send a short note to him on Buckingham Palace headed notepaper: 'I greatly regret that I am unable to give you personally the award which you have so well earned. I now send it to you with my congratulations and my best wishes for your future happiness.'

After the Second World War ended in 1945, Wingate remained in the Army for another thirteen years and was promoted to lieutenant colonel in May 1953. However, a letter to him from General Sir Charles Loewen, dated 14 February 1958, makes it clear that Wingate was being forced to 'retire' against his will and that Army modern-day redundancies are not a new phenomenon. After thanking him for all he had done in the Army and wishing him well, Loewen wrote sympathetically:

All of us have to make the change from full time soldiering to civil life sooner or later. In your case the change has come before the full military career which you had every reason to expect had been fulfilled. I can only say that I am sorry; and that we in the Army Council have tried to be as fair as we can.

Like most other occupations, soldiering has its up and downs; its good patches and its irritating ones. I hope most sincerely that on leaving you will feel that it has been a worthwhile task, carried out in the best of good company, and you will look back on your time in the Army with pride and affection.

As always, a younger generation is coming up to carry on the tasks and traditions that have been yours, and which remain with those still carrying on. I am confident that after leaving, you will continue to support them in any way you can.

Whatever his regrets at leaving the Army may have been, Wingate pursued a second, successful career, putting the skills he had learnt in the Royal Engineers and other Army units to good use by working at the government's Transport and Road Research Laboratory. He also gained an MA from Cambridge, the university where he had studied for his BA some two decades earlier. He retired from his role at the Transport and Road Research Laboratory in October 1978, when he received a letter from the director of the department praising the 'very valuable work' he had carried out in his 'second career'.

Wingate died in Spalding, Lincolnshire, in June 2001, aged eighty-six.

COMPANY QUARTERMASTER-SERGEANT EDWARD KENNETH EVERITT
AWARD: MILITARY MEDAL (MM)
GAZETTED: 4 OCTOBER 1945

Edward Everitt displayed great courage during three clandestine operations to Italy as a wireless operator between 1943 and 1945. He not only showed outstanding bravery evading enemy soldiers, but also when his party was attacked by 700 fascist troops. At one point during this attack, when he and his men were confronted by seventy enemy soldiers, he grabbed a Tommy gun and raced forward, spraying the enemy with bullets and, as they took cover, his party was able to escape.

Everitt had initially served during the Second World War with the Royal Corps of Signals. However, at some point after the SOE came into operation during the summer of 1940, he became attached to the secret service unit. Everitt's MM was announced in the *London Gazette* on 4 October 1943, after his once-confidential recommendation stated:

CQMS Everitt has been infiltrated on three occasions to enemy occupied territory as WT [wireless transmitter] operator. On the first occasion he operated in the Dodecanese area in 1943. In June 1944, he was infiltrated to the Apennines area where he was working as WT operator for a period of over 6 months.

In March 1945, he was again infiltrated to the enemy occupied territory in the Davona area. On all occasions CQMS Everitt proved himself competent as an operator and maintained constant contact with Base despite the many difficult conditions of operating in enemy occupied territory.

In April, 1945, when the mission HQ was attacked by a force of some 700 fascist troops CQMS Everitt displayed considerable initiative and courage in rescuing the mission from an extremely precarious situation. Whilst moving the mission, the party found themselves face to face with some 70 enemy troops who ordered them to surrender. CQMS Everitt with great presence of mind and courage seized his tommy gun and running [ran] forward towards the enemy spraying them with bullets. In front of this unexpected fire the enemy immediately took cover and CQMS Everitt and his party managed to escape.

For his courage under fire and his devotion to duty CQMS Everitt is strongly recommended for an immediate MM.

After the Italian collapse, the SOE in Italy, under the command of Special Operations (M), was renamed No. 1 Special Force and it was tasked with building a large resistance organisation in the cities of northern Italy and in the Alps. Aided by the Italian partisans, they had a great deal of success during the final two years of the war. During the autumn and winter of 1944 the SOE and the partisans conducted numerous guerilla attacks against the German and fascist Italian forces and their supplies. Furthermore, they made isolated attacks in order to sabotage factories, electric power stations and communications, and they provided strategic and tactical support for military operations conducted by the Allied forces. During the spring offensive of 1945 in Italy, the SOE and partisans captured Genoa and other cities without the direct support of the Allied forces.

It is not known what happened to Everitt after the war.

SERGEANT WILLIAM ARTHUR PICKERING
AWARD: MILITARY MEDAL (MM)
GAZETTED: 4 OCTOBER 1945

Bill Pickering was an SOE wireless operator who, after being parachuted into northern Italy in February 1945, spent nearly three months fighting with the partisans towards the end of the Second World War. Despite the death of two officers who were with him, he participated in an epic episode of clandestine warfare that he later recounted in his wartime memoir *The Bandits of Cisterna*. Having lived throughout his time in Italy under the threat of immediate execution if captured, Pickering was originally recommended for an immediate Distinguished Conduct Medal (DCM) but was eventually awarded the MM.

William Arthur 'Bill' Pickering was born in Oldham, Lancashire, on 21 September 1923 and was educated at Manchester Central High School. His father worked as the manager of a plumbing business and he had one younger sister. At the outbreak of hostilities in September 1939 Pickering was approaching his sixteenth birthday and was working as a clerk. He gained an appointment to the Royal Engineers' Cadet Corps in Manchester and subsequently enlisted in the local Defence Corps. By the summer of 1940 he was still under age for military service but, by means of altering his birth certificate, he managed to enlist in the Welch Regiment just two days after his seventeenth birthday. He wrote to tell his parents he had joined up only after the event in case they tried to stop him, and his first wartime role was on aerodrome defence duties at RAF Thetford in Norfolk.

Pickering later transferred to the Royal Corps of Signals, where he qualified as a wireless operator. Driven by a sense of adventure, he volunteered for 'especially dangerous duties', achieving his wish when he was ordered to attend a parachute course at Chesterfield, Derbyshire, in 1942. This was followed by an SOE training course at Fawley Court at Henley-on-Thames, Oxfordshire.

By the end of 1942, Pickering's new SOE comrades were serving in Sicily, Salerno and Anzio, and he was ordered to the Middle East. While serving in Algeria, he transmitted radio messages from British agents in southern France, Italy, Corsica and Sardinia. Furthermore, in Algiers itself, he helped establish the main radio relay station back to London, and it was there that he met Major Malcolm Munthe, an SOE agent who recruited Pickering for a special mission to Sicily in the summer of 1943.

In his memoir, Pickering noted that 'our group was well supplied with jeeps, communications equipment and personal weapons. I was assigned to work with Captains Charles Mackintosh and Gilbert Randall as their radio operator. This time it was my job to put messages into code, so for the first time in the war I actually knew what was going on.'

His mission in Sicily was ended by the Salerno landings of September 1943, when he was embarked for mainland Italy. In January 1944 he was taken by motor torpedo boat (MTB) to the island of Ischia, which he described as 'the main jumping-off point for running agents to and from the west coast of Italy'. Here he taught agents in explosives and radio transmission, prior to joining the opening wave of the Anzio landings in a small team of SOE led by Major Munthe, with whom he had been in Sicily, and Captain Malcolm Gubbins, son of the head of the SOE.

In his memoir, Pickering gave a vivid description of how Munthe and Gubbins seemed oblivious to danger:

Artillery and mortar shells were falling all over the place as we drove along the occasionally cratered road. I could see no pattern to the shelling. The enemy seemed to be sending their stuff in our general direction and the Allies were doing the same back. Munthe overshot our front line and headed for a farm-house in No-Man's-

Land. Mulvey followed. We dashed indoors and I reported our position from the front room. By now the Germans seemed to be concentrating their fire on us, but this failed to impress Munthe. He strolled round the farmyard wearing his green Gordon Highlanders kilt and seemed completely oblivious to the shells which were raining down all around him. Captain Gubbins, in the predominantly red tartan of the Cameron Highlanders, was equally unmoved by the mayhem. Perhaps it is the public school upbringing which prevents an English gentleman from flinching in the face of the enemy. But I did not share their enthusiasm for the job in hand when Munthe urged, 'Come along now, Pickering. There must be a frying pan lying around somewhere.'

I could not believe this was happening to me. We were risking life and limb for a cooked breakfast. Munthe did not appear to recognize the danger. As we wandered in and out of the farm buildings, he pointed to a group of Allied soldiers crawling on their bellies along the trench lines behind us. 'What on earth are they doing?' he asked with genuine incredulity. In my younger days I might have been inclined to reply, 'Acting sensibly, unlike us,' but I held my tongue. On this occasion fortune favoured the brave and we led charmed lives. But we never did find that elusive frying pan.

However, Munthe was seriously wounded a few days later, and Gubbins was killed in action: indeed it was Pickering's duty to signal Sir Colin Gubbins about his son's death. The death of Gubbins and the terrible injuries to Munthe (which ended his war) deeply affected Pickering and he was relieved to be pulled out of the carnage at Anzio. However, a few months later, and having attended the battle training school at San Vito, near Monopoli in southern Italy, he was 'like a coiled spring again' and ready for action once more.

His wish came true on 4 February 1945 when, on a crisp moonlit morning, he was parachuted with five other operatives into the Piedmont province of Italy, some 100 miles behind enemy lines. Five of the six men, including Pickering, were SOE members destined to take part in 'Operation Chariton', while the other man had orders to take part in another mission.

The main role for those taking part in Operation Chariton was to liaise with elements of the Liberation Committee for Occupied Italy and to arrange for supply drops and training for the partisans. They were a colourful bunch, although their rag-tag appearance, including sporting old Italian Army jackets and Nazi trousers, hid a fierce discipline.

The rest of Pickering's team comprised Lieutenant Colonel Max Salvadori, his aide Captain John Keany, Major Adrian Hope and his wireless operator, Corporal 'Busty' Millard. Over the next three months Pickering spent most time with Keany, who 'was courageous to a fault, wanting to fight and engage the enemy at every opportunity. He had a terrific sense of humour and was the life and soul of our party.'

Those hiding the SOE men were taking just as many risks as their secret visitors. Pickering was impressed by the speed and efficiency with which he and his comrades were spirited into the surrounding countryside. Both Pickering and Keany were hidden by an Italian farmer and his wife just outside the village of Monesiglio and only about 400 metres from the occupying German troops. They slept in the house overnight and every day, just before dawn, they would move into a small, stone shed about 200 metres above the house, where they had been shown how they could burrow under a huge pile of dry leaves if they needed to hide at short notice. The farmer's wife came up twice a day to bring the men food, almost in sight of the German garrison, taking terrible risks to make sure that the Britons were well looked after. Every evening after dark, Pickering and Keany would come down to the farmhouse and operate the radio from the attic, transmitting messages to their base in southern Italy. Many of the neighbours had their houses burnt down and their menfolk killed for such acts, but this did not deter their courageous hosts in any way.

After lying low for three weeks, Pickering and Keany moved on to Cisterna d'Asti. Once again, Pickering takes up the story:

Eventually after a two-hour journey, we arrived at a small farm building which was to be our transmission site. One of our guides went 400 yards along the dirt track beyond the farmhouse. The other waited 400 yards short of our destination. There was no sign of the farmer, who had vacated the premises after the leading Partisan had a word in his ear.

As usual I jammed a stone into a loop at the end of 50 feet of copper wire. This was my radio aerial. Then I threw it as high as I could up a tree to maximise the signal strength. The wire was connected to my radio inside the farmhouse and I was in business. I told Bari [his contact point in southern Italy] I was safe and well with Keany and we were ready for any messages. After I had taken down coded gobbledegook for 15 minutes, I handed the pad for Keany to translate into sense. Meanwhile I sent his coded messages back to Bari.

We had been transmitting for another 15 minutes when the balloon went up. Our excitable Partisan friend came running up the road like an Olympic sprinter with his backside on fire. I did not need to be a keen student of the Italian language and its colourful dialects to get the drift of what he was gabbling at 300 words a minute. He had spotted a German direction-finding vehicle and it was heading straight for us. It would be arriving any minute.

Keany grabbed the batteries. I sent another QUG signal [warning of the danger because the enemy was in the vicinity], disconnected the aerial and put the set in my back-pack. We dashed outside, but when I tried to pull the aerial out of the tree, it snagged on one of the branches. The harder I pulled the firmer it became stuck. By now I was sweating, and it had nothing to do with the temperature. Our guide had gone ahead to tell his comrade to run for it. The courageous Keany stayed to cover me. Every second seemed like an eternity and I could feel a wave of mild hysteria starting to grip me. But I managed to pull myself together with the most supreme mental effort. To leave the tell-tale wire behind would spell almost certain death for the farmer and his family. It would also show the Germans they were hot on our heels. So, after regaining my shattered nerves and patching them together, I became cool and detached again for a few vital seconds. I tried to flick the wire upwards away from the branch which was snagging it. At the second attempt, the wire freed itself and fell at my feet. I grabbed it and ran round the side of the farmhouse just as the German lorry's spluttering exhaust came into earshot.

The SOE men survived this and many other scrapes, including an ambush by an estimated sixty German soldiers on one of their hide-outs, before which Pickering had a sixth sense that they were in mortal danger and expressed his concerns to his friend:

Keany said, 'Don't be silly Bill. They couldn't creep up a hill like this without us seeing or hearing them.' To the best of my recollection, those were Keany's last words. I had been standing by his side as we spoke, with my radio transmitter in a pack on my back and my Marlin slung over my shoulder. For no reason I could ever explain I suddenly felt frightened, vulnerable and exposed. I moved two or three paces away from Keany's left side back towards the Calabrian and another Partisan called Tony. As I did so the German sub-machine guns opened up. I flung myself to the ground and saw Keany's chest neatly stitched with a row of bullets. He was flung backwards without making a sound, at least no sound which could be heard above the noise of gunfire. Four other Partisans had been cut down by the initial burst from another sub-machine gun to our right. The rest of us hurled ourselves full length on to our stomachs as the bullets whistled inches overhead.

When Keany was hit I felt the draught from at least three rounds as they zipped past my right ear. At this point all that tedious discipline came into action as army training took over from sheer blind terror and panic. Everything that happened next did so without any conscious pause for thought or consideration. First I loosed off several rounds from my Marlin in the general direction of the enemy guns. I did not expect to hit anybody, but I knew instinctively that a soldier under fire does not aim as accurately as a man whose life is in no danger.

The Calabrian, Tony, and another Partisan named Gino on my left followed my example and we sent a hail of bullets into the hillside below us. Then I motioned for the Calabrian to fire a burst while I scampered round on my hands and knees to get behind him. I fired a burst and he crawled at top speed to the other side of Tony. Then the Calabrian gave covering fire while Tony dashed to the far side of Gino.

In this way, by keeping the Germans' heads down and running like hell, we retreated off the hill. We were reminded to watch our right flank by the sight of the bodies of our lifeless comrades who had been taken in the first burst of fire. As we fell back, the German bullets were getting higher over our heads, so we judged that they were taking more time to move up to the crest of the hill than we were taking to scamper away from it. Whether it was our fear or our geographical advantage which benefited us most was hard to tell, but as we escaped from the immediate danger, we ran into more trouble from an attack on our left flank. Germans with sub-machine guns were hiding behind trees as we ran down the slope. They were 200 yards away but well within firing range. Tony was the first to draw their fire as he ran around Gino. The earth at his feet seemed to leap into life as bullets ripped into it. Immediately, our attention turned from the threat ahead of us and to our right flank to the left side as we pulled back. For a few agonising moments we were pinned down. We knew it was impossible to stay flat on our faces behind what little cover was available. In a few more seconds the Germans ahead of us would have reached the top of the ridge. Then they could pour bullets into us from the other direction.

In the cowboy movies I had watched as a child, this was the time when the 7th Cavalry arrived on the scene with bugles blaring and sabres flashing. On this occasion it was Renato who came to the rescue without any fanfare of trumpets, just his usual calm efficiency.

Although we were pinned down, we could see where our problem lay. A platoon of German soldiers with sub-machine guns and rifles were in a small copse on our left flank 200 yards away. They were firing from behind the cover of the trees.

Renato and his men had got across to the shelter of some trees on our hill a minute or two before us, running at full pelt as soon as the first shots were fired. They had either reached cover before the Germans were in position, or they had run past the danger point with unexpected speed. In either event they were now our saviours as they poured a hail of withering fire into the trees where the Germans were hiding . . .

Once again, Pickering had survived – and had even retained his wireless set – but Keany, of course, had not and the next day the men returned to the scene of the ambush. Keany was lying on his back with a row of six bullet holes neatly across his chest. However, his valuables, including £2,500 worth of Italian lira – a small fortune in those days – were missing. Four partisans had also been shot dead on the hillside. Pickering said that Keany's death had a 'numbing effect' on him, but he also wrote: 'I can only confess that my sorrow at my friend's death was mingled with selfish thanks that I was not lying there in his place.'

After Keany's death, Pickering joined up with Major Hope's mission. From this point onwards, he shared the duties of radio operator with Corporal Millard and also fought alongside the partisans, among whom he became known as 'Inglese Billy' or 'il biondino' (the blond one). By then, supply drops were being made on a regular basis and the partisans were well equipped to harass the German and Italian Republican troops continually.

This resulted in a flurry of ambushes and attacks on major targets such as railway stations. However, one such operation resulted in Hope's death. By April, Pickering noted, the partisans were a force unto themselves, declining to accept a British directive about the difficulties of liberating cities. Pickering was present, under highly dangerous circumstances, at the liberation of Turin, when 'rifles and machine guns were rattling as fierce street fighting took place and bodies were lying around.'

Allied forces reached Turin a day or so later, at the end of April 1945, thereby bringing Pickering's adventure to an end. His recommendation for his gallantry award concluded: 'Throughout his period in the Field this N.C.O. has shown outstanding qualities of courage, determination, and resourcefulness. He has covered many miles in enemy infested territory and during two periods after his two officers were killed, he continued to carry out the mission's activities under circumstances of great danger with exceptional efficiency. In view of his outstanding performance, he is most strongly recommended for the award of the immediate D.C.M.' In fact, he received the MM, which was announced on 4 October 1945.

Ahead of the sale of Pickering's gallantry and service medals in June 2012, David Erskine-Hill, from auctioneers DNW (Dix Noonan Webb), explained that Pickering should have received the higher award of a Distinguished Conduct Medal but did not due to a clerical error: 'He was rightly recommended for an immediate award of the Distinguished Conduct Medal, though an ill-informed senior had this reduced to the Military Medal. Be that as it may, his Military Medal is a great rarity, more so than similar decorations issued to the wartime SAS.'

Pickering was sent his MM and it was accompanied by a letter of congratulation from King George VI.

On New Year's Eve 1945–6 and armed with some festive mistletoe, he met a young Italian woman, Rossana Reboli, at a dance held in the sergeants' mess in Florence. 'I went to a dance in Florence and she was there – and I knew at once she was for me,' he later recalled. On their first proper date at the cinema a few days later, she arrived, not alone, but with her mother, two friends and their two mothers to chaperone her, meaning seven sat down in a line to watch the film. However, he persevered and the couple were married in Cheadle, Greater Manchester, on 11 October 1947, the year after Pickering had been demobilised.

After the war Pickering received a commission in the Army Cadet Force, in which capacity he served for many years and attained the rank of major. He also ran a series of grocery businesses in the Manchester area, before becoming an area manager for Oxfam until his retirement in 1988, aged sixty-five. In his retirement, he wrote his wartime memoir, published in 1991, and represented the Special Forces Club at the unveiling of a memorial to Captain Keany at Cinaglio. In November 2006 Pickering returned once more to Italy and was made an honorary citizen of Cisterna d'Asti. Furthermore, the municipal council made arrangements to have his memoir, *The Bandits of Cisterna*, published in Italian.

Today Pickering is ninety-one; he and his wife, Rossana, who is eighty-seven, celebrated their diamond wedding anniversary in 2007 and have now been married for sixty-seven years. The couple, who are fiercely independent and who holiday abroad every year, have a grown-up son and two grandsons. Pickering still drives and goes to the gym every day, while his wife attends line dancing every week. In an interview at their home in Hindley Green, near Manchester, he said: 'Given what I did, I was lucky to survive the war and I have gone on to have a wonderful life.' He is a keen supporter of Manchester City football club and Wigan rugby league team. According to his wife, Pickering remains unfazed by any danger and was even wheeled off for a triple heart bypass operation singing happily to himself. His wife said: 'In all the time we have been married, I have never known him worried by anything. He's an optimist and I am a pessimist but we seem to get along pretty well nonetheless.'

MAJOR CECIL GERALD MERTON
AWARDS: MILITARY CROSS (MC) AND BAR
GAZETTED: 16 AUGUST 1945 AND 17 JANUARY 1946

'Micky' Merton was awarded an extremely rare Special Forces MC and Bar as one of the original ten members of 'Z' Force, the elite unit attached to British General Staff Intelligence that operated in Burma during the Second World War. 'Z' Force specialised in defensive intelligence and counter-espionage, deploying on foot and, later, by parachute deep into enemy-occupied Burma. Their daring, covert operations behind enemy lines and their brutal encounters with the Japanese are now legendary in the history of the Burma Campaign. Merton, who commanded No. 5 Patrol, was undoubtedly one of the unit's finest patrol leaders and was one of only two men with 'Z' Force to be awarded the MC and Bar. I should point out, of course, that Merton was never a member of the SOE, but I have concluded that his adventures fit more naturally into this chapter than any other. He was, by operating with 'Z' Force, working effectively for the Burmese branch of the SOE.

Cecil Gerald Merton was born in 1909 and educated at Eastbourne College, Sussex, and Cambridge University, where he took a degree in forestry. He arrived in Burma in 1930 and was employed by Foucar Brothers, one of the country's large timber companies. For the next seven years, while working as assistant forest manager, he lived with his Burmese wife in a bamboo bungalow in the jungle. When the Second World War broke out, Merton was on leave in Britain and immediately applied to join the Artists Rifles. However, because of his knowledge of Burma, it was deemed that he would be of more value to the war effort if he returned there. After arriving back in Burma, he spent a further year with Foucars before trying to join the Royal Navy. This attempt failed, but his persistence eventually paid off and he was given a temporary commission in the Burma Rifles.

With his knowledge of the country and its language, Merton was appointed intelligence officer of the 2nd Burma Brigade. In March 1942 he took part in the retreat into India and on reaching Calcutta he was approached by an old friend, J.K. Parry, also of Foucars, who recruited him to join a new experimental intelligence organisation.

The Japanese advance in Burma had been rapid and it had led to widespread confusion. There had been insufficient time for the Allies to organise an intelligence network that could report on where enemy troops were in the country or on their numbers. Ultimately, the enemy plans had to be disrupted and so a decision was taken to recruit volunteers who were prepared to go into enemy-occupied Burma. The demands on these men were high: they had to know the country well, be able to speak the language and already have a network of local contacts. Furthermore, they needed to be able to navigate the deep and often impenetrable jungle and, most importantly, they must be fit, tough and brave.

Initially, it was decided that only ten volunteers should be recruited as an experimental unit, operating in five pairs. Although they would be part of General Staff Intelligence-Z, a specific name had to be given to these volunteers, one that did not attract attention or provide clues as to their identity. The name chosen was 'the Johnnies' and they were to be commanded by Lieutenant Colonel J.P. Shelley. The group's members were mainly recruited from the Forest Department of Burma or the big timber firms. By the beginning of July 1942 all the Johnnies had been selected and were assembled in Delhi. They were: Bertie Castens, Freddie Webster, Sammy Newland and D.W. Rae, all of the Burma Forest Service; Robin Stewart, Dickie Wood, Jimmy Middleton and George 'Red' Parker, all of the Bombay Burma Trading Corporation; and J.K. Parry and

Micky Merton, of Foucar Brothers. It was decided that each patrol would consist of two Johnnies and a minimum of eight men, recruited from among the ex-Burma Riflemen who had escaped into India.

No. 5 Patrol, under Major Parry and Captain Merton, the long-term friends, began the journey to the Chin Hills on 7 August 1942. They arrived in Hakha, the base and starting-point for the patrol, on 3 October 1942. It soon became clear that it was most unlikely that they would ever reach their original target, because although most of the tribes were friendly, those in the extreme south were anti-British and aiding the advancing Japanese. Two weeks later a message was received in Hakha that the enemy was approaching from the south and was only forty miles away. When Parry returned to India on leave, Merton, who had been promoted to the temporary rank of major, took command of No. 5 Patrol. Indeed, his first patrol behind the Japanese lines led to a fleeting encounter with the enemy, which was described by Sir Geoffrey Evans in his book *The Johnnies*:

Simultaneously [Merton and his *havildar* (sergeant), Kya Twe saw] three heads duck down below a ridge about four hundred yards away. They were obviously enemy. Trusting the enemy might think that he and Kya Twe were only scouts from a large force and would not open fire on them, Merton whispered 'Pretend not to have seen anything and we will make for that "dead" ground over there.'

Accordingly they walked with apparent unconcern and on reaching the 'dead' ground made all haste to get away. Picking up the remaining four men of the patrol where they had left them, they marched back to Shurkhua in record time and arrived in a state of complete exhaustion. A few days later reports came in to the effect that two heavily armed Japanese columns, each a hundred strong, had carried out a 'pincer movement' on their old observation post, to capture the mythical British force. 'Still knowing nothing about Wingate's expedition [General Orde Wingate's Column had recently entered Burma], we were very mystified, but nevertheless flattered that we should have been taken so seriously by the Japanese,' was Merton's reaction.

In May 1943 Merton was ordered to return to Calcutta to report on his findings. He was suffering from fever and a swollen face, apparently brought on by having to drink unclean water from the buffalo wallows. Yet by the time he reached the roadhead, 109 miles from Imphal, he had covered, during his first season's work, almost 1,000 miles on foot. In the concluding remarks of his report, Merton highlighted the fact that, due to the scarcity of coolies and absence of roads, the only way to keep patrols properly supplied and equipped was by air, and upon this the success of any subsequent operation would depend. This meant that from then on air became the normal method of supply for the 'Z' Patrols.

Merton's first patrol of the new season began in September 1943, and on the 20th of that month they had their first contact with the enemy. Once again, Evans takes up the story:

Cautiously raising his head, Merton peered through the topmost leaves of a bush and, as he searched the jungle in front, his eyes lit upon the round face of a Japanese only twenty yards away. At that short range he could hardly miss. Raising his Sten-gun in slow motion so that the movement would not give him away, he aimed and pressed the trigger. The only sound was a 'click'. The gun had jammed. Without taking his eyes off the target, Merton whispered to Dum Hpaw Gam [one of his men] – 'Give me a stick' – and on the orderly pressing it into his hand, he rammed it down the barrel to move the offending cartridge. The Japanese had not moved so, reloading, Merton went through the same procedure, but with the same result. Still oblivious of his two narrow escapes from death, his opponent remained in position. In desperation, Merton was about to try a third time when heavy automatic fire broke out behind him, indicating that some of the enemy had worked round to cut off the patrol's line of retreat. Almost simultaneously he heard Parry shout an order to scatter and, abandoning his efforts to shoot the Japanese, he made his way back up the hill through the jungle to rejoin the track further in rear . . . It was now a case of every man for himself . . .

For the ensuing six weeks and until Parry was summoned to India in the middle of November, both he and Merton found themselves involved in a series of sharp engagements on the tracks leading east from Tiddim . . . So close to one another were the opposing forces that a no-man's-land was virtually non-existent, and the patrol either went out with regular Ghurka troops or took part in the defence of some outpost within which they happened to be camping at the time it was attacked. Since this was not the type of operation for which they had been sent and as it was becoming increasingly clear that they could serve no useful purpose by remaining, it was resolved that on Parry's departure Merton should go north and then east towards the foothills overlooking Yazagyo and the northern end of the Kale valley. Here there were only levies and better opportunities would be offered for Merton to carry out patrols into the valley . . .

When Merton and his men next went on operations, they took with them a powerful telescope provided from Calcutta and the next few weeks were spent in careful observation of the enemy positions, their exact location being radioed back to the Royal Air Force to allow periodic bombing raids to take place. Evans describes an important intelligence breakthrough at the end of January 1944:

Visibility was particularly good when he was scanning the valley one afternoon and by chance the telescope was focused on an open space among the trees on the further bank of the river. Up to that moment nothing of interest had been seen and then to his amazement he picked up a light tank scurrying across the clearing to disappear in the trees on the further side. There had never been any reports of enemy tanks in the Kabaw valley, indeed none had been seen in Burma although there had been reports of their presence, and Merton's first reaction was that he must have been mistaken. But when a second appeared, followed by a third and a fourth he was left in no doubt whatsoever. For him this was a thrilling moment. He realised that having spotted first the lorries and now the tanks, he had detected that the Japanese were planning an operation of major importance in the Kabaw valley.

Six weeks later the Japanese marched on Imphal. It was for his courage and leadership during the two campaigning seasons that Merton was awarded the MC. However, due to various delays, this was not announced until 16 August 1945, after his once-confidential recommendation stated: 'Patrolled during the campaigning seasons of 1942–43 and 1943–44 on the Chindwin front in advance of our forward troops, first as Second-in-Command of Major Parry's patrol, and later as a Patrol Leader. In the latter part of the campaigning season of 1943–44, he led a special patrol on Special Force front, carried out numerous daring and dangerous reconnaissances, had a number of clashes with the enemy, and produced much valuable information. Has shown the most consistent gallantry throughout two years' operations, and a complete disregard for his own safety. One of the finest Patrol Leaders in Z Force.'

Following the comprehensive Japanese defeat at the Battle of Imphal, which lasted from early March to early July 1944, and the subsequent Allied advance into Burma, the role of the Johnnies changed. It was decided that future patrols would be parachuted into Burma well ahead of the advancing troops: their task was to report on the Japanese retreat and provide vital information for RAF bombers.

Having undergone a parachute training course, Merton led his patrol on its first operational jump on 26 January 1945. Their specific aim was to locate the position of the wireless transmitter of the Japanese headquarters in Maymyo (now Pyin Oo Lwin). After all the patrol had jumped, and when Merton had taken stock of the position, he was dismayed to find that they had been dropped in the wrong place, and that a major river and range of hills lay between them and their intended destination. Additionally, his second in command, Captain Willy Girsham, one of the new members of 'Z' Force, was injured in the drop, although he eventually recovered sufficiently to complete the mission.

Merton later recounted: 'I had seen this river in the plains, in pre-war days, and then it had been placid and sluggish, and although I expected that in the hills its flow would be much faster, I was dumbfounded when we scrambled down to the bank. It lay at the bottom of a two thousand-foot deep gorge through which it surged and foamed towards some frightening rapids. To make matters worse there was a complete absence of bamboo with which to make a raft and I could see no way of reaching the other side.'

However, they did eventually manage to make it across the river in an improvised raft, though this sank, almost drowning all those on it. Merton and Girsham spent the next six weeks roaming the countryside, picking up and passing back information on the Japanese withdrawal, and located the transmitter in a Buddhist temple twelve miles outside Maymyo. On 22 March 1945 it appeared safe to enter the town of Maymyo. In fact, as they arrived in a small village on the outskirts of the town, they came upon a small colony of Anglo-Burmans who were overjoyed to see a British officer for the first time since 1942.

Knowing that his Burmese wife had gone to live in the region while he was fighting, Merton asked if anybody knew her whereabouts. He was told that she was living in a small hut on the opposite side of the town, so he set out to find her, taking one of the villagers with him as a guide. He later recounted the emotional scene that he came across, telling Evans, the author, how he had walked down a side road towards a small hill on which stood a bungalow, with a small hut on the slope below it. Merton pushed open the gate and entered the garden:

Three children were playing in the garden, two girls and a boy. Surely the biggest must be my eldest daughter, June, and the other little girl my younger daughter. I called out – 'Are you June?' The children looked round startled and prepared to run, so I shouted – 'June, this is your father!' . . . My wife, who was inside, hearing all the noise and wondering what it was all about, looked out of the door. At first, unable to believe her eyes, she stood motionless for a few seconds and then ran towards me. One thousand and eighty-seven days of terrible anxiety and separation were over. At that moment the Japanese, wherever they might be, seemed very remote!

It was for his bravery in late 1944 and early 1945 that Merton was awarded a Bar to his MC, though, as with his initial decoration, the announcement was considerably delayed. It was eventually confirmed on 17 January 1946, after his once-confidential recommendation had stated:

Major Merton led a recce patrol in the Chaungzauk area east of the Chindwin during October and November 1944. In January 1945 he again volunteered to lead a patrol. He undertook a parachute course and was dropped into the area east of Maymyo on 26th January 1945. Unfortunately the patrol was dropped into the wrong area, during a high wind from a great height. The party landed on a rugged hilltop and many of them were hung up in high trees. Major Merton displayed extreme courage and leadership. He worked throughout the night and the following day in extricating his men and rallying the patrol who were dispersed over a large area. He then led them towards Maymyo across the Myitnge River at a most dangerous point, where there were rapids. An improvised raft was constructed and the patrol only narrowly escaped drowning when this sank. Shortly after the crossing the patrol was given away to the enemy, who pursued the patrol for over a fortnight. Major Merton again displayed a very high standard of leadership and with a total disregard for his own safety produced some extremely valuable intelligence.

On 3 May 1945 Rangoon was captured, and by the middle of June the work of the Johnnies came to an end. Field Marshal Bill Slim, who had covered himself in glory during the Burma Campaign, later said: 'The tactical information obtained by these patrols had been of the paramount importance, and there was no other G.S.I. [General Service Intelligence] organisation which produces [produced] intelligence of the same operational importance and with such continuity.'

Operating deep inside Japanese-occupied Burma, for seven months in three successive years, the Johnnies, in company with their loyal Burmese Chins, Kachins and Karens, had carried out a series of highly dangerous missions in a war noted for its savagery. In total, 'Z' Force was awarded one CBE, two Distinguished Service Orders (DSOs), four OBEs, four MBEs, seventeen MCs (with Bars to two) and sixteen Burma Gallantry Medals, making it one of the most highly decorated Special Forces units of the Second World War.

Merton was essentially a civilian who, being called upon to do a wartime job, did it superbly well, with virtually no contact from the outside world and left very much to his own devices. It is not known what happened to Merton and his Burmese family after the war, but he died in Hampstead, north London, on 25 October 1969.

7

POST SECOND WORLD WAR HEROES

In the years after the Second World War, members of the SAS operated all over the world, usually highly secretly and in wars, campaigns and trouble spots. The locations that the Regiment were despatched to included Malaya, Oman, Borneo, Aden, Radfan (in Yemen), Northern Ireland, the Gambia, the Falkland Islands, Bosnia, the Gulf, Somalia, Sierra Leone and Afghanistan. As previously mentioned, Britain has embraced the use of its Special Forces more than any other military power.

There are eight write-ups in this chapter, relating to five different wars, campaigns and trouble spots. Two of the men who feature were awarded decorations – the Military Medal (MM) and MBE respectively – for their courage and service during the Malayan Campaign. The campaign was the result of the 'Malayan Emergency', which involved a guerrilla war between the Commonwealth armed forces and the Malayan National Liberation Army, the military arm of the Malayan Communist Party, from 1948 to 1960.

The next two accounts concern Oman, which was a major trouble spot for the three decades after the Second World War ended. The Middle East nation was oil-rich from the 1950s onwards, but it was also one of the most unstable places on earth, with a series of major revolts beginning in 1957. As the situation became desperate, the Sultan of Oman appealed to Britain for help and the government responded by switching SAS units from Malaya to Oman in 1958. Over the next eighteen years, the SAS fought a 'secret war' against rebel forces that resulted in a series of outstanding acts of gallantry, two of which are highlighted in this chapter. The *largest and most prolonged revolt was named the Dhofar Rebellion and took place from 1962 to 1976: it was sparked by allegations of economic exploitation and dictatorial rule by the Sultan. The enemy was usually referred to simply as the 'Adoo' but, in most cases, the Sultan's forces, bolstered by the SAS, were involved in battles and skirmishes with the Popular Front for the Liberation of the Occupied Arabian Gulf (PFLOAG).*

Next there is a write-up centered on a gallantry medal, the Queen's Gallantry Medal (QGM), awarded for bravery during the Iranian Embassy Siege of 1980. It was this incident, played out in central London in front of live television cameras, that led to a worldwide public fascination with the SAS after the Regiment, once it had been unleashed, dealt with the Arab terrorists swiftly and brutally. I will not enlarge on this incident further in this chapter introduction because the story is told in full in the individual's story.

There are two accounts of courage in Northern Ireland that led to the award of one MM and a Distinguished Conduct Medal (DCM) to two soldiers. 'The Troubles' in Northern Ireland lasted broadly three decades, from 1968 to the peace process of 1998. During this period of intense violence over the partition of Ireland earlier in the century and its resulting sectarian divisions, some 3,500 people lost their lives. During the early years of the Troubles, the SAS had a highly limited intelligence-gathering role in Northern Ireland. It was left largely to the regular Army to tackle the terrorists, patrol the streets and try to act as a peace-keeping force. However, after a series of major terrorist incidents in 1974, Prime Minister Harold Wilson announced that the SAS would be deployed on patrol and surveillance duties in South Armagh – so-called 'bandit country'. The SAS drew up a list of eleven top Provisional IRA (PIRA) leaders in South Armagh whom they planned to hunt down and arrest. During the mid-1970s and the 1980s in particular, the SAS carried out a series of daring and successful operations against the IRA. Sometimes the Special Forces would wait unnoticed for literally weeks in a field or beside a road in order to target a terrorist or an IRA cell. But there were occasional setbacks and failures – for example, when the SAS were themselves ambushed or their cover was blown.

Finally, this chapter deals with a write-up for the First Gulf War that led to the award of the MM to one member of the SAS. The First Gulf War, or Persian War, was a seven-month conflict between Iraq, led by the military dictator President Saddam Hussein, and a coalition of thirty-four countries authorised by the United Nations. It lasted from 2 August 1990, when Kuwait was invaded by Iraq, to 28 February 1991, after the Iraqi Army was routed by the coalition forces, led by the United States. The aim was to restore the Emir of Kuwait to power and to prevent Iraq's further aggression in the Middle East. General Norman Schwarzkopf, the commander-in-chief of the Allied Forces in the Gulf, was not a natural fan of the Special Forces, preferring to rely on conventional warfare. However, Lieutenant General Sir Peter de la Billière, a decorated SAS hero and the British commander in the Gulf, knew their worth. At one point, ambitious plans were studied to try simultaneously to rescue the 3,500 Western hostages in Iraq using Special Forces. Yet, with the hostages split into several groups, such a task was impossible, and in December 1990 most hostages were released.

Initially, Schwarzkopf had hoped Iraqi missiles – hybrids adapted from Soviet-built scuds – would be detected by satellite technology before they were even fired but, from missile testing by the Iraqis on their own land in December 1990, this proved to be unrealistic. Schwarzkopf then hoped that the coalition's vastly superior air power would be able to destroy the missile launchers. However, this too proved impossible – some mobile launchers were moved around Iraq while others were protected by reinforced bunkers. The coalition, therefore, decided to use Special Forces – notably the SAS – to tackle the missile threat. The entire Regiment – other than 'G' Squadron – was committed to the Gulf in the biggest SAS combined operation since the Second World War. They were supported by the SBS and a select team of RAF Special Forces crew. As the coalition built up its strength in the Gulf, Saddam Hussein saw that his army would be unable to match the firepower of his enemy in a land battle. When the coalition started their air bombardment of Iraq – known as 'Operation Desert Storm' – in the early hours of 17 January 1991, Saddam's worst fears came true and he realised his forces were vastly inferior to those of the coalition.

On 18 January Iraq started firing scud missiles into Israel in an attempt to bring the Jewish nation into the war; he hoped that other Arab nations would start supporting Iraq if Israel became part of the coalition. It was time for the SAS to go into action. Over the next two weeks several SAS units were dropped, or made their way, deep behind enemy lines. Some were tasked with attacking targets, others with reconnaissance duties so that the mobile scuds could be destroyed from the air. The first units sent into Iraq were three patrols from 'B' Squadron with call signs Bravo One Zero, Bravo Two Zero and Bravo Three Zero. These eight-man patrols landed behind enemy lines to gather intelligence on the movements of mobile missile launchers and to target the fibre-optic communications that lay in pipelines. It was Bravo Two Zero, led by Sergeant Andy McNab, that was to go down in SAS folklore.

The full-scale ground war began early on 24 February 1991. Coalition forces swept into Iraq and, later, Kuwait. As Iraqi forces fled from Kuwait they started setting fire to oil wells, but by 27 February the emirate had been liberated. The next day, just ten hours after ground troops went into action, President George Bush declared a ceasefire. Coalition fatalities totalled 358, including four members of the SAS. Up to 100,000 Iraqi servicemen are estimated to have died.

Finally, I should point out that men decorated for their bravery in the Falklands War appear in a separate section: Chapter 8.

SERGEANT GEORGE MONK
AWARD: MILITARY MEDAL (MM)
GAZETTED: 15 DECEMBER 1951

George Monk – his surname is sometimes spelt 'Monck' – was awarded the MM for gallantry during the Malayan Campaign, the counter-insurgency action fought by British and Commonwealth armed forces from 1948 to 1960 against the Malayan National Liberation Army, the military arm of the Malayan Communist Party. The recommendation for Monk's decoration described his heroics as a 'brilliant little action' and resulted in the death of two enemy bandits.

Monk was born on 28 June 1922 and enlisted into the Suffolk Regiment in October 1941. During the Second World War he served both at home and in north-west Europe with his regiment and the Royal Artillery, Bedfordshire and Hertfordshire Regiment, and the Royal Warwickshire Regiment. After the war he remained in the Army, serving with the Duke of Wellington's Regiment. However, he transferred to 22 Special Air Service Regiment upon its formation in May 1950.

Monk was mentioned in *The Special Air Service Association's Regimental Gazette* on a number of occasions for his actions during the Malayan Campaign, but it was for an act of bravery in early October 1951 that he was recommended for the Distinguished Conduct Medal (DCM), although this, in fact, led to the award of the MM.

An account of the action appears in J.B. Oldfield's book *The Green Howards in Malaya, 1949–1952*. The author, who had served as a major in the Green Howards (as Alexandra, Princess of Wales's Own Yorkshire Regiment is popularly known), described how, at the end of September, 'A' Company had been in a contact with the enemy, an encounter in which three terrorists were wounded. Intelligence suggested the terrorist gang had moved northwards to the area covered by 'C' Company. With this knowledge, it was agreed to put a platoon from 'C' Company into the South Gemas Forest Reserve in order to try to bring about another firefight in which the enemy would be killed or captured. On 1 October, 8 Platoon, commanded by Monk, entered the jungle equipped with four days' rations. They had marched for an hour and a half, and covered no more than two miles, when the platoon halted. At this point, Corporal Horsefield heard the sound of voices only a short distance away.

Oldfield then goes on to quote from a long account of the day's events that was written at the time by an unidentified military source, though this person was clearly not Monk himself, given that his name was spelt incorrectly throughout. The report said:

Sergeant Monck reconnoitred forward with Corporal Horsefield and discovered that there was in fact an occupied bandit camp immediately in front of them. The ground was not very advantageous, for fifty yards ahead there was a little mound, or an old ant-hill, and then a hollow about fifteen yards wide. The bottom was obviously marshy, but, worse still, it was covered with thick palm, the kind whose leaves are apt to be spikey and through which it is quite impossible to move quietly. Through the jungle on the far side of the hollow could be seen the top of a basha [canvas open-style shelter]. Sergeant Monck brought the platoon up and made them lie down, with the leading section behind the little mound where it could observe across the hollow.

The first thing to do was to find a way round the marshy hollow if possible. Sergeant Monck, therefore, went off to reconnoitre to the left on his own. He found that there was a reasonable approach on that side of the camp, but there was also a sentry there, standing by a dead tree about twenty yards from the camp, so that side was out as far as an unobserved entry into the camp was concerned.

Sergeant Monck now had to decide how he was going to attack. The problem was this: a right or left flank attack would certainly be observed by the sentry, and the occupants of the camp would be able to get away before a shot could be fired at them. On this side of the camp the bandits had obviously trusted to the protection of the marshy hollow to give them warning of anyone approaching, and indeed, the chances of even a single man getting across unobserved under normal circumstances were slight. There was another alternative, and that was to make a wide encircling movement and come into the camp from the back. Sergeant Monck decided against this, however, for the following reasons: first, the gang he was expecting to meet was on the move from 'A' Company's area, and it seemed probable that this gang was only halted temporarily for a meal on the site of one of the numerous old camps in that area; the fact that one sentry was wearing a pack seemed to bear this out; also it was almost certain that if the approach at the rear was good there would also be a sentry there.

It was rather a problem, but Sergeant Monck remembered that just over a year before, 7 Platoon had made a very successful attack on a camp in the Kuala Pilah area, and had completely surprised the occupants of the camp in their bashas, owing to very heavy rain. From what he could see of the sky it looked as if rain was likely, and he therefore decided to wait for a shower of rain to cover the noise of the crossing of the marshy hollow and to make the sentries less alert. If no rain came by 1330 hours he would attack without it.

There was possibly well over an hour to wait, and in the meantime the Chinese Liaison Officer came up to the front and tried to make out what the bandits were saying. He estimated that there were about fifteen of them. This proved to be a very accurate estimate; the majority were, of course, Chinese, but Tamil was spoken by one or two.

One thing astonished the whole platoon, and that was the awful noise they were making. There was no attempt at keeping silence at all; they were talking at the tops of their voices, they were coughing and spitting in the true Eastern fashion, and the fact that they were having a meal was apparent from the clashing of mess-tins together. The unmistakable click-click of mah jhong [a game] tiles could also be heard.

Twice during the period of waiting a plane passed over, and on both occasions there was a shout from the camp for silence; when the plane had gone there was a short blast on a whistle, and the parrot-house chatter started up again. It is difficult to guess exactly why they kept silent when an aircraft passed over for they could not possibly be heard by the people in it. Perhaps it was to hear the whistle of an approaching bomb; certainly the silence was more pregnant when the aeroplane was a Brigand [a dive-bomber] than when it was a Dakota [a transport plane].

At 1325 hours, just as Sergeant Monck was about to attack without the rain, it started to rain, and the platoon attacked. The plan was simple. The assaulting sections were Corporal Horsefield on the left, Corporal Ramsey on the right, Sergeant Monck moving with Corporal Ramsey. Lance-Corporal Fox was to remain as a reserve at the little mound, and when the firing in the camp started he was to fire grenades from the E.Y. rifle over the camp to impede the bandits in flight; two were to be fired half left, two half right, and one centrally. Corporal Ramsey's section, with Sergeant Monck on the right, reached the edge of the camp rather in advance of Corporal Horsefield's section, and while they were waiting for them to come up, Corporal Horsefield's section was spotted by the sentry, who threw a grenade. The section commander immediately opened fire, and Sergeant Monck, Corporal Ramsey and his section charged the camp. As was to be expected, all the occupants were in their bashas, and, except for one who was shot where he lay, the others ran out and from behind trees put up some resistance, throwing in all a total of four grenades. Then Lance-Corporal Fox started firing his E.Y. rifle and bursting his grenades behind the camp. A whistle was blown, and the bandits fled into the jungle in all directions.

When the remainder of the platoon came up a thorough search of the area was made, and three blood trails were found, one leading to a large food dump which contained four cwts. of rice, a side of bacon, and a lot of tinned fish. None of the blood trails could be followed for more than a hundred yards as the heavy rain washed out all traces. In the camp itself, in addition to the dead bandit, fourteen packs were left by the terrorists, together with 400 rounds of .303 ammunition and two Bren magazines. The camp itself was an old one, but the bashas had not been reproofed with the usual attap leaves. Waterproof sheets, which had been camouflaged from the air with leaves and vines, had been used instead.

When wireless contact had been made with the Company base, 8 Platoon were ordered to remain in the area and continue the search for the wounded bandits, and 7 Platoon would join them and carry out the dead bandit and the packs and ammunition.

While Sergeant Monck was speaking on the 68 [radio] set, it was reported to him that a bandit had been seen approaching the camp. The bandit was lost to view for a minute or two, and then reappeared ten yards from the sentry. Unfortunately he spotted the movement of the rifle coming into the aim and dived into the undergrowth, providing only a fleeting target, and he was missed. He must either have been a courier, or one of the gang returning to the camp, oblivious to the attack.

The next day 7 Platoon joined 8 Platoon, and carried out the dead man and the spoils; 8 Platoon continued searching the area and, late in the day, one patrol searching some way from the camp smelt the unmistakable smell of something very dead, and came upon another dead bandit with an American carbine lying by his side; 8 Platoon was then ordered back to the Company base with the second bandit.

The search was not abandoned, however, and 7 Platoon under Second-Lieutenant Tyzack was again sent down to the same area on 3rd October. Two hours after leaving camp the leading man, Corporal Fletcher, came face to face with a lone bandit coming in the opposite direction on the track. Corporal Fletcher immediately opened fire with his carbine and killed him. This man had probably been sent back to look for survivors of the gang, or to see if we had left anything important in the camp.

The area was left fallow for a week, and then once again 8 Platoon went back. Searching further south they investigated a track leading down to the river. As they neared the river the Iban [native guide] said the track had been used that day, and then added, 'There is someone here now.' Going cautiously forward, they heard a man call out in Chinese, which the C.L.O. [communications liaison officer] interpreted as, 'Don't shoot; I'm wounded.' Fearing a trick, Sergeant Monck sent a section round the flank, but when they came up to the man, it proved to be one very emaciated bandit wounded in the leg. He had been in the camp during the attack, and was wounded, but had managed to get to the riverbank where he was found. He had lived for nine days by boiling leaves in a cigarette tin, and his wound, though very messy, had not apparently gone gangrenous. He had no weapon, and none could be found in the area. He stated that he had been deprived of his rifle three months before for a 'misdemeanour', but a photograph in his possession showed him with a Bren gun, so his story sounded somewhat dubious. In due course he stood his trial and was sentenced to five years' penal servitude.

From the documents found in the camp, and from interrogation of the wounded bandit, it was found that this gang was not in fact the one 'A' Company had made contact with, but one which operated in the area of 'A' Company, 1/2nd Gurkha Rifles. They had been living in the same camp for three months and presumably found working in one unit's area, and living in another, extremely satisfactory.

The ten days of targeting terrorists had been successful, but on 6 October 1951 there had been a major setback: a car in which Sir Henry Gurney, the High Commissioner, and his wife were travelling was ambushed on the Gap Road up to Fraser's Hill. Gurney was killed, leading to a massive desire for revenge from the British force in Malaya.

The recommendation for Monk's proposed DCM amounted

to a summary of the lengthy report from which I have already quoted. However, it concluded: 'Sergeant Monk's leadership was faultless, throughout this brilliant little action, and it was entirely due to his great skill, determination and coolness, and above all to his extraordinary patience under the very noses of the enemy, that such a successful conclusion was achieved.' His MM was announced on 15 December 1951.

Monk received many letters of congratulations after news of his gallantry medal was known within the Army. General Sir Charles Keightley told him: 'Your coolness and leadership throughout the action was an inspiration to your men and I am writing to send you my heartiest congratulations. In case you have difficulty in getting an immediate supply of the medal ribbon I am enclosing a small strip which I hope you will find useful . . .'

After his tour of Malaya ended, Monk spent some time as a training sergeant in the Airborne Forces Depot before rejoining the Regiment (SAS) and, once again, serving in Malaya. During his first patrol back in the country, he captured a communist terrorist. At some point too, according to *The Special Air Service Association's Regimental Gazette* for 1954, Monk injured his leg and needed hospital treatment. It recorded: 'Sgt G. Monk, who has been assisting with the Selection Courses whilst his leg recovered from injury is now fit again and will be leaving for Malaya with the next draft.' At this point, Monk was serving with 'D' Squadron and the *Regimental Gazette* for 1957 noted proudly: 'In the years 1955/56 the Squadron has had the lucky but still pleasant distinction of having eliminated more terrorists than any other Squadron in the same period. With a total of 10, including two ranking Party members, our lead is only a narrow one over the New Zealand and Baker Squadrons. (Note from RHQ: since these notes have been received the Kiwis have added to their total. The race is on and the destination of the bottle of whisky [for the most successful squadron in catching terrorists] is in the balance!')

In September 1957 Monk took over 'Q' side of 'D' Squadron, 22 SAS. He was discharged from the Army when his period of engagement ended on 6 October 1963, at which time his conduct was described as 'exemplary'.

It is not known what happened to Monk after he left the Army, but he died in Salford, Greater Manchester, in June 1977.

MAJOR CYRIL HUGH MERCER
AWARD: ORDER OF THE BRITISH EMPIRE (MBE)
GAZETTED: 20 DECEMBER 1957

Hugh Mercer was a relentlessly brave individual who single-handedly made a significant contribution to the development of military parachuting under jungle conditions, partly as a result of trial and error. Nobody knows quite how many times he himself parachuted or abseiled, but most people were surprised that, given the law of averages, his dangerous work never claimed his life.

When the Second World War broke out in 1939, Mercer was serving as a Territorial Army (TA) soldier in the London Rifle Brigade. He was commissioned into the Indian Army in 1940, serving with the Baluch Regiment in Burma until he became a PoW in February 1942. After the war, he transferred to the East Surrey Regiment and served with the 1st Battalion in Greece, Libya and Somaliland. From 1952 to 1954 he was attached to the RAF for ground liaison duties. However, it was Mercer's search for excitement that led to him volunteering for duty with the 22nd Special Air Service in Malaya from 1955 to 1958. This was during the Malayan Campaign, or Malayan Emergency, in which Commonwealth troops were tackling communist insurgents.

It was largely for Mercer's meritorious service in Malaya that he was made an MBE on 20 December 1957, after the recommendation for his honour read:

Major Mercer has been second-in-command of 22 Special Air Service Regiment since February 1955 and his never failing loyalty and enthusiasm have been major factors in determining the success that the Regiment has achieved in many fields of endeavour.

Major Mercer has, in particular, made an outstanding personal contribution to the development of military parachuting under jungle conditions. Very largely due to his imagination and drive, the autonomy of Special Air Service patrols parachuted into the jungle has increased during the last two years from twenty-four hours to fourteen days. In achieving this, Major Mercer, who is thirty-eight years old, has, on eight separate occasions during the past eighteen months, willingly accepted the risk of serious injury in order to satisfy himself as to the safety and efficiency of new equipment by parachuting with it into primary jungle under operational conditions. Furthermore, Major Mercer has conceived the idea for an automatic lowering device for equipment and stores supplied by air to sub-units engaged on jungle operations. This may well alter the whole conception of jungle air supply in that it may be possible to dispense with dropping parcels and thereby avoid much wasted patrol effort and loss of security.

Major Mercer is entirely responsible for all the parachuting activities in the regiment. He has personally organised and despatched all rescue missions, and it has been largely due to his hard work and meticulous attention to detail that the regiment has sustained so few serious parachuting injuries.

An article in *The SAS Regimental Gazette*, No. 33, April 1958, under the heading '22 S.A.S. Regiment' stated:

As we write this another old member of the regiment is on his way home, the Second-in-Command, Major C.H. Mercer, MBE. How he has survived his three years with us nobody really knows for, by all laws and averages, either his chute or his abseil equipment should have failed long ago. The fact that they have always worked has never ceased to amaze us. May they always go on working for him, for the very high standard of efficiency of our special equipment today is largely due to the unremitting vigour with which he has cast himself out of helicopters and aeroplanes over the last three years. We shall always remember him – particularly as we toil painfully up some endless bukit [hill/mountain] carrying the latest form of the 14 day ration!

Mercer's contribution to the SAS ration pack is acknowledged by Philip Warner in his book *The Special Air Service:* 'Experience gained at this time led to the development of the SAS 7–14 day ration, which became the forerunner of the British battle ration. The SAS ration pack was one of the outcomes of Lieutenant Colonel Oliver Brooke's study periods, and owed a great deal to the experience of Major Hugh Mercer.' Warner also highlighted Mercer's achievements in advancing parachute jumping: a successful trial jump into trees resulted in just three men injured out of fifty-four who jumped, then only with minor scrapes. 'It was immediately clear that parachuting into trees was a possibility and probably no more dangerous than landing into the open,' Warner wrote. 'With this knowledge further experiments were conducted and, in consequence, parachuting into trees has become a normal SAS accomplishment. A large contribution to tree parachuting was made by Major Hugh Mercer, ex-Indian Army, ex-Jap PoW, ex-East Surrey, and at the time Second-in-Command 22 SAS . . .'

After returning to Britain, Mercer served as a training major to 23rd London Regiment (TA), which he helped run from 1958 to 1960. He then served as second in command in 21st Special Air Service (Artists), TA, and it was during this time that he fell seriously ill and had to be hospitalised.

Mercer died, after a lengthy illness, in the Queen Alexandra's Military Hospital, Millbank, London, on 23 January 1961, aged only forty-two. He was cremated at Putney Vale Crematorium in south-west London on 30 January 1961 with military honours. His coffin was carried by eight officers, four from the Queen's Surrey Regiment and four from the SAS. In *The Journal of the Queen's Royal Surrey Regiment* his obituary stated: 'He was an enterprising and adventurous chap and his spirit of adventure led him to volunteer for duty with 22nd Special Air Service in Malaya from 1955 to 1958.' It ended: 'The Regiment mourns the loss of a very promising officer and offers deep and sincere sympathy to the widow and family.'

SERGEANT JAMES VULI VAKATALAI
AWARD: MILITARY MEDAL (MM)
GAZETTED: 19 JULY 1976

In the years after the Second World War, a small number of Fijian soldiers who had been recruited into 22 Special Air Service made a significant contribution to the Regiment's work. Two Fijians, Troopers Talaiasi Labalaba and Sekonaia Takavesi, were heroic in their defence of an Omani town during the Battle of Mirbat, part of the Dhofar Rebellion, in 1972. However, they were not the only Fijians to display outstanding bravery in Oman during the SAS's 'secret war', aimed at helping the Sultan of Oman to suppress a revolt from the *Adoo* (enemy) rebels in his country. Step forward Sergeant Jim Vakatalai, who took command when his battalion was ambushed and the Commanding Officer was killed during an attack in western Dhofar. Under heavy fire, Vakatalai personally directed mortar fire on the enemy with devastating effect. Later, he organised the collecting of the wounded and twice went forward to one of the most exposed positions in order to bring back an injured comrade.

Vakatalai was born in Fiji in 1943 and enlisted into the Royal Electrical Mechanical Engineers (REME) at Suva, Fiji, on 13 November 1961. On 25 July 1964 he passed selection to the SAS and served in the Regiment all around the world for the next two and a half decades. During this time he was known affectionately as 'Big Jim Vak' due to his height, formidable stature and the fact that, in the SAS, long Fijian names tended to be abbreviated: similarly Sekonaia Takavesi was 'Tak' or 'Sek' to his comrades, while Talaiasai Labalaba was known as 'Laba'.

The once-confidential recommendation for Vakatalai's MM tells the story of his bravery in some detail, stating:

Sergeant Vakatalai was a member of a Special Air Service Squadron controlling irregular Arab troops in support of the Sultan's Armed Forces (SAF) from September 1974 to January 1975. On 6 January 1975 he was the leader of a 4 man Special Air Service liaison team attached to a company taking part in a battalion attack in Western Dhofar. Vakatalai's party moved forward to join a company on high ground covering the move of the second company across open ground in their front. As this company was moving across the open ground it came across very heavy fire from 60 to 70 enemy in prepared positions using heavy and medium machine guns, mortars and rocket launchers. The company received heavy casualties, including the company commander. When the firing started Vakatalai moved under very heavy fire indeed on to the top of the high ground where he could get a commanding position. Whilst there he came under attack from one of our own jets sustaining 3 bullet holes through his clothing but fortunately remaining unhurt. Seeing that very little direct fire and no indirect fire was being returned he himself directed the 81mm mortar fire on to the enemy. This had a devastating effect and without doubt caused the enemy fire to slacken, enabling those caught in the open ground which included another Special Air Service group to fight their way back out of the killing area. He then took command of all Special Air Service soldiers and organized the return fire.

Once the fire had slackened Sergeant Vakatalai organized the collection of the wounded. He personally twice went forward to the most exposed positions each time returning with a wounded man. On the second occasion a soldier who was helping him to

THE ASHCROFT COLLECTION

ptain (later Major) Leslie 'Iron Man' Callf, of Commando, was decorated twice with the within three months during 1944. He comed being a fine, determined soldier with ng an astute, inspirational leader of men.

Major Cecil 'Micky' Merton was awarded an extremely rare Special Forces MC and Bar as one of the original ten members of 'Z Force', the elite unit attached to British General Staff Intelligence that operated in Burma during the Second World.

c Garland had an extraordinary war, first as a second lieutenant in the Commandos and, later, a flight lieutenant in the RAF. After being shot down, he was a PoW but he escaped to fight h the Partisans in Italy. He was awarded the MC and Bar and the MBE.

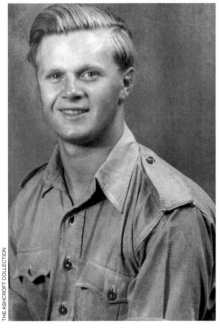

Sergeant Bill Pickering was awarded the MM for repeated courage while serving with the Special Operations Executive (SOE) behind enemy lines in Italy. A wireless operator, he spent nearly three months with the Partisans towards the end of the Second World War.

Second World War veteran Bill Pickering is photographed at his home near Manchester, were he lives with his wife o sixty-seven years, Rossana. Aged ninety-one, he still goes to the gym every day.

The medal group awarded to Sergeant Bill Pickering. His MM, announced on 4 October 1945, said he had shown 'courage, determination, and resourcefulness' while fighting w the Partisans in northern Italy.

Above: Squadron Sergeant Major (later Quartermaster Sergeant) John Taylor is pictured with a camel in the Middle East, believed to be Oman, where he fought with a small number of SAS soldiers in the Battle of Mirbat in 1972. He was awarded the MBE in June 1984.

Right: Sergeant George Monk was awarded the MM for bravery while serving in the Malayan campaign. In October 1951, he took part in 'a brilliant little action' that resulted in the death of two enemy bandits. He later served with the SAS.

Below: Sergeant Jim Vakatalai, a Fijian serving with the SAS, was awarded the MM in July 1976 after showing outstanding bravery while serving in Oman. After an ambush and under a heavy fire, he directed mortar fire at the enemy with devastating effect.

Left: Sergeant (later Captain) Graham Watts, a pseudonym, during undercover work in Northern Ireland at the height of the 'Troubles'. 1973, he was at the hear of an undercover operat that led to the arrest of seventeen alleged leadin IRA men.

Right: Lance Corporal Bill Bentley, a medic, is photographed with his parents at his investiture at Buckingham Palace. He was awarded the MM for gallantry during the Falklands War of 1982 when, under heavy enemy fire, he amputated a comrade's badly tattered leg using a Swiss army knife.

Left: Corporal (later Captain) Ian Bailey, who was awarded the MM for gallantry alongsid Sergeant Ian McKay VC durin the Falklands War of 1982. In the midst of heavy fighting, Bailey received three serious wounds that medics feared would claim his life. Howeve he eventually made a good recovery.

carry a wounded comrade ran when the enemy opened fired leaving Sergeant Vakatalai to carry the wounded man on his back entirely on his own for 100 yards. Once the wounded were under cover he again moved forward under fire, this time to recover weapons. He personally recovered 6 rifles, a radio and an enemy rocket launcher.

This Non Commissioned Officer's gallantry under very heavy fire, his leadership and his quick grasp of the situation in bringing 81mm mortar fire on to the enemy without doubt helped to stabilize the situation and enabled many Sultan's Armed Forces and Special Air Service soldiers caught in the enemy killing ground to fight their way back to cover. Had he not done so, many more would have been killed. His personal example, determination and courage were an inspiration to British and Arab soldiers alike.

Vakatalai retired from the Army in 1985 after twenty-four years' service. Afterwards, he worked in the security industry, including being close protection and surveillance trainer for Total Care Security Ltd (TCS). His biography on the TCS website reads:

Jim served a total of 24 years with the British Army, 21 years of which were served in 22 SAS Regiment. He saw active service in the Far and Middle East . . . During his service he also worked closely with the Foreign and Commonwealth Office in the fight against terrorism. Jim left the SAS as the Chief Instructor of the Counter-Revolutionary Warfare Wing, responsible for the training of the SAS, affiliated Special Forces and Security Agencies in a variety of core specialist security skills including Close Protection, Surveillance, Hostage Rescue, and Close Quarter Shooting Skills.

After making a successful transition into the civilian specialist security sector, Jim has provided Close Protection Teams for Foreign Heads of State, Middle Eastern Royal Families, and Corporate CEO's from Fortune 500 Companies. He has worked

Worldwide in the training and provision of CP Teams for VIPs who have considered themselves and their families to be at risk. Additionally, he has carried out surveillance assignments in the UK, Europe, South America, and the Middle East for commercial companies. He has also been involved in training surveillance skills to a number of UK Government Agencies.

Like his fellow Fijians, Talaiasi Labalaba and Sekonaia Takavesi, Vakatalai, now aged seventy-one, remains one of the Regiment's true legends.

SQUADRON SERGEANT MAJOR (LATER QUARTERMASTER SERGEANT) JOHN JEFFREY TAYLOR
AWARD: ORDER OF THE BRITISH EMPIRE (MBE)
GAZETTED: 16 JUNE 1984

John Taylor, better known as 'Jeff' to his comrades and friends, fought with distinction at the Battle of Mirbat in Oman in 1972. This fierce encounter is often seen as a modern-day Rorke's Drift, the most famous battle of the Anglo-Zulu War of 1879. In both cases, a small, heroic force managed, against all the odds, to fight off a sustained attack from an enemy far superior in numbers. In the case of the Battle of Mirbat, just nine SAS soldiers, with a little support from the Sultan of Oman's Dhofar Gendarmerie (DG), managed to hold off a major onslaught from an estimated 250 *Adoo* (enemy) rebels.

Taylor was born in Barntown, County Wexford, in January 1942 and was educated at the local Barntown National School. Aged just fifteen, he left school to begin a welding apprenticeship at a foundry. As a youth, he played both Gaelic hurling and football to a high standard and was tough on the pitch, mixing with older and bigger schoolboys and students. In 1961, aged nineteen, he moved to London, where he did various jobs in the construction industry, as well as working on the buses. He enjoyed London during the so-called 'Swinging Sixties', but in 1964 he decided to switch careers, considering emigrating to Australia, joining the Merchant Navy or joining the Armed Forces. He opted for this last, enlisting in the Irish Guards early in 1964 and, after basic training, he was posted to Malaya in September of that year. Along with eighteen fellow Guardsmen, he joined No. 9 Company, Irish Guards, who were attached to the 1st Battalion, Scots Guards. For the next three years Taylor was involved in operational tours of duty in mainland Malaya and also in the Borneo confrontation.

It was after completing jungle training that Taylor was deployed on his first tour to the Far East in January 1965 – and it was there that he met up for the first time with the SAS, who were also conducting operations in the region. Indeed, the SAS provided infantry back-up for the battalion's missions deep into the jungle. In August 1965, the battalion began its second tour, this time to Kalabakan in North Borneo and, in September, Taylor was offered the life-changing opportunity that he had been seeking: the opportunity to join the Regiment. In fact, volunteers were being sought to undergo SAS selection with a view to the formation of a new fourth squadron in the SAS, which became 'G' Squadron.

In the first six months of 1966 Taylor completed his selection and continuation training before joining 21 Mobility Troop. The new SAS squadron was deployed on its first operational tour of duty – to the Middle East – in June 1967. In the same year Taylor, who was based at Hereford with the SAS, met a young woman, Helen Davies from Swansea. Helen was doing her nursing training in Hereford Hospital. Their romance led to marriage – appropriately enough, their wedding was held in Hereford – in December 1971.

Soon Taylor was serving in the trouble-torn Middle Eastern nation of Oman. The carefully planned enemy attack that led to the Battle of Mirbat took place on 19 July 1972 and was intended to capture the strategically important town on the

Arabian Sea. During a prolonged firefight, the SAS managed to hold the enemy long enough for air support and reinforcements to arrive. Since they were fighting a 'secret war', only a handful of gallantry medals were given out, including a Distinguished Service Order (DSO) for Mike Kealy, the Commanding Officer. However, it still rankles with many of those serving at the time that two Fijians, Troopers Talaiasi Labalaba and Sekonaia Takavesi, did not receive Victoria Crosses (VCs) for their gallantry. In the former case, it would have needed to be a posthumous award, for Labalaba was killed defending Mirbat, while Takavesi was seriously wounded. Unbelievably, given his relentless bravery, Labalaba was simply Mentioned in Despatches (MiD), while Takavesi received the Distinguished Conduct Medal (DCM).

One of those involved in the close-quarter fighting – at one point the two sides were firing at each other from only twenty metres apart – was Jeff Taylor. He had been sent in advance of his unit, 'G' Squadron, to liaise with 'B' Squadron, as the former was due to take over the duties of defending Mirbat later that very day (19 July). After the *Adoo*'s attack, Taylor fought shoulder to shoulder with the men of 'B' Squadron. The defenders of Mirbat had two pieces of good fortune: first, the heavy cloud lifted, enabling two jets from the Sultan of Oman's Air Force to fly low over the scene, strafing the enemy with cannon fire; and second, an early radio message to the SAS headquarters in Um al Qarif that Mirbat was under attack had been received. Stationed some sixty-five kilometres from Mirbat overnight, the men of 'G' Squadron had been ordered into action. Once the cloud and mist had lifted, they were helicoptered to the edge of Mirbat and, as the aircraft attacked the enemy from the skies, they were fighting their way into the town. It was not long before the *Adoo* was in full retreat, leaving behind between forty and fifty dead and wounded. The bravery of the SAS that day was seen as a turning point in the conflict. Although trouble in Oman flared for many more years, the

Adoo never really recovered from the setback it received at Mirbat and, eventually, the rebel force was defeated. For a longer write-up of the Battle of Mirbat, see my book, *Special Forces Heroes*, first published in 2008.

In the early 1980s Taylor was involved in a role abroad that prevented him from serving in the Falklands Campaign, in which some of his SAS colleagues were killed in a helicopter accident. After the tragedy, in 1982, Taylor was promoted to squadron sergeant major. His MBE was announced in the *London Gazette* on 16 June 1984 in recognition of his outstanding service to the SAS, in general, and his actions at Mirbat, in particular.

General Sir Robert Ford wrote a letter of congratulations to Taylor, saying: 'I am well aware of how much you have done for the S.A.S. over many years and, in particular, of your outstanding work when you took over as Squadron Sergeant-Major after the tragedy in the Falklands Campaign. Your leadership and example have been of the very highest standard and I can think of no one who is more deserving of such an award.'

Taylor ended his SAS career with the rank of regimental quartermaster sergeant; he retired in 1986, aged forty-four, having served with the Regiment, with distinction and courage, for just over twenty years. Next, he returned to Oman, where he served with the Sultan's Special Forces, involved in both training and administration duties, in which he was aided by his knowledge of the Arabic language. However, he returned to the UK after two years and for the next four years worked in Hereford County Council's planning department. After completing his work for the local council, he worked in the security industry in the UK until his retirement in 2001. A keen marathon runner in his youth, Taylor kept fit in his retirement by cycling and walking. He enjoyed travelling extensively and visited the USA, Australia, New Zealand, Africa and many destinations in Europe. Friends said he had a unique personality and style of humour, and he was renowned both for his one-liners and as a confirmed cynic.

Taylor died in August 2011 after a brave battle against a long illness. He was sixty-nine. Much of the information in this write-up – though not, I should stress, any information about Taylor's involvement in the secretive Battle of Mirbat – came in an affectionate obituary published in *Mars & Minerva*, the SAS journal, in June 2012. Written by a comrade, who was also a long-term friend, and signed simply 'Jim D.', the obituary ended: 'Who Dares Wins, Jeff Taylor dared and won many battles and conflicts during his career. We had great times, the best of times together in both civilian and military life. I miss him greatly as he was my friend for the best part of 63 years.'

SERGEANT THOMAS G.C. PALMER
AWARD: QUEEN'S GALLANTRY MEDAL (QGM)
GAZETTED: 22 NOVEMBER 1994

As John Le Carré, the British intelligence officer turned novelist, wrote in the *Sunday Times* on 1 June 1980, just days after the event: 'It had all the ingredients. More than all. In showbiz terms it was over the top. A Bank Holiday, so everyone was at home for the first live political siege to be televised on British soil . . . Before our very eyes the sleeping psychopath in all of us was called to arms, institutionalised, dressed in black and licensed to kill. A bunch of 007s on a tight rein, their violent appetites canalised to the public good, live *on screen* at peak viewing time; and best of all, British.'

Le Carré was, of course, describing the final stages of the Iranian Embassy Siege and how it had transformed the public perception of the SAS overnight. For not only did the incident take place in the heart of London, but it was shown on national television – and the images were soon being beamed across the world. The whole rescue operation took just seventeen minutes

– a brutal, but entirely justified, response to a group of armed Arab terrorists seizing the Iranian Embassy in central London.

The embassy at 16 Prince's Gate, in the midst of London's diplomatic quarter, was taken over by six heavily armed terrorists at 11.32am on Wednesday, 30 April 1980. PC Trevor Lock, a diplomatic protection squad officer, was bundled into the elegant, terraced Georgian building as he was sipping his mid-morning cup of coffee on the pavement. Although some embassy staff managed to escape, twenty-six people, including Lock, were taken hostage by the group, which purported to represent the Democratic Revolutionary Front for the Liberation of Arabistan. The Iraqi-based terrorists were opposed to the rule of Ayatollah Khomeini and were seeking the liberation of the oil-rich province of Khuzestan – which they called Arabistan – from Iran.

The police were soon on the scene, including armed officers from Scotland Yard's D11 unit. The hostages were mostly Iranian, but they also included four Britons. In less than an hour the Metropolitan Police had cleared a two-kilometre-square area around the building. Within hours of the start of the incident, the SAS had been put on standby, although only the home secretary could have asked the Ministry of Defence to order them into action. The SAS had formed an anti-terrorist team more than five years previously and it soon looked as though the siege was going to become their first major challenge.

The police quickly assembled a huge team at the scene and 16 Prince's Gate was soon surrounded by anti-terrorist officers, police marksmen and others. The police moved into the Montessori nursery school at 24 Prince's Gate and established a link with the terrorists. No stone was left unturned: a Farsi interpreter was brought in, along with a psychiatrist with experience of sieges. At around 3pm Willie Whitelaw, the home secretary, chaired a meeting of COBRA (Cabinet Office Briefing Room A), which was attended by several senior Ministry of Defence staff, members of the security and intelligence services and Brigadier Peter de la Billière, the director of the SAS and SAS Group.

Normal phone lines to the Embassy were cut, but an Army field telephone was given to the terrorists so that they could have contact with negotiators outside the building. This had one great advantage for the police and security services – it could not be switched off, so they could hear exactly what was going on in the room where the phone was placed. On the first day, at 2.35pm, the terrorists' leader, Oan, issued his demands: autonomy and recognition for the people of Arabistan and the release of ninety-one Arabistani prisoners. He said that unless the demands were met by noon the next day – 1 May – the group would kill all twenty-six hostages and blow up the embassy.

Scotland Yard had set up a negotiating team to deal with the terrorists and some fifty SAS were drafted into the area, split into two teams – Red and Blue. The Red Team concentrated on the Immediate Action (IA) plan: the ultra-violent action of breaking down the doors and storming the building if shooting started inside or if the negotiators were certain that a hostage, or hostages, were about to be killed. The Blue Team concentrated on the Deliberate Assault Plan (DAP), which was more complicated and involved the SAS – not any action by the terrorists – deciding on when to enter the building.

For five days the instructions from COBRA remained consistent – there was to be no giving in to the terrorists' demands; the negotiators must strive for a peaceful solution; and the SAS were not to be sent in unless a hostage was killed. By Monday, 5 May, the May Bank Holiday, the SAS had been on standby for five days, during which a total of five hostages had been released unharmed. Willie Whitelaw then announced privately that the 'ambassadorial phase' of the siege was over and a firmer line would be taken about the hostages. At 1.31pm, three shots were heard. At 6.50pm, three further shots rang out and, shortly afterwards, the dead body of Abbas Lavasani, the

Iranian Embassy press officer, was pushed out of the front door (in fact, he had died during the earlier round of fire). His body was picked up and placed on a stretcher – all this was shown on live television. Oan, the terrorists' leader who had been codenamed 'Salim' by the SAS, was now making threats to kill a hostage every half hour, or even to kill all the hostages.

By killing one of the hostages, the terrorists had effectively ended all chances of a negotiated settlement. The SAS were committed to action at 6.53pm – as soon as there was proof that a hostage had been killed. Prime Minister Margaret Thatcher's words were: 'The time has come to use the final option.' At 7.07pm, Lieutenant Colonel Michael Rose took control of events on the ground: 'Operation Nimrod' was officially under way.

The SAS's plan was relatively simple – Red Team would deal with the three floors in the top half of the building and Blue Team would go in and clear the basement, ground and first floors. A support group was tasked with pumping CS gas into the building. The first team had to break down the rear garden door; another was to enter the first-floor balcony using frame charges to blast open the windows, which it was believed had been reinforced against terrorists. A third eight-strong team had to abseil forty feet from the roof of the building to gain entry through a second-floor rear window set next to a balcony. Between them, the SAS teams had to search and clear more than fifty rooms on six floors – and they had to reach the hostages before they came to harm. It was feared that, even if things went relatively smoothly, there could be up to forty per cent casualties among the hostages.

At 7.26pm, after the negotiator had been stalling for time in his discussions with Salim, an explosion was heard – the sound of the skylight on the embassy being blown by Red Team. The assault was under way and the SAS was involved in a race against time to prevent the hostages being killed. All the SAS men wore black kit weighing about fifteen kilos and designed for an anti-terrorist role, as well as body armour. They were armed with MP5 German-made machine guns, 9mm Browning pistols and stun grenades. They also wore hoods, respirators and personal radios with earpieces and throat microphones that were tuned to a communal network so that everyone could hear everyone else talking.

Amazingly, Trevor Lock, unknown to his captors, had remained armed throughout the entire siege, but he drew his gun only when the assault on the embassy began. He struggled with Salim during the initial stages of the attack, but was quickly pulled aside by two SAS men, who pumped fifteen bullets into the terrorist leader. There were many other heroics. In the early moments of the siege a sniper had shot one of the terrorists in the telex room with a single bullet, thereby saving the lives of up to fifteen hostages who were with him.

Many men were honoured directly, or indirectly, for their part in the siege. PC Lock was one of two men to be awarded the George Medal, the second highest civil award, and was also honoured with the Freedom of the City of London.

Another was awarded to Sergeant Tommy Palmer, who was born and brought up in Scotland. After a slightly troubled early childhood, Palmer, at sixteen, moved in with his female cousin who, despite being recently married and living in a small house, set him on the straight and narrow. He worked as a coalman but then decided that the Army would be for him. He joined up in 1970 with 33rd Field Squadron, Royal Engineers. He applied to join the SAS in 1973, aged twenty-two, making him at the time one of the youngest ever to apply. His first selection resulted in an injury and the selection team refused to let him continue. However, he was back later that year and passed with flying colours before going on to do his parachute training.

Palmer served in Northern Ireland and did operational tours before and after the embassy siege. He also served in Oman, and the award of the Dhofar Bar covered his service up to 30

September 1976. During the latter stages of this campaign, in which Palmer was present, the SAS provided advisory teams to help train local forces.

On Monday, 5 May 1980, Palmer was part of the eight-man team that had to abseil down the front of the building from the roof. Because of the difficulty of their task, they were instructed to begin a few seconds before the others, once the code words 'Bank robbery' and then, finally, 'London Bridge' had been given. Before this and in preparation for the final assault, explosives had been lowered into place above the skylight and the team of eight were poised on their abseil ropes.

Palmer was on the right-hand rope and his team leader on the left. However, the leader's rope snagged and, though he desperately tried to free it, it would not budge. Palmer had similar bad luck: the rope swayed slightly, involuntarily, towards the embassy, and it was enough to break a pane of glass in the tall, vertical window. At the same time, the police negotiators continued to talk to Salim, promising him that his demands would be met and that a coach was on its way to transport the terrorists and hostages to Heathrow.

During the phone call with the negotiator, Salim claimed to have heard suspicious noises, although the negotiator on the phone tried to convince him nothing significant was going on. As Salim went to check, the sound of breaking glass was heard and so the order to launch the assault was given a few seconds early. It was 7.24pm.

The remaining two abseilers in the first wave went down separate ropes and desperately tried to help Palmer and the team leader down. 'Go, go, go' was the order heard and so the explosive charge above the skylight was detonated. A few seconds later Blue Team's frame charges blew out the first-floor window at the front of the building, followed by stun grenades thrown through the window. By now, the other four abseilers of Romeo Two [the call sign of Palmer's team] had reached the balcony. Palmer, seeing that the curtains had been drawn and that the room was in darkness, kicked out the rest of the glass and threw in two stun grenades.

Palmer tried desperately to free the team leader, but flames were now coming up from the second floor as a result of the stun grenades setting light to the curtains, and so both men were engulfed by flames. Palmer managed to get down his rope to the balcony and then the team leader had his rope cut. Despite falling around twelve feet and having serious burns, he simply got up and carried on.

Palmer and three other men drove through the smashed windows as one and met no gunmen or hostages. There were two doors ahead of them, one of them leading to the small cipher room where the female hostages were supposed to be. The door to this room was locked, but they forcibly opened it and found the four female hostages who by now were hysterical.

The second door led to the landing and stairwell, but again this was locked. Palmer, helped by the team leader, once more forcibly opened the door. It moved only a fraction, however, because the terrorists had blocked it with furniture; despite repeated kicks and shoulder barges it would not move. Palmer then remembered there was a further window on the balcony that led to another room and thought he would try that as a means of entry. By now all the curtains and paint on the windows were on fire. He climbed through this burning mass and felt the intense heat all over. As he reached the balcony he pulled off his respirator and smouldering hood and slapped at his head and shoulders to extinguish the flames. He looked through the left-hand window and saw a figure crouching at the back of this room. Palmer thought that the man had not seen him and began to enter from the balcony. He observed one of the terrorists, Hassan, trying to set light to the carpet, so he took aim and fired. However, his sub-machine gun performed the dreaded 'dead man's click' and no round fired. Hassan shot back with his pistol but missed, giving Palmer time to drop his gun and reach for his Browning pistol, which was in a quick-draw holster strapped to his thigh. Before he could get the pistol out and aim, the terrorist had fled.

Palmer gave chase and saw him run into the telex room where all the male hostages were being kept. As Hassan kept running, Palmer could hear shooting and screaming, and as Hassan ran into the room he made for the far left-hand corner. There, he took out a hand grenade, with his hand positioned to remove the pin. As Palmer entered the room he caught sight of the terrorist and the grenade. In a split second, he shot Hassan dead with a single round. Meanwhile, the other terrorists had shot and killed a hostage before putting their weapons down. Red Team leader spotted the combat jacket of one of the men in the room and, despite protesting he was a student, he was searched and during this a pistol magazine was found. As the terrorist reached for his grenade, one of the SAS men shot him dead.

Meanwhile, on the first floor, Salim was distracted by the noise and confusion and it was with this opportunity that Trevor Lock wrestled him to the ground and held his concealed pistol to his head. While this was going on, two stun grenades had detonated in the room and the SAS burst in. One trooper shouted 'Trevor' and told him to roll out of the way, then Salim was quickly despatched by sub-machine gun.

The main briefing for the operation was to get the hostages out and, amidst the burning and confusion, they were roughly bundled down the stairs, passed from hand to hand along a human chain as the SAS men searched for any clue that a terrorist was hiding amongst them. Suddenly a trooper spotted a fragmentation grenade in a man's hand. However, he could not fire without hitting others in the line of fire as the ammunition was high powered, but he pointed out to the others further down the stairs that there was a 'bad guy' coming down. A trooper below smashed the stock (butt) of his weapon into the back of the terrorist's neck. He tumbled to the bottom of the flight of stairs, where two SAS men riddled him with fire, and as the terrorist released the grenade, the pin fortunately remained in it.

The rest of the hostages were shoved and pushed along the chain and out into the back garden, where they were told to lie face down. They were tied up whilst their identity was checked. A further terrorist, Fowzi Nejad, was found amongst them and taken prisoner: he was the only one to survive (he was subsequently imprisoned and was, eventually, released in November 2008).

The seventeen minutes of action in Operation Nimrod had transformed the reputation of the Regiment because, for the first time, its members had operated in the full glare of the world's media. The rescue had been an overwhelming success: of the twenty-six hostages taken prisoner, five had been released before the assault and one had already been killed when the SAS went in. Of those still in the building, nineteen had been rescued but one had been killed by the terrorists, bringing the overall death toll to just two. Of those who were rescued, two had shotgun wounds.

Willie Whitelaw was quickly on the scene, tears of relief and joy streaming down his face. 'I always knew you would do a good job, but I didn't know it would be this good,' he said. The SAS suffered just one serious injury – third-degree burns to the man who had got caught up in his abseil, but he later made a good recovery from his injuries. The siege was officially declared to be over by Scotland Yard at 8.15pm. That night, while at a barracks, the SAS men who had taken part in the raid were sipping celebratory beers when Margaret Thatcher and her husband, Denis, unexpectedly joined them. 'Gentlemen, there is nothing sweeter than the taste of success, and you boys have got it,' she told them. Palmer had his QGM presented to him by the Queen in a private ceremony at Buckingham Palace in June 1981. (Special Forces decorations are often made secretly long before they are announced officially and publicly in the *London Gazette*.)

Palmer also took part in the Falklands War and, at the end of the hostilities, he and a comrade organised a big party. The two men 'acquired' an Argentine Mercedes wagon, while Palmer persuaded a Royal Naval colleague to supply large quantities of beer. A third source provided steak, rather than Army rations, and the party was a great success.

Palmer had survived the Falklands War unscathed, but he was killed on 8 February 1983, aged just thirty-one, near Lurgan in Northern Ireland. He died after he and another SAS soldier, while on a covert operation, were driving on the M1 and their car overturned and struck an embankment. In his spare time, Palmer had loved to fish and, as a mark of respect, a special Memorial Cup was held in his memory in Hereford for a number of years after his death.

Palmer's posthumous QGM was announced on 11 November 1994, fourteen years after the Iranian Embassy Siege and eleven years after his death in the car crash.

LANCE CORPORAL WILLIAM STUART
AWARD: MILITARY MEDAL (MM)
GAZETTED: 18 SEPTEMBER 1973

William Stuart was decorated after showing outstanding bravery in two separate incidents over the space of just four days in Northern Ireland. At the height of 'the Troubles', he first chased and arrested an IRA commander following a raid on a pub in Lurgan, a town in County Armagh. Just three days later, while out on patrol, he was shot in the right upper arm by an IRA sniper. Although in acute pain, Stuart withdrew his patrol and it was later established that five terrorist gunmen had been at the scene. Although he did not serve with a Special Forces unit, his exceptional bravery means he is fully deserving of a write-up in this book.

Stuart served with the King's Royal Hussars – and his post-war MM is unique to the regiment. His decoration was announced in the *London Gazette* on 18 September 1973, after his recommendation stated:

L/Cpl Stuart of C Squadron 15th/19th Hussars was a member of a troop acting as infantry in Lurgan under Command C Company 3rd Battalion The Royal Regiment of Fusiliers. In the five weeks he had been at Lurgan, L/Cpl Stuart has established a reputation as an outstanding junior NCO maintaining the highest standards of leadership. On two particular occasions he excelled.

On 22nd April 1973 L/Cpl Stuart was with a small patrol, which, acting on information, raided a Public House looking for a man wanted in connection with the murder of at least two members of the security forces and who was known to always be armed. As the patrol of which L/Cpl Stuart was a member arrived at the back of the house four men came running out. L/Cpl Stuart gave chase, and on his own chased the wanted man over 300 metres before arresting him. The man was armed with an automatic pistol. He was the Officer Commanding the local IRA unit. The initiative, physical fitness, courage and quick thinking shown by L/Cpl Stuart were entirely responsible for the capture of this dangerous criminal.

On the evening of the 25th April, L/Cpl Stuart was commanding a patrol in North Street, Lurgan. One single shot was fired by a gunman which shattered L/Cpl Stuart's right upper arm. Despite this severe and painful injury L/Cpl Stuart took control of the situation. He deployed his patrol issuing orders to seal off the area and screen bystanders. He instructed the radio operator to send a contact report and he got one member of the patrol to render first aid. It has since been discovered that there were a total of five terrorist gunmen involved. There can be no doubt that L/Cpl Stuart's quick action prevented further casualties to his patrol. All this was achieved while he himself was in acute pain and bleeding heavily. Despite his own severe wound he kept complete control of the situation, and set a superb example by his calm behaviour. His complete disregard for his own comfort and safety and his devotion to duty are beyond praise. At all times, his main concern was the safety of his own men and counter action against the terrorists. L/Cpl Stuart's actions were in accordance with the highest traditions of his Regiment and the British Army.

As part of the surgery on his arm, Stuart had to have his shattered limb reconstructed using parts of his own leg. Stuart served with the 15/19th Hussars from 1970 to 1975 then, after leaving the Army because of his serious injuries, he worked as a pipe fitter; however, as a civilian he continued to be troubled from acute pain in the arm that had been shattered by a terrorist's bullet.

Stuart, a divorced father of two who was also a grandfather, died at his home in Newcastle-upon-Tyne on 17 April 1997, aged forty-eight. At the time, those close to him attributed his death to the wounds he had received from the sniper's bullet twenty-four years earlier. His funeral was attended by more than 500 people and both his family and his former colleagues were generous in their praise.

His brother, who asked not to be identified by his first name, told his local paper: 'If it wasn't for the injury he would still be in the Army today. He loved the Army and was a soldier through and through.'

His mother added: 'When he was shot I was angry with the IRA, but I don't feel anything now. He said the Irish were just normal people. Some would give him a cup of tea while others would spit in his face, but he didn't hate them. He was very modest and didn't really talk about his time in Northern Ireland at all. He was just doing the job he loved.'

Major James Walls, who at the time of Stuart's death was Commanding Officer of the Light Dragoons at Fenham Barracks, Newcastle, said: 'We were all deeply shocked to hear about his death. He joined us in 1970 as a trooper and I was regimental sergeant major. He became part of the team

255

immediately and was an excellent athlete. He had a very pleasing nature and he was always ready to give advice. He only made lance corporal because of his injury but there's no doubt he would have risen to a high rank had he been able to continue his Army career.'

Stuart's local paper, the *Evening Chronicle*, hailed him as a hero in its comment pages, saying:

> William Stuart paid a high price for his courage. In the blood-soaked Ulster of 24 years ago his army career and his life were shattered by an IRA bullet just days after he had shown bravery above and beyond the call of duty. Royalty, top brass and the nation – in the shape of the Military Medal – paid tribute to this man of steel forced back into civilian life, yet another casualty of Northern Ireland. Now he is dead, aged just 48, and there is every chance that the high impact bullet which smashed his arm a quarter of a century ago left him with a tragic legacy which was to trigger that premature death. Lance Corporal Stuart – to all but those who knew him – is now just another name on the roll call of waste. For those who did [know him], he was a hero in the truest sense of the word and for them the memory will long live on.

SERGEANT (LATER CAPTAIN) GRAHAM WATTS*
AWARD: DISTINGUISHED CONDUCT MEDAL (DCM)
GAZETTED**:

Graham Watts is a pseudonym requested by the individual concerned because of his crucial role in what was almost certainly the most successful surveillance coup during the whole period of 'the Troubles'. Watts was at the heart of an undercover operation that virtually wiped out the complete Provisional IRA

* Name change for security reasons
** Date removed for security reasons

command structure in Belfast at the time through the arrest of seventeen of its leading members. Among those seized were the entire hierarchy of the IRA's Belfast Brigade and arguably the three most wanted men in the city at the time: Gerry Adams (Officer Commanding), Brendan Hughes (Operations Officer) and Tom Cahill (Finance Officer). Watts' award was the first DCM to any member of the Special Forces in Northern Ireland. Furthermore, the whole surveillance operation of the summer of 1973 is recounted in an astonishing interview with the undercover operative following his retirement from the Army.

The son of a lorry driver, Watts was educated at the local primary and secondary-modern schools before leaving school at fifteen. He joined the Army as a junior soldier and then worked his way up the ranks as a private from the age of seventeen. In 1972 he, then a sergeant, and two corporals from his regiment were seconded to serve in Northern Ireland. Early the following year Watts welcomed the opportunity to join 14 Intelligence Company on its inception. He worked for '14 Int', as it was commonly known, as a plainclothes, undercover operator, seeking to obtain information on the IRA leadership and its members. He provided me with a fascinating account of the events that took place on 19 July 1973:

> By mid 1973 we were building up the first comprehensive picture of the IRA. But there were still huge gaps in our picture; we had photographs of many suspects but we didn't know their names. And we had many names, but no photographs to put them to. And there were others who were no more than rumours – no picture, no name. The organisation was recruiting in record numbers and it was our job to find out what it was up to. It was a long-winded process compiling the data, but these were the days before all of the sneaky kit today's intelligence people use. We took photos of suspects then asked the regular Army to stop them at road-blocks and check them out. Or we would take the photos to the RUC and Special Branch to see if they could put names and

details to the mug shots.

When we identified a 'player', or even if we just had a name or photo, we gave him a code; C3, B2, D1 etc. The white-haired, stooping old man I was watching was C5. There were four of us on his tail and we swapped around often to prevent him suspecting anything. I took over the observation as C5 entered the Falls Road. It looked promising.

C5 was on foot and I was sitting in my car, a grey Triumph Dolomite, from where I could see him amble up the road in front of the red-bricked terraced housing. The road was wide and busy, I knew I didn't stick out and was confident that C5 wouldn't get too close to me. The car, like me, was meant to be anonymous and blend in to the city. I watched C5 as he slowly made his way up the road towards the Beehive and I started to sense that he would go to the pub where our men in the OP [observation post] opposite would pick him up. If he went to the pub, I doubted we would get anything out of it. It could be a frustrating business: I was 24 and wanted action. But I was trained enough to know that patience brought results. I'd get my action later.

However, C5 didn't go as far as the pub, he stopped only a few houses short and let himself into the terrace through a poorly maintained front door. Things were looking up. Perhaps we might get a result. Even if we identified some more players, put a couple more pieces in our picture, it would be a success. However, what we all hoped for was a major bust, lifting some of the IRA's top men. The man we really wanted, who was on the top of our list, was just known as A1. We had no other details, but he was dangerous, ruthless, the heartbeat of the Provisionals. Chances were we had his photo or name, but without confirmation these pieces of information were useless. The IRA was bombing, shooting, maiming and beating with an increasing intensity. That year, forty-two British soldiers had been killed, as had seven policemen and five members of the Ulster Defence Regiment, a regiment of the British Army that recruited almost exclusively from Ulster's Protestant population.

The IRA had lost eighteen known members, many killed while bomb-making. There had been riots in Belfast and in Londonderry, Northern Ireland's second city, where Catholics held a majority. Just the year before, thirteen Catholic civil rights' marchers were shot dead by British army paratroopers (another victim died later) during 'Bloody Sunday' in Londonderry. The IRA retaliated by killing nine civilians in a car bomb attack in Belfast, 'Black Friday'. And so it continued, with acts of atrocity focusing the eyes of the world's media on the north-west tip of Europe, to an island that could trace the roots of its present acrimony back hundreds of years. The violence was not, and never had been, the preserve of the Republican contingent. The RUC, Army and terrorists loyal to the British Government all had skeletons in their closets. But working for the British Government meant we were after the IRA. It was becoming increasingly organised and sophisticated, and was spreading its tentacles not only within its communities in Ireland, but across the Atlantic to the United States and across Europe to sympathetic regimes and other terrorist organisations. Earlier that month, customs investigators in Bremen, [West] Germany, announced they had seized a huge consignment of weapons, including 5,000 rifles, which were destined for the IRA.

But the IRA warlords were not easy to find in their urban jungle, even if we had photos and positive ID. The leaders of the Provisionals lost themselves in the Catholic areas with sympathetic communities. They changed identities and appearance, moved often and practised effective evasion technique – especially A1, who remained a mystery. It was a war of wits and patience.

We were told that no act of terror from the IRA in Belfast went ahead without the express say-so of A1. To lift him would be a major propaganda coup for us, not that we'd get any credit – our presence was top secret. But the RUC and the regular Army would consider it a major boost in the fight against the IRA terrorists who were demanding an end to British rule in the six-state province and [to] be joined with the Republic south.

I settled down in my car, watching the house where C5 had

gone. I rotated my head to take in the surroundings. I had to remain 'situation aware', as the Army jargon goes. It looked like a scene from Coronation Street; but I knew the Rovers Return and the Beehive had little in common. I felt my gun, a standard 9mm Browning, which was tucked into my belt. I checked my rear-view mirror and for a moment was taken aback. But it was only my hair. I'd grown it long for the job – in an effort to blend in. But, of course, to blend in properly you couldn't just grow your hair long, you had to have it styled in the latest fashion. My shoulder length black locks were nipped and tucked and gelled into a style that never really caught on – it was in stark contrast to my shaven-headed squaddie cut. When I signed up, the Light Infantry would seriously have had to consider my chosen career if I had known what haircut I would be sporting eight years later. But detail was crucial and I could live with the embarrassment.

For a while nothing happened at the house and I reported [via radio] the lack of movement back to my boss. He was from the Welsh Guards and we had gone through training together and were mates – we worked well as a team on these types of operations.

Then another character arrived at the house. He looked shifty, nervous and was hiding his face. But then he scooted off past the house towards the Beehive and I sighed. It was like getting a bite when fishing, but then immediately losing the fish. But, strangely, he stopped before the pub and walked back down the road from where he had come. He passed the house again and carried on for fifty metres down the road. I could tell something was up, he was checking out the locality before knocking on the door. I sensed an IRA Brigade meeting was going ahead. Sure enough, the man returned quickly to the house, knocked on the [front] door, then turned to look out across the road. Moments later the door opened and in he went. I reported back to base and said I didn't recognise the suspect.

'Keep me informed, Graham,' Harry instructed. I knew he'd be checking the description I'd given him against known and suspected 'players', to see if we could make a cursory ID. The visitor was an undistinguished chap: smart casual dress, longish brown hair, clean-shaven, just under six foot tall. Not much to go on.

Then it happened again, another dodgy-looking, steely-faced man walked towards the house. He was tall, thin, bearded and bespectacled and he certainly wasn't out for a summer stroll. He followed the same routine as the first visitor. He crossed the wide, busy road, then walked up and down looking in all directions. I was not worth a second glance, my haircut seemed to be working. Then he, too, knocked on the door, then looked out before quickly being ushered inside. I sent the commentary to Harry [over the radio].

Then another suspicious-behaving character arrived and followed the same routine as the first two. I was certain I had a Brigade meeting on my hands. It was quite probable the length of people's lives was being determined inside the house. They could be drawing up a hit list, arguing about whom to kill, where to plant the bomb and whether to warn the authorities about it. They could be discussing our role in the game of terror they were determined to continue. Whatever was going on I knew these were 'players' we had to lift – Harry had confirmed my suspicions. He had no method of proving the identities of the mystery men, but he had enough intelligence to be sure this gathering would be worth disrupting. When I felt that all who were going to turn up had arrived, I advised Harry to get the regular Army in and let the RUC in on it. We could not be involved in the actual raid – we had to remain undercover. What made things more dangerous for us was that the gung-ho lads in the 'Green Army' [uniformed British Army or security forces] were not aware we were on the ground. It never seemed to link the intelligence it received with Special Forces, I think the squaddies put it down to informants – informants whom we had only just begun recruiting. Although we were at war with the IRA, our main enemy was the Green Army. After all, we looked just like the locals with our trendy haircuts – they could quite legitimately have shot us dead because we were always armed.

My adrenaline began to flow as I waited for the Army to raid the house opposite me. I had given the house number and description to Harry over the radio. It looked like being a straightforward lift. I envisaged no problems. After all the intense training, I was more confident that operations would go smoothly, without incident. However, my faith was soon to be bruised – by an enormous cock-up. After only a few minutes' wait, the second battalion of the Light Infantry, together with the RUC, began to descend on the Falls Road. Through the wing mirrors of my car I could see the armoured vehicles as they trundled towards me. About twenty personnel arrived at the scene. The troops wore jungle camouflage that had the opposite effect of the designer's intention in the brick and concrete city by making the Army stick out like a sore thumb. But automatic rifles were at the ready and there was a satisfying look of thoroughness to the approach. But then, to my abject horror, the troops began to raid the wrong house. I couldn't believe it; they were cordoning off the house next door to the meeting.

'Harry, they're doing the wrong f***ing house,' I yelled into my radio. 'They've f***ing gone next door.'

Somewhere in the line of communication the house number I had given was changed. Either that or the lieutenant in charge had some form of numerical dyslexia. It was a cock-up on the scale of the 'Bay of Pigs' invasion.

'Get them in the right f***ing house, Harry,' I yelled. I was frantic and furious, and I repeated the correct address. Harry said he'd get the Army in the right house, but he had no direct contact with the ground troops. I watched aghast as the Green Army surrounded the wrong house and cleared the area. I knew the procedure and was aware that, because I was parked so close, they would check me out. Then I could flash my ID and tell the fools what they'd done. But I waited and waited and no one approached me – another cock-up. I banged my steering wheel in frustration and waited for Harry to get word through. Eventually the Green Army, having searched an empty house, left the area. I watched the right house for signs of the players fleeing, but nothing was happening.

Harry told me to stay and keep watch and said the Army would return and do the lift properly. I wasn't going to hold my breath – I just hoped the guilty party was getting a suitable bollocking from someone suitably important. The results of weeks of work, tracking, time, and effort was in the balance. If the IRA got wind of the cock-up – or surmised it later – it would be a marvellous piece of propaganda for the organisation. I didn't take my eyes off the front of the house. No one left through the front door and Harry informed me no one had left though the back exit, where one of the team was in position. All were inside; there was a chance we could still get a result. It could well have been that those in the house, if they were aware of the botched raid next door, might not have taken any notice, assuming they were not the only people being naughty on the Falls Road that day. As time went on, my confidence returned and I became sure that the lift could still be carried out, but the Green Army would have to be careful – just in case there was an ambush or booby traps.

But then luck again swung to the terrorists – I'd been clocked by a look-out. F***. He was walking across the road towards me. I enabled [over the radio] Harry to listen in to the exchange I sensed would follow. The man rolling towards me was squat and youngish, a new recruit I guessed. His hair was dark, face stern. He wore dirty blue jeans and a crinkled shirt with the sleeves rolled up. I didn't think he was carrying [a gun], but I checked my weapon again. He was making a beeline for me and he spoke as he approached the car. He announced that he was from the 'Civil Defence Community' – a synonym for Provisional IRA.

'I don't want anything to do with your f***ing Irish s***,' I bellowed at him. There was no point in trying to put on an accent to disguise my West Country roots; if he had only half a brain he would have seen through it. 'My boss is doing some business round the corner, I'm waiting for him,' I explained.

'What f***ing business?' the look-out screamed in my face.

'F***ing insurance,' I returned, with equal volume. 'I don't give a s*** about your Irish s***, I don't f***ing want to be here. F*** off.'

'F***ing watch it,' he warned, before storming off. My cover was shot to pieces and I fully expected the look-out to dash to the house and inform those inside of my presence. But, remarkably, he seemed to buy my lie and then wandered off. I assumed he was still watching me, to see what I did.

Then, within thirty seconds, I saw Bill, one of my team, dressed in shirt, tie and carrying a briefcase, walking towards the passenger door. An insurance salesman. Nice one, Harry.

Bill opened the door and got in. I drove off quickly. It was obvious he was as pissed off as I was.

'What the f*** happened?' I asked.

'Chinese f***ing whispers.'

'F***.'

'They're still going ahead with the raid,' Bill said. 'The RUC are determined. You've got to drop me off and get to the safe house at the edge of the city. Your cover is blown.'

'He might have bought the lie,' I tried.

'Got to assume he knows – he will after the raid, anyway.'

I grudgingly admitted what I knew was the truth and dropped off Bill before leaving for a secret address.

I had never known frustration like it. I had done everything properly and we'd got lucky – then it all went pear-shaped, my cover was blown and I had no idea of knowing how the raid finally went. When I reached the address in a safe, Protestant area of Belfast suburbia, I sat in my car with the radio waiting for news. Harry would let me know how it went as soon as he could. But I waited and waited . . . nothing. I wanted to do something, I wanted to be involved, but I was stuck right out of the way.

Then the radio crackled into life. Harry spoke.

'Success Graham,' he announced. I could almost see his chest puffing up with pride. 'We've basically lifted the IRA's Army

Council. We couldn't have had a better result. But we've really set the cat amongst the pigeons. The other IRA players we've been tailing are fleeing the city in droves; to the border and to Derry. There's a brown Mark II Cortina heading your way out to "Green One". Four big guys in the car, we need them tailing. Get to it, Graham.'

He gave me the registration number as I headed for Green One, the road leading west out of Belfast towards Derry. I was back in the action and Harry had sounded excited; it looked like we'd hit the jackpot. I was guided to the target car by Harry and picked up the Cortina as it left the city on the motorway – Green One. I had the entire street plan of Belfast in my head – thanks to the intense memory training I had received – but I had no idea what roads lay out of the city. And with manpower stretched I was the only one following the targets. This was not a scenario we had planned for. As a result, training was [later] changed. But I didn't care much for procedure as I left the slip road in pursuit of people who it had to be assumed were IRA terrorists. This was action, this was what it was all about. Me, undercover, a car chase, after terrorists dedicated to a war against the British Government – fantastic. But, like so many things, a real car chase is not what is portrayed in the flicks. And nor was my devotion to the Queen. The IRA opposed the monarchy, and the terrorists' political wing, Sinn Fein, later refused to take up its seats in the Palace of Westminster because it would not swear allegiance to Her Majesty. I had no opinion about the Queen; I fought because it was my job. But later in my career I was to meet Elizabeth II in an official capacity and she impressed me greatly.

Car chases and Hollywood directors have obviously not coincided in their short pasts because the reality is not speed and jumps and skids and sirens. It is a discreet business, full of subtle manoeuvres and tactics. It was probably just as well the car chase was not a high-speed affair, as my Dolomite was no racing machine.

When the Cortina pulled on to the motorway, it adopted the

tactics I expected and slowed down to about 30mph – slower than even the heavy lorries. Following the car was not easy; if the driver sensed he was being tailed he could pull off the route and lose himself. I kept a long way behind at first, hiding the Dolomite behind lorries when I could. But driving so slowly meant I could be spotted easily, and because I was the only one in pursuit, I had to keep overtaking the Cortina at speed then coming off the road and rejoining again behind the car.

I kept Harry informed, but he could offer no support – resources were at full stretch as the IRA members ran scared from the capital. I knew I'd have to keep on the car's tail in unfamiliar territory until an Army unit could be summoned to stop the vehicle and lift its occupants. The three-lane road was busy and, while this helped conceal me from the targets, it hampered my attempts to find the car when I rejoined the road after overtaking. I confirmed there were four suspects in the car, the two in the back were broad shouldered types and I had to assume they had weapons. The IRA had been buying arms in great numbers and, more importantly, operatives were being trained to use them.

Once more I turned off the road and circled a roundabout until the Cortina had passed me again on its painfully slow mission to Derry. As I neared the coastal town, I became keener for Army support. I didn't know the place, and to enter it alone could put me at risk. Then I heard the crackle of the radio and Harry told me to change frequency and talk in a chopper [helicopter] to the target. I flicked over channels and got in touch with the pilot who was only minutes away. He stayed out of the way until the Army units had caught up and I could see them through my rear view mirror. Then the chopper swooped in above me and picked up the target car. The Cortina driver sped up a bit, to try and tell if it was his car the chopper was homing in on. The four occupants were soon in no doubt they were the targets as three Army vehicles surrounded the car and forced it to the side of the road. The Army also decided to pull me in, which was fair and efficient. The chopper landed in a field by the road. The soldiers burst from the Army truck and approached the Cortina with weapons raised and at the ready. As I was watching, the lift of a rifle was pushed through the open window in my car and in to the side of my head. An angry face grimaced at me and swore.

'All right, all right,' I said, while trying to watch the real action as the targets were searched, then marched to the helicopter. When they were out of view, I told the squaddie threatening me who I was and showed him my ID card. He was soon satisfied, took away his gun from my stylish hair and allowed me to radio back to Harry to give him the good news.

Back at base a party was in full swing. All the top brass from the Army and RUC were there, showering us with champagne. The IRA's heart had been ripped out; Belfast's most important terrorists were captured. And plenty of other smaller fish had been picked up too, including the four I followed out of the city. That day a total of sixteen IRA staff was lifted. Harry was ecstatic and we tried to hammer out who was responsible for the day's earlier cock-up. The RUC officers at the party were particularly pleased. The four picked up in the house were men they had been after for months – they were suspected of being behind all the bombings and killings carried out in Belfast in the name of Republicanism over the previous few years.

So delighted was the RUC about the capture of these men it offered to take us down town to its Springfield Road barracks and have a look at the terrorists for ourselves. Harry and I took them up on the offer. I thought at that moment how the lookout, who had approached me in the Falls Road, must have been kicking himself. We were driven to Springfield Road by an RUC officer and with us was a Special Branch officer with a keen interest in the arrests. After security checks, we were shown in to the building that was just off the Falls Road. We were guided to a small viewing room and from behind the one-way glass we watched as the suspects were put into position for our perusal. The Special Branch officer began to tell us who they were.

'That one there,' he said, pointing at a sorry looking figure, 'is

Brendan Hughes. Nasty character. Like all of them he's a murderer, terrorist and IRA leader. His speciality is bombing. The next is Owen Coogan, Brigade intelligence officer [later the alleged director of operations]. Then there's Tom Cahill, thirty-eight years old, can't get much higher than him in the IRA. See his face, the scars: that's from when the Official IRA tried to assassinate him two years ago. They shot him in the head and chest. The Provisionals and the Officials are quite happy to try and kill each other off. His brother, Joe, is in prison for gun-running. And the bearded one is Gerry Adams, Brigade Commander. He's been interned before, even had secret talks with the British Government about a peace prospect. We've been after him for over a year. He's the biggest catch.'

Harry and I smiled in satisfaction, then Harry said to me: 'We knew of them all, at least by reputation. Gerry Adams is A1. He was on our records all the time, but he's an expert at evasion. He's been in hiding since the peace talks went to pot just over a year ago.' This bust put our presence in Northern Ireland on the map, but the war was not over and nor was my involvement in it . . .

Watts was worried that his undercover identity had now been blown because he had been seen close up by an IRA member. He went on leave and, when he returned about three weeks later, he had changed his hairstyle and was wearing very different clothes. However, in an exclusive interview near his West Country home, he revealed just how close he came to being shot dead just weeks after the operation to detain the IRA suspects:

I was floating around on surveillance duties trying to keep off the Falls Road, but then the 2ic [second in command] asked me to reconnoitre two or three men outside the Beehive pub. I didn't want to do it [in case he was recognised] but I agreed and drove past two or three men outside the pub to see if I recognised them.

It was about 4 o'clock in the afternoon. A car [of IRA men]

picked me up and followed me. I radioed [discreetly using his Army radio] that I was being followed. I was driving a brand new Triumph Dolomite – a different vehicle to three weeks earlier. When I stopped my car, this guy [IRA man] touched my car's back end with his. Then he pulled alongside my car and the man in the back aimed his SMG [sub-machine gun] at me from only a few feet away. I was so close I could hear the working parts of the gun moving forward, but it didn't pick up a round or fire because the magazine clearly wasn't in properly. This sometimes happened with SMGs. The driver was already speeding off and so I instinctively chased after him. I knew that, because I had radioed that I was being followed, other [Army] cars would be closing in. At the time, the adrenaline was flowing and I stayed cool and calm. We chased the car to a football ground nearby, where the men we were after abandoned their vehicle and ran off. It was only when I got back to base, and had to write up my report on what had happened, that it hit me how close I had come to being killed. If the SMG hadn't jammed, I would have been dead.

During the whole period of the Troubles, only eighteen DCMs were awarded and, of these, very few of them to members of the Special Forces. Watts' award was announced after his recommendation stated [once again, his surname has been changed at his request]:

On 19 July 1973 he [Sergeant Watts] was tasked with following a prominent I.R.A. suspect, which he did successfully to a house in the Falls Road. Following a period of observation, Sergeant Watts determined that in all likelihood a senior I.R.A. Brigade meeting was taking place.

He chose to stay in his vehicle and report by radio the movements of those entering and leaving the property with only a 9mm pistol for protection. Sergeant Watts' appreciation of the situation resulted in the fast moving operation that followed, the aim of which was to arrest all suspects at the house under observation.

During one particularly dangerous phase of the operation Sergeant Watts was spotted and challenged by an I.R.A. suspect acting as lookout. Remaining calm throughout the encounter he waited until the lookout had re-entered the building and then, knowing his cover was most likely blown, had the presence of mind to move to a safe-house and wait while the Green Army raided the house and arrested the occupants.

Those arrested proved to be of the utmost significance and triggered other senior I.R.A. members to flee the city. One vehicle containing four suspected terrorists was reported to be heading in Sergeant Watts' direction. He was tasked with following this vehicle until the Green Army could close in on it and apprehend the suspects, this he did with great skill.

By locating the Brigade meeting and choosing to stay in a location of extreme danger while relaying vital information back to his superiors, Sergeant Watts showed bravery and skill that cannot be understated [underestimated]. The significance of the outcome of these operations in the province cannot be overstated.

After he was nearly shot, Watts could no longer work undercover in Northern Ireland, as he had been 'rumbled' by the IRA, although he was later involved in training other undercover operators. However, he continued to have a distinguished and lengthy career in the Army. In the late 1980s he received a short-term commission, serving as a lieutenant and, later, a captain.

Watts, now in his mid-sixties, retired from the Army in 1992 after more than thirty years' service and has done various jobs since.

TROOPER ROBERT GASPARE CONSIGLIO
AWARD: MILITARY MEDAL (MM)
GAZETTED: 20 NOVEMBER 1991

Trooper Robert 'Bob' Consiglio was one of the eight members of the ill-fated Bravo Two Zero patrol that has become one of the most notorious episodes in Special Forces history. The daring exploits of the SAS team were originally made famous by Andy McNab's international best-selling book *Bravo Two Zero*, and since then others have published their accounts of events. In the aftermath of the mission, its members have not always seen eye to eye, but they have all consistently agreed on one thing: that Bob Consiglio was a tough, courageous soldier whose bravery and self-sacrifice undoubtedly gave the other members of the team a better chance of escaping the Iraqis.

'Bravo Two Zero' was the call sign of the eight-man SAS patrol deployed behind enemy lines during the First Gulf War in January 1991. At this time, prior to the coalition ground invasion of Iraq, 'B' Squadron, 22 SAS, was stationed at a forward operating base (FOB) in Saudi Arabia. The aim of the mission was to gather intelligence and find a good lying-up position (LUP) from which to set up an observation post (OP) above the main supply route (MSR) between Baghdad, the Iraqi capital, and the north-west of the country. If possible, too, the patrol was tasked with destroying Iraqi scud-missile launchers – likely to target Israel – along the 160-mile stretch of the MSR. The eight-man patrol was led by Sergeant Andy McNab (a pseudonym) and the other members of the team included Corporal Chris 'Geordie' Ryan (a pseudonym) and Trooper Bob Consiglio.

Consiglio was born in Lausanne, Switzerland, on 13 April 1966. He enlisted into the Royal Marines on 19 April 1983, just six days after his seventeenth birthday. After serving with the Marines for five years, he successfully applied to the SAS. In January 1991 Consiglio was the youngest member of the Bravo Two Zero patrol, aged twenty-four.

On the night of 22/23 January, Consiglio and his seven comrades were transported into Iraqi air space by an RAF Chinook helicopter. After being dropped off without Land Rovers, the eight men made their way to the proposed location of the OP. It was soon discovered that they had a major communications problem, which meant that they could not receive or relay messages on the patrol's radio. In short, they were essentially on their own.

On 24 January the patrol was compromised when its members were spotted, first by a young goat herder and, later, by a bulldozer driver. This, in turn, led to a firefight with Iraqi soldiers in armoured personnel carriers (APCs). Realising their plight, the patrol hoped to be picked up at their infiltration point – the standard procedure in the event of an emergency or no radio contact was that the helicopter would return to this spot every twenty-four hours. However, there was no rendezvous and, rather than head south on foot to Saudi Arabia, the patrol decided to walk north towards the Syrian border. This was a longer route, but they concluded it meant the Iraqis were less likely to be looking for them in this area.

On the night of 24/25 January, while McNab was trying to contact a passing coalition aircraft using equipment he had with him, the patrol inadvertently became split into two groups, the smaller one comprising three men, including Ryan, who by this point were armed only with rifles and pistols. By then, too, the weather had taken a turn for the worse and, by the evening of 25 January, one of the three men was suffering from hypothermia. At some point that evening, this man lost contact with the other two and died shortly afterwards, aged thirty-six. On 26 January, after again being compromised, Ryan and his comrade split up and the latter was captured by the Iraqis.

By this time, McNab's group of five were having better fortune. McNab and Consiglio staged a stunt that enabled them to commandeer a yellow taxi on the evening of 26 January. However, in the early hours of the 27th, and by now close to the Syrian border, they came into contact with armed civilians and local police. Once again, as the bullets flew, the men broke up and Consiglio became separated from his comrades. However, as he was surrounded and the enemy closed in, he refused to surrender, firing until the very end and thereby helping the others to make good their escape.

This is not the place to re-tell the Bravo Two Zero story in tens of thousands of words: McNab and others who were there have already done just that. Suffice to say that a second man died of hypothermia. Like McNab, three others were all captured and brutally tortured by the Iraqis, although they were eventually freed at the end of the war. Ryan was the only one to make it to safety, reaching the Syrian border and thereby claiming an escape of some 180 miles.

For some time, as the ground war raged, it was not known what had happened to Consiglio. Indeed, in a letter to his mother dated 1 March 1991, a senior officer wrote:

I have purposely delayed writing this letter in the hope that I might be able to give you better news. Sadly, this is not the case.

Bob was a member of a patrol from the regiment. The patrol's mission was to report on Iraqi positions some considerable distance behind enemy lines. On the second day of their deployment the patrol was attacked by a large group of enemy and there was a fierce exchange of gunfire. The patrol managed to get away without injury but they lost their backpacks containing the radios. At this stage the weather turned and conditions for the subsequent 3 days were appalling with rain, snow and freezing temperatures. The enemy also followed up and throughout the night attempted to capture the patrol that at some point became split. A large and detailed air search was immediately instigated but to date only one man has been recovered. At the time of writing I have absolutely no idea where Bob is; he is listed as Missing in Action.

All the relevant details have now been passed to the International Committee of the Red Cross and should they be granted access to the Iraqi Government, then perhaps we might learn more. We are vigorously pursuing any lead that might help us locate Bob but I would be less than honest if I didn't say that the longer we hear nothing, the less chance there is of survival.

I hope you will forgive me for writing an identical letter to the other six [missing men's] next-of-kin but I believe you should all know the broad facts as they stand at present. If the situation becomes clearer then you will be amongst the first to be told . . .

However, within just seventeen days, the senior officer had written a second letter to Consiglio's mother confirming her son had, in fact, been killed in action. His second letter contained a more detailed account of the mission:

When I wrote to you at the beginning of the month, I had hoped that my foreboding might be proved wrong and that somehow Robert might have 'returned from the grave.' Sadly, this was not to be and it was only when I saw his body return home today that I realised just how final it now is.

As I mentioned in my previous letter Robert was a member of a patrol from the regiment which was inserted by helicopter some 187 miles behind enemy lines. Their mission was to report on the movement of Iraqi Scud Missiles; a mission of the utmost strategic importance. On the second day they were compromised and chased by the enemy. During the pursuit they were forced to ditch their bergens [framed rucksacks]. It was at this point that the weather turned and for the next 5 days there was driving rain, snow and sleet. During that first night on the run the patrol split but with both halves heading for Syria approximately 195 kms to the North. Robert was with the larger part of the patrol and all went well until 27th January when they reached a point just 5 miles from Syria. Unfortunately, they ran into an enemy position and there was a fierce exchange of gunfire. Robert was not seen again after this contact, which split the patrol still further. Although we will never know for sure, I believe Robert died as a result of a gunshot wound received during that contact on approximately 27th January.

It is pointless me telling you what a magnificent soldier your son was and what a bright future he had with the Regiment. As his mother, you will of course know all this. Robert was all those things and more. Perhaps the highest compliment I can pay is that he was a professional soldier who died a soldier's death, fighting with his friends for a cause that he believed in.

I have just been handed 2 gold sovereigns that were with Robert's military clothes that he left behind in Saudi Arabia. Ten of these gold coins were issued to each man to use as 'escape money' in the event of having to escape whilst behind enemy lines. He must have kept 2 aside as mementos. Rather than return them to the Bank, I thought you might like to keep one: I will give the other to his father.

On behalf of the Regiment please accept our sympathy on the loss of your son. He was a fine soldier and companion and we grieve with you.

Lieutenant General Sir Peter de la Billière, the commander-in-chief of the British forces during the Gulf War and who had himself served in the SAS for many years, also wrote to Consiglio's mother. In a letter dated 4 April 1991, he said:

I cannot write about the details of his death, but the operation on which he was participating was most important to the success of the campaign; Robert understood this. He died upholding the full traditions of his Regiment. Throughout preparation and during operations Robert proved himself a fine, brave and resolute soldier who won the confidence, respect and admiration of his friends and comrades . . . The war was fought for a just, and honourable cause. Robert gave his life to this cause, so that it could be brought to a successful conclusion. Robert is a man to be proud of – I am proud of him and I know you and your family will remember him for the hero he is.

In his book *Bravo Two Zero*, McNab wrote fondly of

Consiglio and was pleased that he was awarded a posthumous MM. McNab said of his comrade's brave death:

> Either he made his choice or it was made for him, but he went forward like a man possessed and tried to fight his way out of the contact. In doing so he drew a fearsome amount of enemy fire, and this diversion, without a doubt, helped the rest of us get away. He was hit in the head by a round that came out through his stomach and ignited a white phosphorous grenade in his webbing. He died instantly.
>
> As is the custom, we held a dead man's auction. All the men's kit was sold off to the highest bidder, and the proceeds given to the next of kin or squadron funds. The practice is not macabre; it's just the culture within the Regiment. If you worried about people getting hurt and killed you'd spend your life on anti-depressants . . . Bob [Consiglio] had a big Mexican sombrero in his locker at work, a typical tourist souvenir that I knew for a fact had only cost him ten dollars because I had been there when he bought it. I took the piss out of him on many occasions for wasting his money on such a bit of tat. At the auction, however, some idiot parted with more than a hundred quid for it. I kept it at home for a while, then took it to his grave with some MM ribbon for him and 'Legs' [like Consiglio, one of McNab's comrades nicknamed 'Legs', was also awarded a posthumous MM].

McNab himself was awarded the Distinguished Conduct Medal (DCM) for his bravery in Iraq, on top of the MM that he had already received for courage in Northern Ireland. Ryan was the third member of the patrol to receive the MM.

Others have paid warm tribute to Consiglio. In his book *The One That Got Away*, Chris Ryan told of the moment that he learned Consiglio had died: 'Bob Consiglio had gone. I felt very sad about Bob, good, tough little guy that he was – and immediately I wanted to know what had happened to him.'

Later, Ryan compared Consiglio's action favourably with any act of bravery ever performed by an SAS soldier:

> In more contemporary terms perhaps the single most selfless act of bravery was performed by a man called Bob Consiglio who, at 22 years old [in fact, he was 24], was the youngest member of Bravo Two Zero patrol where I served in the Gulf War. It was 1991 and the group he was assigned to had become splintered on the run for the Syrian border. Consiglio became estranged from the rest of the men and found himself alone. He would have known that he was going to run out of ammunition and stood little chance but he decided to stand and fight, giving the others enough time to escape . . .

8

FALKLANDS WAR HEROES

On 2 April 1982 Argentina invaded the Falkland Islands, the South Atlantic territories that had been under British sovereignty since 1833. The next day the separate British dependency of South Georgia, 800 miles away, was also invaded, although it had already been occupied by Argentinian scrap-metal dealers the previous month. Britain's team of Foreign Office ministers, headed by Lord Carrington, resigned after being caught wrong-footed by Argentina's claim to 'liberate' the Malvinas (as the islands are known in South America). The Falkland Islands are 8,000 miles from the UK, but it was soon resolved by Margaret Thatcher, the prime minister, that they would have to be recaptured – if necessary by force.

A senior SAS officer first learnt about the invasion through a BBC news flash. He immediately told one of the Regiment's squadrons to be ready to move. He also telephoned Brigadier Julian Thompson, in charge of 3 Commando Brigade – the likely spearhead of any British counter-attack – and offered the services of the SAS. The day after the invasion, 'D' Squadron was assembled at the Regiment's headquarters. The following day – 4 April – the men were given a general briefing about the conditions they were likely to encounter in the Falklands. One officer, with typical understatement, described it as 'just like the Brecon Beacons in a wet winter'. The truth was that the SAS were going to have to go to war in the wet and bitter cold of the Falklands or the numbing blizzards of South Georgia.

Both Peter de la Billière, then a brigadier, and a senior SAS officer argued for members of the Regiment to be included in the Task Force that would be sent to the Falklands, and by early April members of the SAS and SBS were on their way to the South

Atlantic. The Special Forces deployed repeatedly and effectively against the enemy. Twenty SAS members were killed during the Falklands War, including Captain John Hamilton, who was awarded a posthumous Military Cross (MC) for his courage on West Falkland when, despite being heavily outnumbered, he fought a spirited gun battle after his observation post above Port Howard was discovered. Hamilton, who had been in the SAS for just over a year, died from severe gunshot injuries on 10 June 1982.

Argentina's military government, led by General Leopoldo Galtieri, had totally misjudged Britain's determination to keep the Falkland Islands, and surrendered on 14 June 1982. The conflict had lasted seventy-four days, during which more than 900 people were killed and 1,800 injured on both sides. Neither side had formally declared war on the other.

Some people may question why the Falklands War and write-ups on non-Special Forces men have been included in a book concentrating on the activities of Special Forces operatives. My answer to this is simple: 'Operation Corporate' was a highly specialised operation involving the sort of amphibious landings for which the SAS and SBS had long been famous. Furthermore, by the time the British Armed Forces arrived in the Falklands, the islands were in Argentine hands. This meant that all operations in and around the Falklands involved being in enemy-held territory and, at times when the SAS was involved, deep behind enemy lines. I am, however, fully aware that the liberation of the islands essentially involved a massive contribution from Britain's conventional forces, and the last thing I would want to do would be to play down that immense effort in any way. What I will say with confidence is that every one of the courageous men who features in this chapter is fully worthy of his place in a book dealing with the special operations of Britain's Armed Forces.

CORPORAL (LATER CAPTAIN) IAN BAILEY
AWARD: MILITARY MEDAL (MM)
GAZETTED: 8 OCTOBER 1982

Ian Bailey was a twenty-two-year-old corporal when he charged with fixed bayonet and grenade at an elevated Argentine position on Mount Longdon at the height of the battle to regain the Falkland Islands. At Bailey's side during his initial charge was Sergeant Ian McKay, one of only two men to be awarded (both posthumously) the Victoria Cross (VC) for their gallantry during the conflict. Despite being wounded three times during the firefight that claimed McKay's life, Bailey served for a further twenty years in the Parachute Regiment and it was only some time after he left the Army in 2009 that he became aware of still having an Argentine bullet and shrapnel in his body as a result of his wartime wounds from the summer of 1982.

Born in Staffordshire and the eldest of four children, Bailey came from a family with strong military roots. His grandfather had fought in both world wars, being awarded the MM in the First World War, while his father had served with the 16/5th Lancers as a tank driver and wireless operator. His family moved to north Wales when Bailey was a young boy and, after attending local schools, he enlisted, aged sixteen, as a boy soldier in the Infantry Junior Leaders Battalion (IJLB). He graduated from there after a year as the boy regimental sergeant major. He then went to Depot Para in January 1978, passing out in April the same year. He was posted to the 3rd Battalion, Parachute Regiment, based in Germany, the following month, beginning his career as a private.

Bailey was serving as a corporal with 3 Para when he and his comrades were transported to the Falkland Islands as part of the Task Force. He took part in the action at Mount Longdon in June 1982, which claimed more lives than any other battle during the Falklands War. The mountain was some five miles to the west of the capital, Port Stanley, on the island of East

Falkland. A vivid description of the battle appears in Martin Middlebrook's book *The Falklands War* (now published by Pen and Sword Books but previously known by the title *Operation Corporate: The Story of the Falklands War, 1982*), in which Bailey and others were interviewed about their wartime experiences. As part of the advance on Port Stanley, and of a three-pronged attack, 3 Para was given the objective of reclaiming Mont Longdon, which lay within a large government-owned property that was leased to a local sheep farmer. Of the units involved in the three-pronged assault, 3 Para's began first, with Lieutenant Colonel Hew Pike concluding that the best way of attack was frontally at its west end. The plan was that 'A' Company on the left would try to seize a feature that was codenamed 'Wing Forward'. It was intended that this would, in turn, act as a fire-support base for another attack by 'B' Company on the main Longdon Mountain, on which two parts were codenamed 'Fly Half' and 'Full Back'. Finally, it was intended that 'C' Company would move up if, as was hoped, there was a collapse by Longdon's Argentine defenders, part of the conscripted and overburdened 7 Regiment.

On 11 June 1982 the Paras moved off after dusk for the approach march to the Start Line, when the British artillery were firing no more than the normal evening harassment. Bailey was given a role as a section commander in 'B' Company, which, along with 'A' Company, reached the Start Line some fifteen minutes later. In an interview with Middlebrook for his book, Bailey said:

> We were only on the Start Line a few minutes. I went round the lads and checked everybody and had a joke with my mates. The lads were quiet, each man whispering to their own very good friends, having a last drag. It was a time for being with your own mates. They knew some of them were going to get killed. For some reason, most of them fixed bayonets; I put mine on and looked round to find all the others were putting theirs on too.

We stepped over the stream and set off. It was a very clear night, cool, but it didn't feel cold; there was too much adrenalin flowing. We knew we had got a punch-up on our hands. It was uphill, a fairly steep gradient, lots of rocks, tufts of grass, holes where you could break your ankle easily – just like a good training area. You could see 200 or 300 metres ahead of you. As we went up, we were funnelled together into a space between the main Mount Longdon and a large separate rock. At one time, we were shoulder to shoulder, so we tried to spread out, some men waiting while others moved on faster. That was only about twenty feet from their main position but that first position turned out to be empty.

At this point, everyone was trying to be as quiet as possible as they approached well-constructed and heavily manned defences, but this ploy was ruined when Corporal Milne, a section commander in 'B' Company's left forward platoon, stepped on a mine, severely injuring his leg. The explosion, coupled with Milne's agonising screams, informed the Argentinians that the battle they had been anticipating was about to begin. 'B' Company came under fire before it reached the main Argentinian positions and the Paras found themselves forced into a vulnerable series of steep and narrow rock channels. From their vantage points further up the mountains, the Argentinians could fire their weapons and toss grenades. Furthermore, it was not possible to bring the British artillery close enough to engage the Argentinians who had opened fire on the Paras.

Once again Bailey, in his interview with Middlebrook, takes up the story:

Then we got the first grenades; they were just bouncing down the side of the rock face. We thought they were rocks falling, until the first one exploded. One bloke caught some shrapnel in the backside. He was the first one in the section to get injured, not badly but enough to put him out of the fighting. The small-arms fire followed soon after. People were getting down into cover again then. Because we had got funnelled, we weren't really working by sections now; the nearest private soldier to you just stuck with you. Corporal McLaughlin, the other leading section commander, was ahead of me now. He and his men were getting the small-arms fire. It was keeping his group pinned down but no one was being hit in either of our sections. There was a lot of fire on the right, where 6 Platoon was going up but it was quiet on the left where 4 Platoon was coming up after hitting the minefield.

My men started firing their '66s' [hand-held 66mm anti-tank rockets]. Whoever was in the best position to spot targets fired; the others passed spare rockets to them. It was a very good bunker weapon; there wasn't going to be a lot left of you if your bunker or sangar [a small, raised, protected structure for observation or used as a firing-point] was hit by one of those. We could see their positions by now, up above us, possibly thirty feet or so away, we could even see them moving, dark shapes. Their fire was sparse to start with but then it intensified. Some of them were very disciplined, firing, moving back into cover, then coming out again and firing again or throwing grenades.

The next cover to get forward to was in some rocks with one of their positions in the middle of it. Corporal McLaughlin's GPMG [General Purpose Machine Gun] gave us cover and we put about four grenades and an '84' round into the position, which was a trench with a stone wall around it and a tent, which was blown over. We went round and on, myself and whichever 'toms' [private soldiers in the Parachute Regiment] were available, and the two men with the '84' launcher. It was all over very quickly. We ran across, firing at the same time. Just as we went round the corner, we found one Argentinian just a few feet away. Private Meredith and I both fired with our rifles and killed him. The rest of the post – two men – were already dead, killed by the grenades or the '84' shrapnel. We put more rounds into them, to make sure they were dead and weren't going anywhere; that was normal practice.

Elsewhere on the mountain, men from 'B' Company were having a tougher time of it. Lieutenant Bickerdyke's 4 Platoon had become pinned down by one of the heavy machine guns and was largely out of contact with the company commander. However, three men from 5 Platoon put the enemy machine gun out of action, thereby freeing 4 Platoon to rejoin the fray. With the advance route on the left under a formidable fire, Bickerdyke eased 4 Platoon to the right and two of his sections became intermingled with 5 Platoon. However, their progress became blocked by a second heavy machine gun and this, in turn, caused some casualties. Bickerdyke himself was thrown backwards after being hit in the thigh.

The next phase of the action was led by Sergeant McKay, with some of his men from 4 Platoon and with Corporal Bailey's section from 5 Platoon. Once again, Bailey describes the thick of the action:

> Ian and I had a talk and decided the aim was to get across to the next cover, which was thirty to thirty-five metres away. There were some Argentinian positions there but we didn't know the exact location. He shouted out to the other corporals to give covering fire, three machine-guns altogether, then we – Sergeant McKay, myself and three private soldiers to the left of us – set off. As we were moving across the open ground, two of the privates were killed by rifle or machine-gun fire almost at once; the other private got across and into cover. We grenaded the first position and went past it without stopping, just firing into it, and that's when I got shot from one of the other positions which was about ten feet away. I think it was a rifle. I got hit in the hip and went down. Sergeant McKay was still going on to the next position but there was no one else with him. The last I saw of him, he was just going on, running towards the remaining positions in that group. I was lying on my back and I listened to men calling to each other. They were trying to find out what was happening but, when they called out to Sergeant McKay, there

was no reply. I got shot again soon after that, by bullets in the neck and hand.

After the battle, Bailey was found lying on the ground, badly injured as a result of three separate rifle bullets. He was eventually stretchered down the mountain and given first aid for separate injuries to his neck, hip and hand. After being treated at the company and regimental aid posts, he was deemed unlikely to survive his injures. However, he was later transported by Wessex helicopter to a hospital ship, SS *Uganda*, where he underwent seven operations. Later, when back in the UK, he was treated at an RAF hospital in Wroughton, Wiltshire. His unit, 'B' Company, had suffered heavy casualties in the battle to recapture the Falklands: forty-nine injured and twenty-seven dead.

Bailey was discharged from hospital in September 1982 and resumed his military career. His MM was announced on 8 October 1982, when his short citation read: 'In the early hours of 12th June 1982, the 3rd Battalion The Parachute Regiment assaulted enemy positions on Mount Longdon, eight kilometres to the West of Port Stanley on the Island of East Falkland. Corporal Bailey's Section were tasked to aid a Platoon pinned down by heavy automatic fire.

'Under covering fire, together with Sergeant McKay, he attacked the enemy's position with grenades. Whilst closing on the enemy, Corporal Bailey was wounded. His brave actions helped to destroy the enemy and relieve the pressure on the Platoon that was pinned down.'

The posthumous award of McKay's VC was announced in the *London Gazette* on the same day as Bailey's MM. This longer citation provides an insight into Bailey's courage as well as that displayed by McKay and it concluded:

The enemy fire was still both heavy and accurate, and the position of the platoons was becoming increasingly hazardous. Taking Sergeant McKay, a Corporal [Bailey] and a few others, and covered by supporting machine gun fire, the Platoon Commander moved forward to reconnoitre the enemy positions but was hit by a bullet in the leg, and command devolved upon Sergeant McKay.

It was clear that instant action was needed if the advance was not to falter and increasing casualties to ensue. Sergeant McKay decided to convert this reconnaissance into an attack in order to eliminate the enemy positions. He was in no doubt of the strength and deployment of the enemy as he undertook this attack. He issued orders, and taking three men with him, broke cover and charged the enemy position.

The assault was met by a hail of fire. The Corporal [Bailey] was seriously wounded, a Private killed and another wounded. Despite these losses Sergeant McKay, with complete disregard for his own safety, continued to charge the enemy position alone. On reaching it he despatched the enemy with grenades, thereby relieving the position of beleaguered 4 and 5 Platoons, who were now able to redeploy with relative safety. Sergeant McKay, however, was killed at the moment of victory, his body falling on the bunker.

Without doubt Sergeant McKay's action retrieved a most dangerous situation and was instrumental in ensuring the success of the attack. His was a coolly calculated act, the dangers of which must have been too apparent to him beforehand. Undeterred he performed with outstanding selflessness, perseverance and courage. With a complete disregard for his own safety, he displayed courage and leadership of the highest order, and was an inspiration to all those around him.

Bailey had known McKay prior to the battle in which the sergeant died, although Bailey was in 5 Platoon while McKay served with 4 Platoon. 'I knew Ian to be a good footballer and always smart. We would pass the time of day, but we did not know each other well,' he said. Bailey had not realised that McKay had been killed on Mount Longdon until he was returning home on the hospital ship.

However, McKay's body was later exhumed from the

Falkland Islands and brought back to England, where it was re-interred with full military honours at Aldershot Military Cemetery in Hampshire. Bailey, though still recovering from his wounds, was one of the pall-bearers. He also took part in the London Victory Parade organised by the City of London on 12 October 1982, when 300,000 people lined the one-mile route to pay their respects to those servicemen who had taken part in the war. Bailey received his gallantry medal from the Queen at an investiture at Buckingham Palace in January 1983, which was attended by his parents. Furthermore, when he was shot, his 'dog tag' identification disc had been lost on Mount Longdon. Yet in 1983, as the Royal Engineers cleared the battlefield, they found the bloodied tag and it was returned to Bailey.

In an interview at his home in the south-east, Bailey told how he made an emotional return to Mount Longdon, as part of an Army exercise, in 1998: 'I walked the route that we had taken sixteen years earlier. It enabled me to look at it from every angle and to see if we had done anything wrong. But, with all the information we had at the time, there was no way we could have launched the attack any better.'

During a distinguished Army career, Bailey was involved in training programmes for the Royal Marines, Royal Irish Home Service and the Parachute Regiment. In 2000 he received a commission as a captain, but he resigned it three years later and retired from the Army due to the injury to his neck and the possible fusion of his spine. By then, Bailey had served for nearly twenty-seven years, including completing tours in Northern Ireland and Kosovo. However, the severe wounds he had received on Mount Longdon affected his military career and they were eventually responsible for his decision to resign his commission. Shortly after leaving the Army in 2003, he began to have problems with the bullet wound to his hip opening up and, after seeing a medical consultant, was amazed to learn that he still had the head of an Argentinian bullet, as well as numerous smaller fragments of shrapnel, lodged inside him. In June 2009 the wound required an operation to remove the metal debris and, in order to undergo the surgery, Bailey had to resign from his senior job within the security industry in Nigeria. During the operation, the bullet and forty-two tiny pieces of shrapnel were all removed.

Bailey said:

> On leaving the Army in 2003, I started to have problems with discharge from my hip injury. On referral to a consultant it was found that I had numerous bits of shrapnel in my hip. Over the next six years the discharge became more frequent and the pain more intense, culminating when I went into hospital to have them removed. This took some three hours on the operating table and some five days in hospital. They found many bits of shrapnel including the head of the bullet. These offending items had been in my body since June 1982 and no one had bothered to mention it! My injuries remain a bone of contention between the Army and me: I was shot three times serving my country, and left with long-term problems, yet I only receive a small military pension.

Since leaving the Army, he has worked in the security industry, spending time in Iraq, Nigeria, Afghanistan, Libya and London. However, this career was ended in the summer of 2014 by a heart ailment. Today, aged fifty-four, Bailey remains married to the woman who was his fiancée at the time of the Falklands War, and they have two grown-up children, a son and daughter.

I am particularly delighted to have Bailey's medal group in my collection of decorations for, in 1989, I had purchased the VC of Ian McKay. It means the gallantry medals of these two courageous men can, appropriately, lie side by side, just as the two men fought shoulder to shoulder more than thirty years ago.

LANCE CORPORAL MARTIN WILLIAM LESTER BENTLEY
AWARD: MILITARY MEDAL (MM)
GAZETTED: 8 NOVEMBER 1982

Bill Bentley was decorated for outstanding bravery at the battle for Goose Green during the Falklands War. During the peak of the fighting, he made his way to a forward slope to help a seriously wounded comrade. Seeing the extent of the injuries, Bentley amputated the man's badly tattered leg using a Swiss Army knife despite facing accurate enemy machine-gun and rifle fire.

The son of a bus conductor and one of ten children, Bentley was born in the north-west of England. After moving to Chorlton-cum-Hardy, Greater Manchester, in 1960, he was educated at Chorlton Park Junior School and nearby Wilbraham Technical High School. In April 1970, when still only fifteen, he joined the Junior Leaders' Regiment of the Royal Armoured Corps as a boy soldier. He became a keen and talented sportsman and was awarded his regimental colours for cross-country skiing and represented the regiment at the national judo championships. By the summer of 1972 he achieved the rank of junior squadron sergeant major and in August was chosen as 'Best soldier passing out to a Cavalry Regiment'. He subsequently passed out as a trooper in the 14/20th King's Hussars, where he was also awarded his regimental colours for cross-country skiing. From 1973 to 1976, Bentley was attached to the Parachute Squadron of the Royal Armoured Corps and during this time his postings included Malaya, Sharjah, Cyprus, Norway, Germany and Northern Ireland. His skiing and shooting skills were such that he was selected for the national biathlon squad.

Of his time in Cyprus, during the 1974 conflict between Greece and Turkey, Bentley wrote: 'Under the command of [then] Lt. Rod Hine, I was involved in the evacuation of Archbishop Makarios from Paphos. Later we were cut off behind the Turkish lines, in Kyrenia for ca. [approximately] one month, we were the last group to be brought out. Later still, I was the driver of one of two armoured escort vehicles which brought Rauf Denktasch [the senior Turkish Cypriot politician] into the Ledra Palace Hotel, Nicosia to sign the "cessations of hostilities" agreement.'

In 1976–7 Bentley was attached to 22 SAS, where he completed the selection course and all other training but, not seeing eye to eye with some of the training staff, he opted to return to the 14/20th King's Hussars. In 1978 he was a divisional white-water canoeing champion, while serving in the British Army of the Rhine (BAOR), before completing another tour of Northern Ireland. In 1979 he left the Army, only to re-enlist later the same year with 2 Para, with whom he conducted yet a further tour of Northern Ireland and, later, became a regimental medical assistant. Still supremely fit, Bentley represented his new regiment in the Northern Ireland judo championships and also came eighth in the open-international Mourne Mountains Marathon in County Down.

During the Falklands War, Bentley – a member of the Regimental Aid Post – served as a combat medic carrying out a dangerous role, which involved spending a great deal of time in and around the battlefield. Captain Steve Hughes, the medical officer for the 2nd Battalion of the Parachute Regiment, kept a diary throughout the conflict, extracts of which appear in Max Arthur's book *Above All, Courage: Personal Stories from the Falklands War*. Some of the accounts provide a fascinating insight into the role that Bentley and others performed during the Battle for Goose Green. Hughes wrote on 27 May 1982: 'The CO outlined a six-phase battalion plan to take the Goose Green/Darwin isthmus, with the initial fire support of HMS *Arrow*. We all retired away from Camilla Creek House [holding position] until start time to make our individual preparations . . .'

On 28 May, Hughes wrote:

I got the lads up at 01:20 after spending a freezing night . . . We brewed up, packed up and moved close into Camilla House, moving off behind Battalion Main Headquarters just after 02:00. Moving with the medical kit divided amongst us, in our bergens . . . Around the area of Burntside House we came under mortar and artillery fire, quite close, for about ninety minutes . . . We were also under fire from a sniper/snipers on the right of the track and at one stage a round whistled inches above my head. It was at this stage that D Company took casualties and we were asked to move forward . . .

About 11.00 . . . Soon after, we came under heavy bombardment in the gully, with shells whistling not twenty feet overhead. The rear slope position saved our bacon . . . Shrapnel casualties drifted in, the smoke and cordite streamed through our position doing its damnedest to fog us out at times . . . One lad came in almost in tears. He was okay but his mucker, Private 'Chopsey' Gray, was pinned down, dying on the forward slope with his leg blown half off. I knew I had to send a medic forward. It was difficult to ask, I felt almost as if I ought to do it myself, but knew that was out of the question. Bill [Lance-Corporal Bentley] accepted the task without qualm. Together with a stretcher party he precariously made his way onto the forward slope to Gray. He completed the partial amputation with his clasp knife and was able to stem the blood loss with a tourniquet. They were then able to bring him into the RAP [Regimental Aid Post]. He had no veins visible anywhere, he had lost so much blood.

Hughes told in his diary how Bentley was in action again with Captain John Greenhalgh: 'at dusk, he [Greenhalgh] had, remarkably, taken his Scout onto the forward slope to drop off Lance-Corporal Bentley and to pick up casualties. He had flown, guided by lads on the ground, by a radio version of the "Golden Shot" – "left a bit, right a bit" and "here".'

Bentley filled the helicopter, including his place, with casualties, having to make his way back from the battlefield on foot. He later reported the bravery and flying skills of the pilot, Greenhalgh, for which Greenhalgh was awarded the Distinguished Flying Cross (DFC). Hughes noted how on 29 May, the Argentine force surrendered its position, adding: 'A television news crew choppered in and tried to film the tragic spectacle of our dead. I sent Bill [Bentley] to see them off.'

Hughes' immensely high opinion of Bentley was revealed in his diary entry for 1 June 1982:

> I travelled into Darwin to visit A Company and Lance-Corporal Bentley. He is having second thoughts about leaving the Army. It would seem a shame now to lose all the ground we've made in terms of experience – we must consolidate. I must try and keep him. Bill's performance has been nothing short of outstanding. He is both a soldier and a very brave man. From the first time we came under fire he stayed cool and set an example to those around him, including me. He has a calming influence, projected not least by his immense practical sense. If there was nothing else to do whilst we were under shell-fire in the gully, Bill was brewing up! Understandably, just his presence instils confidence in all those around him and the others have come on immeasurably.

Bentley's MM was announced in the *London Gazette* on 8 November 1982, when his citation stated:

> Lance Corporal Bentley was a member of the Regimental Aid Post of the Second Battalion The Parachute Regiment throughout the Falkland Islands campaign. During the battle for Port Darwin and Goose Green on 28th/29th May it was of tremendous credit to the Regimental Aid Post that none of the Battalion's thirty four wounded died. This credit belongs to none more than Lance Corporal Bentley. From the first moment that the Regimental Aid Post came under mortar and artillery fire Lance Corporal Bentley's qualities manifested themselves. His courage and presence of mind in carrying out his job acted as an inspiration,

not only to the other medical orderlies, but to all those who came in contact with him. With an immense pack of medical kit on his back Lance Corporal Bentley was to be found wherever the casualties were thickest. Regardless of enemy shell and mortar fire he not only dealt with his casualties in a calm reassuring manner, but boosted their morale with a continuous lighthearted banter.

Typical of his sustained performance during the course of the battle was when a soldier had his lower leg blown off by a mortar bomb. Lance Corporal Bentley, still with heavy pack, ran forward onto a forward slope position and, although under persistent enemy fire, calmly and efficiently carried out the emergency medical treatment that undoubtedly saved the soldier's life.

This incident is just one of many that epitomises the qualities of this brave, resourceful and exceptional man. He acted in, and beyond, the finest traditions of The Parachute Regiment.

After being contacted for this book, Bill Bentley generously provided a previously unpublished account that he had written about his experiences at Goose Green. I am reproducing part of his work, with his permission, because it provides a vivid picture of just how tough the situation was at Goose Green, where Colonel 'H' Jones was killed in an action for which he later received a posthumous VC.

Moving along a track towards Goose Green we could hear and even feel the incredible rush of the shells, which were being fired by our ships and artillery, passing overhead in support of our advance. The track was the only practical approach route from our direction. Suddenly we heard what turned out to be horses galloping. Perhaps it was this that also alerted the Argentinians, either way, within seconds, we came under heavy and accurate enemy artillery fire, the shoe was now on the other foot [previously the Argentinians had been under fire]. Clearly our approach along the track had been anticipated and a 'defensive fire plan' had obviously been measured up in anticipation of our arrival. We were now in 'the killing zone' and someone had to give the command to spread out. Not an easy decision, as one could just as well assume that the sides of the track had also been mined. After a short wait, I am an impatient beggar, I, as a lance corporal, took the initiative over my many superiors and gave the order to spread out. Which was just as well as the track became a death trap just a few seconds later. Whether the sides of the track were mined, we will never know: perhaps the frozen ground had prevented a complete disaster. Soon Dr [Captain Steve] Hughes took control and we moved forward into dead ground. At least my comrades had started to realise that I was not a bullshitter and I started to quickly gain the respect of the young soldiers and the commanders alike.

Ahead of us on the upward slope, the battle was in full swing and casualties were being brought in to us at the Regimental Aid Post, which was no more than a group of medics and a doctor, all with rucksacks full of medical supplies. One young soldier had been shot in his water bottle, which had exploded, probably breaking his hip. Another [wounded soldier], we could not identify his injury and so I persuaded the PT [Physical Training Corps] Sgt, who was leading a stretcher-bearer team, to shine his torch onto the casualty. The PT Sgt was horrified at the thought of lighting up the darkness while the battle raged just ahead of and above us. Using his own body to screen the light from the direction of the battle, he did as I had requested. We were then able to identify that this young man had also been shot in his webbing, the bullet had ripped through his equipment, travelled along the inside of his belt and had come to rest exactly in his navel. Clearly the lad was shocked and bruised but, as I could find no injury and there were obviously no broken bones, I wanted to send him back to his platoon. After all, they were in the heat of the battle. My boss, Dr Steve Hughes, was more sympathetic and sent the lad back to Ajax Bay for a proper check up. (This young man rejoined us before the battle for Wireless Ridge where he was then killed). The battle moved forward ahead of us but we remained in the dead ground where it was much more realistic to treat the casualties than on the battlefield itself.

During quiet moments, we tried to take a nap but the bitter cold made this almost impossible. As dawn broke, we went forward to search for our missing comrades. Along with the Reverend David Cooper, our padre, I carried in our first dead body. The soldier, a friend of mine, had been shot through the head, the bullets had ripped the back of his head off and literally blown his brain out. While carrying his body back into the lines, in a poncho, his head kept banging against my knee and giving off a 'hollow echo' a sound that is not easy to forget.

I went out again, this time, with Mark James [name changed]. Mark and I decided to split up, the area to cover was considerable and time was critical to the survival of our comrades. I soon became aware of someone sitting or crouching, about a hundred metres ahead of me. Looking for cover I suddenly saw a trench ahead of me and ran to it and jumped in. In the bottom of the trench there was obviously someone hiding under a poncho. Instinctively, I fired a long burst of Sub Machine Gun [SMG], luckily, past my own feet into who or whatever was under the poncho. Climbing out, it was as if I was stood on a water-bed with lumps in it. I guess shocked, I sprang back out and moved forward to another trench. Here there was a severely wounded Argentinian soldier who was unconscious [and dying]. Again moving forward, towards the first person that I had seen, I realised that he was also an Argentinian soldier. I moved quickly and cautiously towards him and, as he had made no aggressive gestures, I was also not aggressive. In front of me was a young Argentinian soldier, he had been shot through the leg and was in deep shock. The better side of me, or my training, now took over. The youngster had no weapon at hand and so I hoisted him up over my shoulder, a classical fireman's lift, and carried him into our own lines. Looking back this was quite a risk as he would have been looking down onto my bayonet and it would have been fairly easy for him to have drawn it and stabbed me in the back.

One of the medics indicated to me that another missing friend of mine was 'over there'. I found him alongside another body lying next to his. It was obvious that my friend had been injured first and that the youngster had gone to his aid. The shell dressing and the position of the bodies were unmistakable. They had then both obviously taken a prolonged burst of machine-gun fire that had made a real mess. Out of respect for the youngster, I chose to carry him in first. Lying down next to him, I took his arms up over my shoulders and staggered to my feet, as I did this the youngster just rolled to the side and back to the ground. I was still holding one of his arms over my shoulder. Spreading my own poncho out on the ground, I rolled his body onto it and dragged him back towards the rest of the medics. Somebody came out to meet me and helped me drag the body the rest of the way. I desperately needed a rest, we had now been moving in extreme conditions for about fifty hours. I had to ask two other medics to go out and bring in my friend while I had a brew and tried to take a nap.

I was awoken to obvious confusion. Dr Hughes was getting ready to go forward and attend to Lt Col Jones who had been shot. The RSM [Regimental Sergeant Major] would brief us and I should bring up the rest of the medics at the double. The RSM asked us to take forward as much ammunition and weaponry as possible so I stashed my SMG and grabbed a GPMG [general-purpose machine gun] and as much ammo as I could carry. My own load was well in excess of 120 lbs, my trench-mate Dawson [name changed] was similarly loaded. We two went on ahead of the others. 'Just follow the track' were our only instructions. Upon reaching the crest of the hill, we became aware of a Pucara fighter aircraft bearing down upon us. I immediately opened fire from the hip with the GPMG but got a stoppage [gun jammed]. Dawson dashed to help me but fell to the ground like a stone. The Pucara flew past us and I moved to help Dawson. Luckily, he had not been wounded but had tripped and was winded by the weight of his load landing on top of him. We looked for the Pucara which was, by now, shooting down one of our helicopters about half a mile away. Immediately upon arrival at 'A Company's lines' we were relieved of our extra weapons and ammunition and so, I for one, now felt naked with only my SMG and at the very next opportunity took an SLR [self-loading rifle] from the dead marine, Cpl Geoff Hunt [name changed]. Several other medics followed suit.

We found Dr Hughes: Colonel Jones was already dead. Others desperately needed our services and, having assisted a couple of casualties, I became aware that one of the young platoon medics, Greg [name changed], with whom I had become very close during the training on the MV [merchant vessel] *Norland*, needed help. Greg had been shot some hours earlier and had lost a lot of blood and, although he had been patched up by others, he was in danger of also freezing to death when we found him. Dawson ripped open his own shirt and placed an infusion bag against his naked body to try to take off the chill, while I placed the infusion needle into Greg's arm. It was a moment desperately full of emotion that I can only compare with the delivery of my own two daughters into this world. We evacuated Greg on the next available helicopter, regardless of medical priorities. Greg survived as did, luckily, all other casualties who were alive when we reached them. Another young platoon medic, Arthur [name changed], had been shot through the head. A squirt of his brain was visible on the back of his head, like toothpaste that had been squeezed out of a tube. I did not consider that he could survive and told Phil Barnes [name changed] to give him 'a lot of morphine' but Dr Hughes thought that he could 'have a chance' and, with help from Phil and Mark James, he also survived. Thanks to all of them, Arthur Jones is today still a valued friend of ours.

The day passed with moments of intense action and quiet moments. During a heavy barrage, I found myself sharing a shell crater with our padre, what a guy! If anything put me off him it was the extra long spade that he carried, just in case he had to 'dig a quick grave'. He always had a story or a quick joke like 'not being fussy about who I have to bury' and 'I would be proud to do you the favour'! Thanks, padre.

Steadily the row of our own bodies grew and at some point my good friend Bertie's [name changed] [dead] body was brought in. I confess that I broke down and cried. We were not getting any useful medical re-supplies: we were all dead tired, hungry, even eating biscuits from the pockets of the dead, friend and foe alike, and the ammunition was running out. Their artillery had us pinpointed, the colonel was dead along with a growing list of officers and men, things were looking pretty desperate.

Fred [name changed], a friend of mine, came staggering down from the crest of the hill towards us, his bayonet still fixed and he told Dr Hughes that yet another platoon medic, Jim Lang [name changed], and another friend Peter Plant [name changed], were injured on the other side of the hill. Doc [Hughes] looked at me and I heard myself volunteering. Fred led me through our own front line, through a gap in a stone wall, where he suddenly opened fire on two enemy soldiers. I also breeched the gap and opened fire. By the time I came up level with Fred, he was thrusting his bayonet into the second soldier, the first was already most definitely dead. We moved on to the forward slope down a small depression to a point where Fred could point out the casualties to me. It was about twenty-five metres to them, fully exposed to the enemy down in Goose Green. I told Fred to await the rescue party and then to creep over to us on my signal. I crept over to Jim [Lang] and Peter [Plant]. Peter told me to look after Jim who 'is in a bad way'. Jim had gone back to rescue Peter who had been shot through the arm and, in doing so, had himself been hit 'full on' by a mortar bomb which had shattered one leg, broken the other and he was full of fragmentation. I quickly decided it would not be possible to deal with all of this on the spot, and so opted to amputate the shattered leg. By now, somebody had become aware of my presence and bullets were 'pfloping' into the soft ground around us. I placed a tourniquet on Jim's leg and severed the remains of his lower leg with my Swiss Army knife so that I could place a stump bandage. Jim just cringed into the ground, which was already soaked with his own blood. The sweet sickly smell, mixed with the cordite, burnt flesh and fresh earth, is unforgettable. The incoming fire was, by now, increasing and so, turning to help Peter, I gave the signal to Fred to come and get Jim. A young captain had, however, taken command of the rescue party and he had decided to rush in, grab the wounded and bolt for cover, which is exactly what happened. If a plan works it was the right plan on the day!

When the enemy saw a group of men rushing from cover, all hell broke loose. The ground around us exploded. I remember placing Jim's severed leg on the stretcher then suddenly they were all ten metres ahead of me. The ground between us erupted, it was alive! I decided to play dead where I was. After what seemed to be an eternity, the rescue party reached safety and the incoming fire faded away. I slowly gathered my equipment together and as many of the 'left behind' weapons from the rescue party as I could carry and, in the now oncoming dusk, made my way back up the hill. I became concerned that I did not know the password to re-enter our lines. This, however, was not a problem: the lads had seen everything that had happened and welcomed me with open arms. When I asked 'what is the password?' somebody said: 'Who cares? When we challenge "who goes there?", if the answer is "qua?", we shoot the bastard!' I arrived back over the hill in time to see Jim and Peter waiting for a helicopter evacuation. When the helicopter landed, we placed Jim's stretcher in the pod on the outside of the chopper but we could not get the lid to close. Realising that Jim still had his webbing on and the spade that he had been carrying was preventing the pod lid from closing, I sat Jim up to remove his shoulder harness and that's when Jim saw his own leg lying across the end of the stretcher. He stared at me, or rather through me. I gave him a hug, assured him he'd be okay, pressed him back down, closed the pod and waved to the pilot to take off. Enemy artillery had seen the helicopter landing and were again making things most uncomfortable.

Bentley left the Army in 1983 and for the next year worked mostly in America for Prince Bandar bin Sultan, the Saudi ambassador to the United States. In 1985 he returned to the UK where, for the next five years, he served in the Duke of Lancaster's Own Yeomanry. He finally ended his time in the military in 1990, having by then completed three separate stints and accumulated a total of seventeen years' service.

After leaving the Army for the final time, he moved to Germany in 1990, marrying for the first time. He has two daughters by his first wife, a German, but the relationship ended in divorce. Bentley later remarried, again a German woman, who had three sons from a previous relationship. Since moving to Germany, Bentley, who will be sixty in the New Year (2015), first worked collecting the cash from casinos and then trained as a gas and water fitter. More recently, he became a property surveyor and, finally, an energy consultant. However, Bentley was forced to give up this role in 2011 after many years of ill-health and he now lives, with his second wife, on a smallholding and off his Army pension.

In a telephone interview from his home outside Berlin, Bentley played down any suggestion that he had been brave during the Falklands War: 'People talk about courage but if you are not afraid you don't need courage. Personally, I was never afraid. Sure, I knew I was taking risks but they were calculated risks and so I just got on with it. I never did anything that I considered to be foolhardy. I have never felt fear for myself though I have felt it for my family.'

CORPORAL (LATER COLONEL) THOMAS JAMES CAMP
AWARD: MILITARY MEDAL (MM)
GAZETTED: 8 OCTOBER 1982

Tom Camp was remarkable in that he served in the British Army for more than thirty-one years, during which time he was awarded a gallantry medal as a corporal yet, later, rose to become a lieutenant colonel. His MM was gained during the Falklands War, during a fierce firefight to recapture Darwin Hill on East Falkland.

Camp joined the Army in September 1973 as a junior leader at Oswestry, Shropshire. From 1975 to 1982 he served as a Junior Non Commissioned Officer (JNCO) with the 2nd Battalion, Parachute Regiment. During this period he was deployed to Northern Ireland, the USA, Norway and, finally, to the Falklands War as part of 'Operation Corporate'. It was during the heavy fighting on East Falkland that he displayed outstanding courage.

His MM was announced on 8 October 1982, when his citation stated:

> In the early hours of 28th May, the 2nd Battalion The Parachute Regiment were ordered to attack enemy positions in the area of Port Darwin on the island of East Falkland. The enemy were well entrenched in strength on Darwin Hill and fierce fighting ensued.
>
> Corporal Camp was leading his Section when they came under fire from an enemy bunker: continuing under fire he moved forward and hurled grenades into the bunker. He then manoeuvred his men into positions from where their anti-tank rockets and section machine gun were able to engage and destroy the enemy position.
>
> Thereafter, he successfully led his men in further assaults on well defended enemy positions. His courage and leadership in action were outstanding.

After being selected for a commission, Camp attended the Royal Military Academy, Sandhurst. From 1984 to 1987, now a lieutenant, he served with 29 Commando Royal Artillery, with deployments to Norway and Denmark. By 1987 he was a captain and was posted to 19 Field Regiment Royal Artillery in Dortmund, West Germany, serving as a forward observation officer, adjutant and headquarters battery commander. Next, he deployed to Northern Ireland and then to British Army Training Unit Suffield (BATUS) in Alberta, Canada.

After attending the Army Staff Course at Camberley, Surrey, he joined Headquarters 1st Armoured Division as it moved to Saudi Arabia as part of the initial deployment for 'Operation Granby' during the First Gulf War. After the liberation of Kuwait, Camp was Divisional Operations Officer at Verden, in Germany, from 1991 to 1992. In 1993 he assumed command of 88 (Arracan) Battery of 4 Field Regiment, Royal Artillery in Osnabrück, Germany. He returned with his battery to Northern Ireland in 1994, where he was responsible for Army support to the Royal Ulster Constabulary (RUC) within the New Lodge area of north Belfast. He was Mentioned in Despatches (MiD) for his courageous work in New Lodge.

In September 1994 Camp was promoted to lieutenant colonel and he joined the directing staff at the Army Staff College, Camberley; it meant he was returning to Sandhurst eleven years after being commissioned. In March 1996 he became the directing lieutenant colonel of 'A' Wing at the Army Junior Division at Camberley, where he was responsible for overseeing the initial staff training of seventy Army captains. Camp commanded the 5th Battalion, Royal Irish Regiment, in Ballykelly, Northern Ireland, from August 1997 to September 1999, where he was responsible for Army support to RUC police divisions. Next, he was posted as a Plans Officer to Nato's Joint Headquarters Centre (JHC) in Heidelberg, Germany, as they moved to Kosovo for KFOR 2 (Kosovo Force 2), where he served in Pristina. On promotion to full colonel in January 2002, he assumed his final post of deputy commander and Chief of Staff, HQ British Forces Gibraltar. He retired from the Army on 18 April 2005 after thirty-one years and six months of service, during which he had worn a total of six different cap badges.

It is not known what happened to Camp after he left the Army.

COMPANY SERGEANT MAJOR (LATER CAPTAIN) WILLIAM MCINTOSH NICOL
AWARD: DISTINGUISHED CONDUCT MEDAL (DCM)
GAZETTED: 8 OCTOBER 1982

William 'Bill' Nicol received one of just eight DCMs awarded for the Falklands War during a distinguished career with the Security Forces spanning almost forty years. His decoration was made for his bravery during the Battle of Tumbledown Mountain in the final stages of the conflict in June 1982. Nicol was shot and injured while rescuing a mortally wounded comrade, showing great composure under heavy fire and then refusing to be evacuated, despite his injuries. The close-quarter night battle was later immortalised by the BBC in its 1988 film *Tumbledown*.

Nicol was born on 16 December 1945 in Falkirk, a town in the Central Lowlands of Scotland. The youngest of three children, he was made a ward of court, aged just five, and brought up in children's homes. Having seen potential in the young boy, Nicol's local town council sent him to Elmfield Rudolf Steiner School in Stourbridge, Worcestershire, where he boarded from the ages of eleven to fifteen. After leaving school in 1961, he joined the Army as a boy soldier, but he was earmarked for likely promotion and was sent to the Infantry Junior Leaders' Battalion (IJLB) at Oswestry, Shropshire, where future Non Commissioned Officers (NCOs) were trained.

Nicol had initially joined the Scots Guards and he served with the unit in Malaysia and Borneo during the 'Confrontation' with Indonesia from 1963 to 1967. Having earned a reputation as a fine, practical soldier, he was selected to become an instructor at the Royal School of Jungle Warfare in Johor Baru from 1968 to 1970. During this time, Nicol and his fellow instructors were training Americans, Australians and New Zealanders who were about to fight in Vietnam. To this day, he considers jungle warfare to be his forte.

Next, Nicol served in Belize and Northern Ireland; from 1977 to 1980 he was posted to Dungannon, County Tyrone, part of the infamous 'murder triangle'. His job was to train the local Ulster Defence Regiment (UDR) – an initial two-year posting that was extended by a further year. After completing this role, he served in Ballymurphy, a staunchly nationalist area of Belfast, with his own unit.

Nicol sailed for the South Atlantic on 12 May 1982 following the outbreak of the Falklands War and after two weeks of unit training in Sennybridge, South Wales. By then he was married with a young son. He was on board the *Queen Elizabeth II*, originally a liner but requisitioned as a troopship, as part of the 5th Infantry Brigade and 'Operation Corporate'.

The official Ministry of Defence account of the war noted:

After landing at San Carlos on 2 June, the 2nd Battalion Scots Guards was taken in HMS *Intrepid*, three days later, to Bluff Cove, a settlement not 25 kms from [Port] Stanley. There the Battalion dug in, in appalling weather and awaited the expected order to move forward to Stanley. In the week the Battalion was there, good intelligence was received from the recce platoon in a covert patrol base well forward in Port Harriet House. This intelligence subsequently had a profound effect on the Brigade plan for the advance on Stanley. During this week the disastrous Skyhawk raid occurred against the *Sir Galahad* and *Sir Tristram,* dealing a sad blow to the Welsh Guards [who took heavy casualties]. If there was any consolation in this attack, the Battalion accounted for certainly two, if not three, enemy planes with small arms fire.

During the night 11/12 June, 3 Commando Brigade took Mount Longdon, Two Sisters and Mount Harriet. The 5 Infantry Brigade plan then was for the Battalion to take Mount Tumbledown from the west and, when firm, to provide fire support for 1/7 Gurkhas to assault Mount William. The Welsh Guards were subsequently to be prepared to take Sapper Hill.

The Battalion plan was for a silent night attack in three phases. The fire plan was to include fighter ground attack, five batteries of 105 mm Light Guns and Naval Gun fire from HMS *Active* and *Yarmouth*. The mortars of 42 Commando 1/7 Gurkhas were also available. Each phase was to involve a Company attack on a different part of the objective. Phase 1 was for G Company to take the first part of Tumbledown. Thirty minutes before G Company crossed the start line, there was to be a diversionary attack from the obvious southerly approach. Phase II involved Left Flank moving through and assaulting the main part of the mountain, and in Phase III Right Flank would secure the final part.

Nicol was one of the first on the scene when the Left Flank's No. 13 Platoon ran into serious opposition during the assault on Mount Tumbledown on 13 June. He later described his experiences in Martin Middlebrook's book *The Falklands War* (previously known by the title *Operation Corporate: The Falklands War, 1982*):

When we came under fire, everyone went to ground and was returning fire. There was a staggering amount of noise. I had gone off 'floating' around the left leading the platoon, doing what I saw as a company sergeant-major's job, giving the boys encouragement – not that they needed it. They shouted for me and I went across to [Guardsman] Tanbini and tried to pull him back into cover; if I had tried to lift him, we would have both been exposed and hit. I suggested that he tried to push back with his feet, while I pulled him, but he said, 'Sir, I've been shot' – typical Guardsman, the way he addressed me as 'Sir' – and then he died.

Someone else was screaming for me then. It was the platoon sergeant [John Simeon], he had been badly shot in the thigh. I jumped up and ran across to him and, as I got to him, I was hit. I was just about to kneel down beside him when the bullet hit the centre of my rifle which was across the front of the centre of my stomach in the approved manner, ready for action. If I hadn't been holding that rifle in the manner in which I had been teaching people for years, I would be dead by now. The bullet ricocheted off the barrel and went through my right hand. Tanbini, John Simeon and I had all been shot in one line by the same sniper, I think. I had just received a letter from my wife to say she was pregnant and this went through my mind. I thought I was going to be next. There was nothing I could do about it. That sniper was good; I would like to have met him.

In short, even though Nicol had almost been shot dead by the enemy sniper, he could not, as a professional soldier, hide his admiration for the man's shooting skills.

The official Ministry of Defence (MoD) account of the incident continued:

At approximately 0230 hrs, artillery rounds landed accurately in front of the right forward platoon and the platoon commander, together with the company commander and company head-quarters, led an attack on the forward enemy positions. This assault was successful and the momentum of the attack was maintained. About eight enemy were killed with grenades, rifles and bayonets. The company commander himself killed two and bayoneted a third. Although one section commander, L/Sgt C. Mitchell, was killed, the assault continued up the hill, with sangars and bunkers being taken at the point of the bayonet. The demands of clearing these positions and guarding prisoners resulted in only seven men of Left Flank reaching the top of the mountain and the end of their objective. Below them were the lights of [Port] Stanley and enemy running away. Of these seven, three including Lt Mitchell, were immediately cut down by machine gun fire from Right Flank's objective.

By about 8.15am, Tumbledown was in the hands of the 2nd Battalion Scots Guards, although eight men had been killed and forty-three wounded.

At the time, Nicol also spoke about his admiration for (then) Major John Kiszely, the company commander of Left Flank and the man who recommended him for his DCM. At the point when Nicol was injured, Kiszely was away from his unit, having also required treatment for his own wound. Nicol said: 'The citation came as a total surprise. As far as I was concerned, I was just doing my job.'

Nicol returned from the Falklands on 10 August 1982 and his twin daughters were born shortly afterwards. His DCM was announced less than two months later – on 8 October 1982 – and singled out three separate acts of bravery spanning nine days:

WO2 Nicol was the CSM [company sergeant major] of Left Flank, 2nd Battalion Scots Guards throughout the campaign in the Falkland Islands. During this time he maintained exemplary standards of personal courage and leadership which inspired similar standards in all members of his company. Three particular occasions stand out: On 6th June, after a 6 hour sea voyage at night in open boats in which most men were completely soaked, the Battalion was ordered to occupy defensive positions on high ground in freezing rain and sleet. Due to CSM Nicol's efforts, although a number of exposure casualties were taken in other companies, none occurred in Left Flank.

On 8th June some 12 enemy aircraft involved in an attack on shipping at Fitzroy flew in three sorties at low level over the Company's positions at Bluff Cove. No warning of the enemy aircraft was received but, despite this CSM Nicol so rapidly and skilfully organised and controlled his company in firing rifles and machine guns, moving from sangar to sangar with no thought for his own safety, that 2 or 3 enemy aircraft were brought down by the Battalion.

On 14th June at Tumbledown Mountain, his company were ordered to take a strong enemy position as part of a Battalion night attack.

After the initial assault, the company came under constant and devastating machine gun and sniper fire. One of the platoon sergeants was wounded, and CSM Nicol went forward under accurate sniper fire to rescue him. Wounded in the hand while doing so, he continued to tend the dying sergeant.

He remained cool and calm under heavy fire encouraging and exhorting his men and, at the same time, advising one of the young platoon commanders how to defeat a seemingly impregnable enemy position.

He remained unperturbed by the weight of enemy small arms, artillery and mortar fire thus instilling great confidence in men who might well have been frightened. He refused to be evacuated himself, until all the other casualties in the company (26 in all) had been evacuated. CSM Nicol's distinguished conduct and conspicuous personal bravery throughout the campaign and in particular on the three occasions described proved an inspiration and example to all ranks and have made an outstanding contribution to his company's exceptional achievements.

In the spring of 1984 Nicol was with the Scots Guards in Cyprus before, once again, being posted to Northern Ireland, this time serving with the Northern Ireland Training Advisory Team in County Down.

Nicol left the British Army in 1986 in the rank of captain after twenty-five years' service and went to live and work in Northern Ireland. He continues to be feted for his bravery in the Falklands. In June 2012, in an interview with his local paper to mark the thirtieth anniversary of the Falklands War, he described the scene when he was involved in the action that led to him being awarded the DCM. 'The place was just a blaze of tracer. I've never seen anything like that in my life. Never seen it in a war movie. It was unbelievable,' he recalled.

Nicol intends to retire from his current job later this year (2014), after his sixty-ninth birthday. Speaking at his home in Northern Ireland, where he still lives with his wife, he said: 'I have been very fortunate. I have had a marvellous life.'

SELECT BIBLIOGRAPHY

Almonds-Windmill, Lorna, *Gentleman Jim: The Wartime Story of a Founder of the SAS and Special Forces*, Constable, London, 2001

Arthur, Max, *Above All, Courage: Personal Stories from the Falklands War*, Cassell, London, 1985 (extract printed with permission)

Ashcroft, Michael, *Special Forces Heroes*, Headline Review, London, 2008

Asher, Michael, *The Regiment: The Real Story of the SAS*, Viking, London, 2007

Bailey, Roderick, *Forgotten Voices of the Secret War*, Ebury Press, London, 2008

Brown, George A., *Commando Gallantry Awards of World War II*, Self-published, 1991

Byrne, J.V., *The General Salutes a Soldier*, Robert Hale, London, 1986 (extract printed with permission)

Coburn, Mike, *Soldier Five: The Real Truth About the Bravo Two Zero Mission*, Mainstream Publishing, Edinburgh, 2004

Cowles, Virginia, *The Phantom Major: The Story of David Stirling and the S.A.S. Regiment*, originally published by William Collins Sons & Co., Glasgow, 1958; republished by Pen and Sword Books, Barnsley (South Yorkshire), 2010 (extract printed with permission)

Darman, Peter, *A–Z of the SAS*, Sidgwick & Jackson, London, 1992

Devins (Jr), Joseph H., *The Vaagso Raid: The Commando Attack That Changed the Course of World War II*, Chilton, Massachusetts, 1968

Evans, (Lt Gen. Sir) Geoffrey, *The Johnnies*, originally published by Cassell, London, 1964; republished by the Orion Publishing Group, London (all attempts at tracing the copyright holder have been unsuccessful)

Eyre, Philip, *Those Who Dared*, Token, Honiton (Devon), 2002

Farran, Roy, *Winged Dagger: Adventures on Special Service*, originally published by Collins, London, 1948; republished by the Orion Publishing Group, London (all attempts at tracing the copyright holder have been unsuccessful)

Friedlander, Gerhart, and Turner, Keith, *Rudi's Story: The diary and wartime experiences of Rudolf Friedlaender*, Jedburgh Publishing, London, 2006

Gage, Jack, *Greek Adventure*, Unie-Volkspers, Cape Town (South Africa), 1950

Geraghty, Tony, *Who Dares Wins: The Story of the SAS 1950–1992*, Time Warner, London, 1980

Harrison, D.I., *These Men Are Dangerous: The S.A.S. at War*, originally published by Cassell, London, 1957; republished by the Orion Publishing Group, London (extract © D. I. Harrison 1957 printed with permission)

Hoe, Alan, *David Stirling: The Authorised Biography of the Founder of the SAS*, Little, Brown, London, 1992

James, Malcolm, *Born of the Desert: With the SAS in North Africa*, Collins, London, 1945

Keyes, Elizabeth, *Geoffrey Keyes V.C. of the Rommel Raid*, George Newnes, London, 1956

Kofod-Hansen, Mogens, *'Andy' – A Portrait of Major Anders Lassen, the Dane Who Was Posthumously Awarded the Victoria Cross in the Second World War*, Self-published, 1989

Ladd, James D., *SBS: The Invisible Raiders*, Book Club Associates, London, 1983

Langley, Mike, *Anders Lassen, VC, MC of the SAS*, New English Library, London, 1988

Lloyd Owen, (Major General) David, *Providence Their Guide: The Long Range Desert Group 1940–1945*, Pen and Sword Books, Barnsley (South Yorkshire), 2000 (extract printed with permission)

Lodwick, John, *Raiders from the Sea: The Story of the Special Boat Service in WWII*, Greenhill Books, London, 1990

Lovat, Lord, *March Past*, Weidenfeld & Nicolson, London, 1978

Maclean, Fitzroy, *Eastern Approaches*, Jonathan Cape, London, 1949

McClean, Stewart, *SAS: The History of the Special Raiding Squadron 'Paddy's Men'*, Spellmount, Stroud (Gloucestershire), 2006

McCrery, Nigel, *The Complete History of the SAS*, Carlton Books, London, 2003 (extract printed with permission)

McHarg, Ian, *Litani River*, Self-published, 2011

McManners, Hugh, *Falklands Commando*, William Kimber, London, 1984

McNab, Andy, *Bravo Two Zero*, Bantam Press, London, 1993

Middlebrook, Martin, *Operation Corporate: The Falklands War, 1982*, Viking, London, 1985 (extract printed with permission)

Mills-Roberts, (Brigadier) Derek, *Clash By Night: A Commando Chronicle*, William Kimber, London, 1956

Morgan, Mike, *Daggers Drawn: Real Heroes of the SAS & SBS*, Spellmount, Stroud (Gloucestershire), 2000 (extract printed with permission)

Mortimer, Gavin, *Stirling's Men: The Inside History of the SAS in World War II*, Weidenfeld & Nicolson, London, 2004

Mortimer, Gavin, *The Daring Dozen*, Osprey, Oxford, 2012

Mortimer, Gavin, *The SAS In World War II*, Osprey, Oxford, 2011

Mortimer, Gavin, *The SBS In World War II*, Osprey, Oxford, 2013

Neillands, Robin, *The Dieppe Raid: The Story of the Disastrous 1942 Expedition*, Aurum Press, London, 2005

Oldfield, (Major) J.B., *The Green Howards in Malaya, 1949–1952*, Gale and Polden, Aldershot (Hampshire), 1953

Owen, James, *Commando: Winning World War II Behind Enemy Lines*, Little, Brown, London, 2012

Parker, John, *SBS: The Inside Story of the Special Boat Service*, Headline, London, 1997

Pickering, William, and Hart, Alan, *The Bandits of Cisterna*, Leo Cooper, London, 1991

Ryan, Chris, *The One That Got Away*, Century, London, 1995

SAS War Diary 1941–1945, Extraordinary Editions, London, 2011

Saunders, Hilary St George, *The Green Beret: The Story of the Commandos 1940–1945*, Michael Joseph, London, 1949

Scholey, Pete, *SAS Heroes*, Osprey, Oxford, 2008

Seymour, William, *British Special Forces*, originally published by Sidgwick & Jackson, London, 1985; republished by Pen and Sword Books, Barnsley (South Yorkshire), 2006 (extract printed with permission)

Stevens, Gordon, *The Originals: The Secret History of the Birth of the SAS In Their Own Words*, Ebury Press, London, 2005

Stilwell, Alexander, *Special Forces In Action*, Pen and Sword Books, Barnsley (South Yorkshire), 2007

Taylor, Peter, *Brits: The War Against the IRA*, Bloomsbury Publishing, London, 2001

Tudor, Malcolm, *SOE in Italy 1940–1945*, Emilia Publishing, Newtown (Powys), 2011

Warner, Philip, *The Special Air Service*, William Kimber, London, 1971

Young, (Brigadier) Peter, *Storm from the Sea*, William Kimber, London, 1958

INDEX